W9-BIS-940

195-

INTERNATIONAL ORGANIZATIONS AND ENVIRONMENTAL POLICY

Recent Titles in
Contributions in Political Science

Environmental Policies in the Third World: A Comparative Analysis
O. P. Dwivedi and Dhirendra K. Vajpeyi, editors

Social Justice in the Ancient World
K. D. Irani and Morris Silver, editors

Securing the Covenant: United States-Israel Relations After the Cold War
Bernard Reich

Why the Cold War Ended: A Range of Interpretations
Ralph Summy and Michael E. Salla, editors

Presidential Leadership and Civil Rights Policy
James W. Riddlesperger, Jr. and Donald W. Jackson, editors

The Eagle and the Peacock: U.S. Foreign Policy Toward India Since Independence
M. Srinivas Chary

Japan's Role in the Post-Cold War World
Richard D. Leitch, Jr., Akira Kato, and Martin E. Weinstein

Botswana's Search for Autonomy in Southern Africa
Richard Dale

Contested Terrain: Power, Politics, and Participation in Suburbia
Marc L. Silver and Martin Melkonian, editors

After Authoritarianism: Democracy or Disorder?
Daniel N. Nelson, editor

Ethics and Statecraft: The Moral Dimension of International Affairs
Cathal J. Nolan, editor

Social Security Programs: A Cross-Cultural Comparative Perspective
John Dixon and Robert P. Scheurell, editors

INTERNATIONAL ORGANIZATIONS AND ENVIRONMENTAL POLICY

Edited by
Robert V. Bartlett,
Priya A. Kurian,
and Madhu Malik

Prepared under the auspices
of the Policy Studies Organization

Stuart S. Nagel,
Publications Coordinator

Contributions in Political Science, Number 355

GREENWOOD PRESS
Westport, Connecticut • London

HC
79
E5
I57
1995

Library of Congress Cataloging-in-Publication Data

International organizations and environmental policy / edited by
    Robert V. Bartlett, Priya A. Kurian, and Madhu Malik.
        p.   cm.—(Contributions in political science, ISSN 0147–1066
    ; no. 355)
    Includes bibliographical references and index.
    ISBN 0–313–29623–5 (alk. paper)
    1. Environmental policy.   2. International agencies.
    3. Environmental policy—International cooperation.   I. Bartlett,
    Robert V.   II. Kurian, Priya A.   III. Malik, Madhu.   IV. Series:
    Contributions in political science ; no. 355.
    HC79.E5I57   1995
    363.7'0526—dc20   94–47417

British Library Cataloguing in Publication Data is available.

Library of Congress Catalog Card Number: 94–47417
ISBN: 0–313–29623–5
ISSN: 0147–1066

First published in 1995

Greenwood Press, 88 Post Road West, Westport, CT 06881
An imprint of Greenwood Publishing Group, Inc.

Printed in the United States of America

The paper used in this book complies with the
Permanent Paper Standard issued by the National
Information Standards Organization (Z39.48–1984).

10 9 8 7 6 5 4 3 2 1

Contents

Tables and Figures

TABLES

FIGURES

Acknowledgments

We thank many people for their time and effort in making this volume possible. First of all, thanks to the authors of this book for responding appropriately to various comments and suggestions, for their assistance in offering helpful reactions, comments, and ideas about the overall volume and various chapters, and also for their good humor.

A group whose assistance we especially want to acknowledge includes several distinguished scholars who served as an editorial board for this project. Their contributions included offering advice about the planning and execution of the book and reviewing numerous proposals and draft manuscripts: Lynton K. Caldwell, Kenneth Dahlberg, Philippe G. Le Prestre, Marvin S. Soroos, John McCormick, and Kenneth Hanf. Four of them made the ultimate commitment by becoming contributors themselves. We also thank several other scholars who reviewed individual proposals and draft manuscripts: Stefanie Rixecker, Laura Strohm, Dennis Pirages, Christopher Joyner, Roger Coate, Donald Puchala, Rosemary O'Leary, Lester Milbrath, Thomas Malone, Henry Lambright, Kai Lee, Elaine Sharp, Ronnie Lipschutz, Mukund Untawale, Peter Zwick, Richard Kozicki, Vicki L. Golich, and Richard Kraus.

Indispensible secretarial assistance was provided at crucial times by Claire Windler, Mary Rapier, and Betty Hartman. Caroline Orth ably corrected bibliographic references during final editing.

Robert V. Bartlett
Priya A. Kurian
Madhu Malik
March 1995

Acronyms

AOSIS	Alliance of Small Island and Low-lying States
ASEAN	Association of Southeast Asian Nations
BAPMoN	Background Air Pollution Monitoring System
BEUC	European Bureau of Consumers' Union
CCOL	Coordinating Committee on the Ozone Layer
CFC	Chlorofluorocarbon
CIS	Commonwealth of Independent States
COP	Conference of the Parties
EA	Environmental assessment
EC	European Community
ECOSOC	Economic and Social Council
ECSC	European Coal and Steel Community
EEA	European Environment Agency
EEB	European Environmental Bureau
EIA	Environmental impact assessment
EMEP	Cooperative Program for the Monitoring and Evaluation of the Long-Range Transmission of Air Pollutants in Europe
EPA	Environmental Protection Agency
EU	European Union
FAO	Food and Agriculture Organization
FCCC	Framework Convention on Climate Change
GARP	Global Atmospheric Research Program
GATT	General Agreement on Tariffs and Trade
GEF	Global Environment Facility
GEMS	Global Environmental Monitoring System
GESAMP	Group of Experts on the Scientific Aspects of Marine Pollution
GO_3OS	Global Ozone Observing System
IAEA	International Atomic Energy Agency

IBPGR	International Board for Plant Genetic Resources
ICI	Imperial Chemical Industries
ICPD	International Conference on Population and Development
ICSU	International Council of Scientific Unions
IEL	International environmental law
IEP	International environmental policy
IGO	Intergovernmental organization
IGOSS	Integrated Global Ocean Services System
IL	International law
ILO	International Labor Organization
IMO	International Meterological Organization
INC	Intergovernmental Negotiating Committee
INGO	International nongovernmental organization
IO	International organization
IPCC	Intergovernmental Panel on Climate Change
IR	International relations
IUCN	International Union for Conservation of Nature and Natural Resources
IWC	International Whaling Commission
MAP	Mediterranean Action Plan
MDB	Multilateral development bank
MNC	Multinational corporation
NACE	North American Environment Commission
NAFTA	North American Free Trade Agreement
NASA	National Aeronautics and Space Administration
NATO	North Atlantic Treaty Organization
NEAP	National environmental action plan
NGO	Nongovernmental organization
OAS	Organization of American States
OAU	Organization of African Unity
ODS	Ozone-depleting substance
OECD	Organization for Economic Cooperation and Development
SBI	Subsidiary Body for Implementation
SBST	Subsidiary Body for Scientific and Technological Advice
SCOPE	Scientific Committee on Problems of the Environment
SEA	Single European Act
SORG	Stratospheric Ozone Review Group
TRIPs	Trade related intellectual property rights
UN	United Nations
UNCED	United Nations Conference on Environment and Development
UNCLOS	United Nations Conference on the Law of the Sea
UNDP	United Nations Development Programme
UNECE	United Nations Economic Commission for Europe

UNEP	United Nations Environment Programme
UNESCO	United Nations Educational, Scientific, and Cultural Organization
UNFPA	United Nations Fund for Population Activities
UNTS	United Nations Treaty Series
USAID	United States Agency for International Development
WCRP	World Climate Research Program
WHO	World Health Organization
WMO	World Meteorological Organization
WRI	World Resources Institute
WWF	World Wildlife Fund

1

International Environmental Policy: Redesigning the Agenda for Theory and Practice?

Priya A. Kurian, Robert V. Bartlett, and Madhu Malik

> Any piecemeal introduction of innovative forms of social choice into a world of ecologically irrational mechanisms is perilous. . . . Systems have a remarkable capacity to frustrate structural change. . . . [They] therefore compound their ecological irrationality by securing their own perpetuation. (Dryzek, 1987: 245)

International environmental policy and politics have in the last two decades increasingly centered on making possible the twin goals of economic development and environmental protection. The tantalizing idea of "sustainable development," carrying with it the promise of delivering both goals, has held policymakers, scholars, activists, and parts of the general public in thrall especially since 1987 when the Brundtland Commission gave it wide currency. And, despite sustainable development meaning different things to different people, or perhaps because of this attractive ambiguity that allows it to mean all things to all people, the 1992 United Nations Conference on Environment and Development held in Rio de Janeiro found governments and nongovernmental organizations (NGOs) continuing to pay homage to this term. But the rhetoric of sustainable development cannot be an adequate substitute for meaningful policy. To grapple successfully with environmental policy issues, new and creative ways of dealing with policy and administration are needed. New knowledge, new theories, and a fundamental shift in values are required if international environmental policy is ever to deal satisfactorily with the environmental dilemmas facing the world today. More than anything else, politics and institutions must adapt to new situations created by the global environmental problematique[1]; they must be ecologically rational.

In the domestic context of only one country's environmental problems, there is some evidence that policy processes can be ecologically rational (see Bartlett, 1986a, 1990; Dryzek, 1987). To what extent is it possible to frame or even think about international environmental policy that has ecological rationality at its core? Are our social, economic, and political institutions capable of learning? How do we understand the role, functions, and performances of the international organization—one of the primary actors bringing about the changes necessary for ensuring environmental protection in the long term? And how do political and ideological conflicts obstruct or undermine the ability of international organizations (IOs) to promote international environmental cooperation?

The pressing nature of global environmental issues, their centrality to any discussion of development and economic growth, and the willingness of governments of the industrialized and industrializing worlds to wrestle, however adequately, with the complexities involved in tackling environmental problems are factors that necessarily shape the policy-making process. And, increasingly, the role of international organizations in framing the environmental agenda of the world is coming into sharper focus. This role of IOs has begun to receive more attention in the scholarly literature as well (Porter and Brown, 1991; Haas, Keohane, and Levy, 1993). An important contribution of IOs to environmental policy-making and implementation processes lies in forging political and technical consensus about the nature of environmental threats and thereby establishing appropriate issues on the global agenda (Haas, Keohane, and Levy, 1993). IOs view themselves as being in the business of global governance, and as such, they tend to define the international policy agenda in holistic terms in order to reflect the "interdependencies among global processes and problems" (Ruggie, 1979-80:518). Through their ability to define the issues that constitute the collective policy agenda, IOs have been able to address the global problematique by initiating policies to address new areas of concern and by drawing attention to interdependencies and mutual vulnerabilities among issues (Ruggie, 1979-80).

What is surprising, however, is the dearth of both theoretical and empirical scholarship—with some prominent exceptions—on international organizations of all kinds. To begin to think seriously about international environmental policy, we need to understand better how such organizations function and, especially, the roles they now play in the environmental policy arena. Although there is no shortage of roles prescribed for international organizations in the literature, we need to move beyond a mere recognition that IOs are a significant feature of global politics. We need to focus on the qualitative participation of international organizations in global politics in order better to understand the nature and scope of those roles in international environmental policy and politics. Ecologically rational international environmental policy is certain to require extensive involvement of international organizations, including many yet to be created, in ways yet to be envisioned. And institutional and administrative change on this degree and scale will require fundamental reorientation, which will hinge on social, political, economic, and cultural changes.

International organizations are usually analyzed in the context of international relations (Claude, 1957), but this scholarship has ignored many of the most interesting questions about IOs.   Indeed, much of the literature vacillates between being purely normative or purely empirical, neither of particular use for international environmental policy.   It has virtually ignored the environmental problematique and has made only a few contributions to understanding international environmental policy development.   To understand the roles, functions, limitations, and potential of international organizations in environmental policymaking, we need to appreciate the broader context in which they act and the internal influences on their action—only part of which is addressed in traditional international relations scholarship.

Borrowing the concept of equilibrium from economic theory, Liska (1957:15) analyzed IOs "as part of a dynamic interplay of institutional, military-political, and socio-economic factors and pressures constituting a multiple equilibrium." The advantages of this concept were twofold: first, it placed developments in international cooperation among the broader forces at work in the international system, and second, it served as a tool for analyzing the internal forces at work within specific IOs.   Yet, more complex questions remain unaddressed. In the international realm, does policy determine politics as it often does domestically (Lowi, 1972)?   To what extent do economic, social, and cultural factors shape the functioning of IOs?   How do dominant societal myths, metaphors, and models structure the institutions we create? What political forces internal to international organizations prove significant for international environmental policy development?

We speculate in this chapter about answers to these questions and suggest an analytical framework for critically evaluating the place of IOs in international environmental policy.   Other chapters in this book address the pressing need to reconceptualize the agenda for international environmental policy theory and practice by bridging the gap between normative and empirical research.

INTERNATIONAL ORGANIZATIONS AND ECOLOGICAL RATIONALITY

Working over time, an array of forces woven together in complex patterns, not all of which are easily comprehensible, has resulted in systems, institutions, beliefs, values, and practices that work against ecological rationality. Notions of rationality vary, and popular understanding of rationality tends to view it in terms of economic or technical rationality, where the efficient achievement of a goal or a plurality of goals is the measure of the degree of rationality in, for example, a practice or an institution. Quite distinct from this is ecological rationality, "the rationality of biogeochemical systems, their integrity, maintenance, reproduction, evolution..., an order of interdependence, the interdependence of the biotic community." At heart, "it is a way of thinking about actions, about organizations, and about ultimate ends or values" (Bartlett, 1986a:234, 229). Functional ecological rationality[2] is evident in decisions and actions that result in maintaining a sustainable relationship between humans and the environment. Economic and technical, as well as social, legal, and political rationalities,[3] are indeed relevant and even necessary, but it is critical that ecological rationality have lexical priority in the (re)designing of institutions and values (Dryzek, 1987). It is ecological rationality that allows the "preservation and maintenance of ecological life support capability [that] makes possible the preservation and improvement of decision structures and, hence, political rationality and all other forms of rationality" (Bartlett, 1986a:235; see also Dryzek, 1987). Especially in the context of the ecological scarcity (Ophuls and Boyan, 1992) that frames the global reality today, ecological rationality necessarily needs to take priority to attain some form of steady-state society. This commitment to ecologically rational thinking requires in turn that the politically expedient foci of governments and institutions on the short term be replaced by a longer term perspective.

How, then, can IOs contribute to ecological rationality in the global system of governance, and how can ecological rationality be imbedded in IOs? Indeed, is ecological rationality at all useful in understanding the structures, functioning, and interactions of IOs?

For a long time, the rhetoric of states—still the most significant actors in the international arena—has played down the immensity of the environmental problematique. Environmental protection and sustenance has been, at best, one among many goals, an indulgence to be "grafted on to a growth economy" (Walker, 1989:32). Given the context in which international organizations have been created and must function—characterized by the preeminence and dominance of military power, national sovereignty, and economic rationality—perhaps it is not surprising that most have subscribed to an assessment of environmental issues that minimizes their seriousness and coherency.

International organizations were established and have evolved in the context of the modern system of nations, a system that is linked by the imperative of economic growth. Although some IOs have clearly delineated technical functions of knowledge generation and dissemination (the World Meteorological Organization, for example), the functions and goals of even the most seemingly innocuous agencies are framed by the politics of the global economy (see Chapter 5). It is a politics driven by the perceived need of states, as well as other units of the economy, such as multinational corporations, for economic growth. Technological developments and an increase in the desire for material welfare spurred the creation of IOs in order to govern and manage increased interaction and collaboration between people and institutions (Mitrany, 1943). Yet, as Redclift (1987:56) points out, "The concentration on growth has served to obscure the fact that resource depletion and unsustainable development are a direct consequence of growth itself." Indeed, the social, environmental, and ethical dimensions of sustainability are too often ignored in the debate on development.

Both capitalist and socialist systems are based on notions of resource abundance and, consequently, have focused efforts on maximum exploitation of nature. The political-economic paths that different nations have chosen are driven in large part by their search for maximum efficiency and consequent (economic and political) success (Ellul, 1964:183-84). The pressures of economic systems are such that, even in the unlikely event of nations wishing to stay out of the scramble for growth, they cannot do so; the coercive reality of survival and the interdependence of all nations ensure the continuation of an environmentally destructive system (Walker, 1989; Redclift, 1987). Furthermore, the increasing globalization and integration of markets exert a strong universalizing as well as centralizing force, resulting in the intertwining of economic and ecological interdependence (Hurrell and Kingsbury, 1992b; MacNeill, Winsemius, and Yakushiji, 1991). The problem finally remains as much the "system" as the nature of the state itself. It is fundamental to today's "technological society" that states be agents of centralization (Ellul, 1964:194). And, indeed, the modern administrative-bureaucratic state, with all its centralizing tendencies, is at the very root of the environmental problematique (Paehlke and Torgerson, 1990).

Weberian notions of bureaucracy saw the bureaucratic organization as a means to a greater rationalization of systems of production. The centralized hierarchical form, specialization of knowledge, and division of labor which characterize bureaucracies, as well as their persistence and ability to survive, are also the fundamental characteristics of the administrative state. The state goes beyond being merely a collection of organizations, of course. The modern administrative state refers to the entire society that is dominated by administrative institutions, hierarchical organizational forms, bureaucracies, and norms and values that go toward maintaining these institutions. Thus, the administrative state represents not just structure, but also the means and the process of taking and implementing decisions. Despite the currency and power of popular myths about the evils and incapacities of bureaucracies, and the ascendancy of "New Right" antibureaucratic ideology in both politics and social science scholarship, nowhere is the administrative state withering away.

Given the need to survive in a capitalistic world economic system, the state has always sacrificed the environment for economic growth (Walker, 1989). In a system that operates with a focus on the short term—indeed one that punishes planning and decisionmaking that veer from this norm—the state necessarily commits to the status quo. Governments, thus, "react to symptoms but seldom to causes which tend to be regarded with suspicion as possibly leading to 'subversive' changes" (King and Schneider, 1991:4). Indeed, the emergence of the environmental movement is itself a token of the failings of the administrative state which can be seen as largely responsible for creating and perpetuating the environmental crises the world faces today (Paehlke and Torgerson, 1990).

Just as nation states have inhered in themselves the contradictory roles of creating and maintaining economic growth while ensuring ecological balance through the management of resources (Walker, 1989; Redclift, 1987), so too do we find international organizations today caught in the bind of conflicting demands and expectations. Organizations that are primarily financial, such as the World Bank and the International Monetary Fund (IMF), are now called on to foster environmental protection. And even those IOs with exclusively environmental mandates, such as the United Nations Environment Programme (UNEP), find themselves having to pirouette in a world arena marked by tensions caused more by nations' perceived need for economic growth than by resulting environmental degradation. IOs are at least partly extensions of, and certainly modeled after, the successful organs of the administrative state. Most IOs are structured hierarchically with effective power concentrated at the top, thus affecting decisionmaking processes. Centralized decisionmaking and functioning, based on narrow notions of expertise and technocratism, are both undemocratic and exclusionary, offering little scope for the flexibility, openness, and non-compartmentalization critical to environmentally rational administration and policy (Paehlke and Torgerson, 1990:292-99).

Although international organizations share the commonality of being part of an interconnected global administrative system,[4] it would be wrong to assume that they are all alike. International organizations differ in the settings in which they operate, the power they wield, the forms of behavior through which power is exercised, their mandates, their structure and functions, their competence, and their significance to international environmental policy (E. Haas, 1990:63-96). As Feld and Jordan (1988:203) point out, "The domestic politics of member states interact directly on both the states' foreign policies and policies and politics of [intergovernmental organizations]," and this is especially evident in organizations dealing with aid and development (see Chapter 7). The diversity of IOs makes it difficult to generalize about their abilities to play effective and meaningful roles in the international environmental policy arena. It is conceivable, however, that in spite of the pressures of traditional concerns of sovereignty, economic growth, and so on, international organizations can "learn to think" ecologically (Taylor, 1984).[5] One manifestation of social learning of international institutions and IOs is the development of "heterarchy," or a decentralized structuring of institutions (Caldwell, 1988). Furthermore, IOs can contribute to greater ecological rationality in the global systems by paying greater attention to the potential effects of multilateral management when designing optimal responses to global problems.

To what extent, then, can organizations learn to be ecologically rational? Under what conditions are they capable of adopting strategies that are ecologically rational? Drawing on Selznik (1957), Taylor (1984:252) identifies four conditions necessary to institutionalize precarious organizational values and bring about change in bureaucratic thinking: "(1) a group inside the organization committed to the value, (2) goals clear enough to provide guidance for action, (3) autonomy and power for this group so that they can protect the value, and (4) outside support for the inside group's goals." One example of the potential for changing the thinking of *some* international organizations may be seen in the European Union, especially in its dealings with ozone depletion (see Chapters 3, 4, and 11). As scientific evidence grew confirming both the cause and the significance of the ozone hole, the political and environmental importance of the issue also expanded. Bureaucrats and environmental organizations worked within individual member states while UNEP, the United States, and sections of the world scientific community provided the external pressure to get the European Community[6] to commit to reduction in chlorofluorocarbon (CFC) use. In the same way, the capacity of the World Bank to learn environmental values has been facilitated by the increasing significance of its own Environment Department, the massive lobbying efforts of environmental organizations, the salience given to the environment by the media, and the World Bank's acknowledgement of the link between its developmental goals and environmental protection (see Chapters 6 and 7).

Less publicized and thus less acknowledged is the potential for IOs to change the thinking of national agencies. Change and learning may be fomented by international organizations both directly and indirectly. IOs have the potential to influence the behavior of national agencies and to shape national policy responses by performing three distinct functions: promoting concern about environmental threats among governments, enhancing the contractual environment by providing negotiating forums and disseminating information, and building national political and administrative capacity (Haas, Keohane, and Levy, 1993). International civil servants, furthermore, often participate in informal networks and linkages with national bureaucracies and political institutions that serve as channels of influence to bring about change. Thus, IOs can potentially develop and foster certain behaviors and actions that may prove key to bringing about policy change in the direction of more environmentally sound decisionmaking by national governments. UNEP's catalytic role in ozone control and reduction illustrates the central role an IO can play in providing leadership and mobilizing international consensus on environmental issues (Benedick, 1991a; see also Chapters 10 and 11). UNEP helped facilitate research on ozone and undertook "diplomatic groundwork" prior to signing the Vienna Convention and Montreal Protocol, both of which were crucial to the relative rapidity with which the negotiations proceeded (Benedick, 1991a:148). In addition, international organizations, in accordance with their different mandates, may foster issue linkages between political arenas that have an impact on national policies (see Chapter 13). Finally, international organizations such as the IMF and the World Bank may bring about change directly in national policies by their requirements for structural adjustments in order to qualify for loans and aid. The structural adjustment conditions, of course, are driven by notions of economic rationality and may prove environmentally disastrous in the long run. But such IOs may also increasingly require environmental protection and safeguards as a prerequisite to qualify for loans (see Chapter 6).

It is in this context that we may recognize environmental impact assessment (EIA) as an example of the kinds of reforms that are required over the next several decades to institutionalize "precarious" values (Taylor, 1984; Bartlett, 1990). Certainly, EIA has been adopted increasingly by international organizations as an integral part of the decision-making procedures. The Framework Convention on Climate Change, formulated by the Intergovernmental Negotiating Committee, requires all signatories to undertake environmental assessments of projects potentially affecting climate (see Chapter 12). The World Bank has required EIA of major projects on an ad hoc basis since 1984 and, more recently, has made it mandatory for all projects likely to have a significant impact on the environment (see Chapter 6). Agenda 21, one of the three principal official agreements achieved at the United Nations Conference on Environment and Development at Rio in June 1992, although not binding on nations, endorses the adoption and greater use of EIA (see Chapter 2).

But environmental impact assessment is only one potential mechanism or reform that might force international organizations to contribute to more ecologically rational international environmental policy. International organizations in addition to the World Bank and other funding agencies are in the process of changing the norms that govern their behavior, EIA being only one means for forcing and securing such change (see Chapters 2 and 4). Indeed, a primary focus of this book is an exploration of institutional change through organizational learning.

MYTHS, MODELS, AND METAPHORS

The push for economic growth alone does not explain away the paradox that, in the face of massive increase in knowledge about environmental problems and their causes, humans still adamantly cling to ways of life that are fundamentally unsustainable. As important as the institutionalized commitment to economic growth are the dominant belief systems—the myths and metaphors that frame our thinking, mold our actions, and provide the (often unacknowledged) foundations to the institutions we create. Myths are "the best term for those descriptions of the world every society provides to the people growing up in it, descriptions that locate them in the world and within their society. . . . [M]yths are shorthand, the things we never learned but we all know" (Dunlap, 1988:ix). The way we deal with the environmental problematique, thus, is shaped to a large degree by our conceptions of nature and environment—conceptions that are shaped by our cultural myths. It is an unfortunate reality that the representatives of nation-states who determine much international environmental policy, and some IO officials themselves, exemplify by and large a fairly simplistic understanding of environment as primarily a resource available for human consumption and utilization. At the same time, scientists, environmentalists, and others who do have a deeper understanding of the complex meanings of the environment are often limited by their relatively superficial appreciation for international politics and the real and potential role of international organizations in making environmental policy.

The term "myths," of course, has multiple meanings that can become more complex (and confusing) when considered together. As Brennan (1989:1-2) points out, "Myth as distortion or lie; myth as mythology, legend, or oral tradition; myth as literature *per se*; myth as shibboleth—all of these meanings are present at different times in the writing of modern political culture." In the realm of international environmental policy, a number of concepts and ideas may be best understood as myths in the sense of both distortion and legend that often have impeded the formulation of effective and meaningful international environmental policy. The legalistic notion of absolute national sovereignty, for instance, is a myth, a fiction that has hindered both the formulation and implementation of environmentally rational policy.[7] It can come in the way of appropriate international and transnational action to deal with environmental problems—problems that may not only be beyond the scope of individual national action but that may also go against the short-term political and economic interests of a country. National sovereignty manifests itself in the reluctance of states to contribute financially to international organizations, to sign and ratify international agreements, and to implement such agreements. Yet in the context of today's global economy and close economic links between various nations, absolute national sovereignty is both irrelevant and impractical (see Chapter 2; also King and Schneider, 1991). It still is a concept, however, that remains politically expedient for national governments, evoking as it does powerful emotions of patriotism and identity. It is this that makes sovereignty critical to the discussion of environmental policy generally, while hindering effective policymaking in a myriad of ways.

If the existence of absolute national sovereignty is a troublesome myth, equally problematic is the myth that international law (IL) does not exist as *law* because it is not formally, directly, coercively enforceable (see Chapter 9). The notion of the nonexistence of IL takes on a mythical life of its own, freshly reconstructed with each repetition of the idea. Debate on the source of obligation of international law, for example, has resulted in relegating the often intangible realities of law to the status of legal fiction, thus undermining the role it can play in environmental policy (Morgenthau, 1973; Hoffman, 1985). This reification of sovereignty and denial of the realities of international law are, unfortunately, advanced by both scholars and politicians.

Yet another example of a belief that has taken on mythic, even religious, proportions is a faith in science and technology as the source of solutions to all problems (Ehrenfeld, 1980). One consequence of technological and scientific "progress," for example, may be seen in the dilemmas posed by the "population problem" that the world faces today. Advances in medical technology and effective international public health measures, organized in part through the World Health Organization (WHO), have been responsible for the dramatically falling death rates that more than compensate for the slower decrease in birthrate. The optimism generated by science and technology—and by the "successes" of IOs such as the Food and Agricultural Organization (FAO) and the development agencies—has long fed the faith that humans' basic needs would be met without artificially limiting "exploding" populations. Population growth, of course, is but one example of the larger problematique technology poses for environmental protection and policy. Indeed, the notion of "sustainable development" itself is a myth that comes out of this blind faith in science and technology (Worster, 1993). Far from reflecting a real appreciation of what is truly sustainable, too often the availability of particular technologies is what influences the kind of projects and programs that get supported by international organizations, *irrespective* of their suitability to local conditions and needs (see Chapter 6). It is indeed a fundamental characteristic of the technological society that whether something is done is determined more by whether it can be done rather than by careful deliberation of whether it should be done (Ellul, 1964). Moreover, as Redclift (1987:51) argues, "Technology is not simply a means to harness nature in industrial society, it is also the instrument through which people can become alienated from nature."

Other important myths structure and direct interpretations of reality. For example, the rhetorical characterization that places all industrializing or nonindustrial countries in the Third World or the "South" and all industrialized countries in the First World or the "North" conveys a false notion of homogeneity within each such category. This portrayal of countries so vastly diverse in their cultures and socioeconomic and political realities in such dichotomized terms creates an oversimplified, fictitious notion of uniformity that comes in the way of formulating effective international environmental policy. There is also the myth that the benefits of economic development trickle down from the rich to the poor, from the North to the South. Yet, as the Green Revolution in India and elsewhere has shown, technological advances in agriculture and commensurate increase in food production continue to benefit the rich at the expense of the poor. Of poverty, malnutrition, and oppression, there is little sign of diminution (King and Schneider, 1991:24, 56).

In all this—in the creation of environmental problems of often indefinable magnitude, in humanity's gradual understanding of the earth as a biosphere, and in the development of possible (often partial) ecologically rational solutions to the environmental problematique—science and technology have played a powerful role. Critical to a realization of the profound implications science and technology hold for our understanding of the environmental problematique—and for the concept of sustainable development—is an appreciation of the intersections of science, culture, and our notions of nature.

SITUATING INTERNATIONAL ORGANIZATIONS: NATURE AND CULTURE

Can "development" be sustainable? Can we allow science and technology to sweep us indefinitely along in economic and political conquests of the unknown and yet allow the simultaneous survival of Nature? Most fundamental of all, whose values, cultures, and ideas of Nature should govern in defining sustainable development? Worster (1993:143) points out that sustainable development may be a dead-end road. Without an acknowledgement that the "progressive, secular, and materialist philosophy on which modern life rests . . . is deeply flawed and ultimately destructive to ourselves," environmental goals of saving biodiversity and the earth itself from human onslaught will never be attained. It is precisely this recognition that appears to be missing from the rhetoric of sustainable development. As Caldwell points out:

> [A] literal explanation of the word sustainable, unmodified, tells nothing about what is sustained other than the process of development, and says nothing about the level of environmental conditions to be sustained for how long, or at what cost, and to whom. (1990a:182)

Indeed, the logic of international politics is founded on unstated beliefs in climatic stability, resource abundance, and the ability of science to deliver knowledge and techniques needed for human survival (Orr, 1992:48). Missing is an understanding of the limits of the biosphere; to exceed these limits will inevitably result in a fundamentally unsustainable relationship between humans and Nature.

Our approach to environmental policy is framed significantly by the way that we conceptualize nature. Nature, seen in moral, religious, and aesthetic terms, requires and demands a policy approach sharply distinct from nature as merely a resource for human use or a subject for scientific investigation. Nature with a capital "N," symbolizing power and beauty, is far removed from "the environment" which has meant "the physical and biotic resource base for human sustenance and survival" (Sagoff, 1991:5-6). The profound impacts of humans on nature has been a consequence of, among other things, both modernity and the rise of modern science—the systematic, organized pursuit of research and the linkage of such research to technological development. With modernity has come the sense of displacement for the individual, the alienation from land which provided an identity, and a replacement of kinship and community (*gemeinschaft*) with the challenge of individual isolation in a modern society (*gessellschaft*) (Toennies, 1971). This is not to say that all premodern communities necessarily had sustainable relationships with nature.[8] History tells us otherwise. But certainly, modernity has brought additional burdens to humans' relationship with the environment, burdens that contribute to the mounting environmental crises of the modern era (Orr, 1979, 1992).

Modern science (and technology) has revealed itself as a two-headed creature with the potential to do both enormous good and profound evil. Caldwell distinguishes between the ability to invent and develop advanced technology and the ability to control it:

> Technological innovation depends on imagination, observation, intellectual
> and manual dexterity and particularly on a certain kind of aggressiveness
> or compulsion to dominate or control the elements of the environment.
> Control of the technology, on the other hand, is fundamentally self-
> control. It involves a special kind of imagination called foresight and
> requires prudence and restraint. (1972:88)

It is this lack of control, this absence of self-control in the use of technology, that manifests itself in the uncritical assurance and unexamined optimism with which technology is wielded. Encouraged by international funding agencies, such as the World Bank, the IMF, and the United Nations Development Programme (UNDP), Third World countries have set about constructing mammoth projects (the Aswan Dam in Egypt and the Sardar Sarovar Project in India, for example) that reveal yet again humanity's arrogant attempts to control a nature that can wreak both death and destruction. Nature is increasingly manipulated using science-based technologies; underlying this is a notion of nature as merely a thing to be utilized for humans' ends of wealth, security, and power.

Missing from this utilitarian conception of nature is an understanding of the functioning of the biosphere that consists of all life and the environment that supports it. Margulis and Lovelock (1974) have argued in their Gaian hypothesis that the earth is like a living organism that is to a high degree self-regulating and self-sustaining, with homeostatic capacities to withstand onslaughts on its integrity (also Lovelock, 1986). Human activity, although often self-destructive, is unlikely to affect fatally the survival of earth's biosphere itself, although it may change it profoundly. Harkening back to the notion that all things are interconnected in nature, the hypothesis offers a unifying interpretation of the organic and inorganic aspects of earth. Understanding Gaia and respecting it may prove to be the first step to an ethical and moral approach to our dealings with the environment (Caldwell, 1990a:54).

And it is the work of IOs over the last century that we have to thank for much of our understanding of global ecosystems (Caldwell, 1972).

At the same time, the temptation to subscribe to a naive environmentalism where nature is assumed to be "stable, balanced, homeostatic, self-healing, purifying, and benign, while modern humanity, in contrast, is assumed to be environmentally unstable, unbalanced, disequilibrating, self-wounding, corrupting and malign" needs to be avoided (Cronon, 1993:10). Underlying such a dualism are powerful metaphors enjoying cultural sanctity, where it is assumed that

> ideal nature is essentially without history as we know it . . . . that natural time is cyclical time, while the time of modern humanity is linear. Time's cycle is the proof of nature's self-healing homeostasis and equilibrium, while time's arrow is the proof of humanity's self-corrupting instability and disequilibrium. Humanity's arrow is the fall while nature's cycle is salvation. (Cronon, 1993:10)

Thus, superficial understandings of nature's inherent capacity for stability can result in human actions and behaviors that can be fundamentally unsustainable, while being culturally inappropriate (Cronon, 1993:14). The Gaia hypothesis, while suggesting that nature is self-correcting, also makes clear that nature's homeostatic processes are unlikely to be cognizant of issues of human survival. To what extent, if any, do we see a popular advent of such an understanding of nature?

> The idea that conservationists could never attain their long-term goals without paying attention to the needs of human populations, and that economic developers could not bring sustainable gains without facing up to the ecological conditions and the conservation requirements of the environments being affected by development, has been widely accepted by the conservation community. . . . [But] although many ecologists and conservationists have moved toward recognition of economic and social needs, relatively few economists and engineers have moved to recognize ecological limits or conservation needs. (Dasmann, 1988: 281-82)

Many actions and publications of international organizations such as the World Wildlife Fund (WWF), the United Nations Educational, Scientific, and Cultural Organization (UNESCO), UNEP, and FAO reflect this awareness of the interaction between human and ecological goals,[9] but it is far from being the guiding principles for the international financial and trade organizations and others.

POLICY ANALYSIS AND INTERNATIONAL ENVIRONMENTAL POLICY LITERATURE

Most of the scholarship on international organizations and environmental policy reflects a relatively limited appreciation for the politics of policy. During the post-World War II era, IO scholars did make initial moves toward policy sciences as reflected in their interest in process over structure, but they failed to pursue further inquiry and research in this direction (Rochester, 1986). More recent IO scholarship, in the 1980s and 1990s, has paid more serious attention to the contributions that IOs have made, and can make, in formulating and implementing international public policy (Jacobson, 1979; Dahlberg et al., 1985; Soroos, 1986; Untawale, 1990; Nagel, 1991). Much of the literature, however, has focused on describing events, taking a relatively atheoretical approach to international environmental issues.

An overemphasis on the structure of international organizations, the power play between nations using IOs as their fora, and on cooperation through the institutionalization of various regimes has resulted in ignoring the substantive policies produced or neglected. As a result, the field of IO scholarship has been dominated by empirical research at the expense of theoretical reexamination and new theorizing. Another important deficiency in IO scholarship is lack of serious attention to the effects of IOs in the processes of multilateral environmental management. There remains a tendency to ignore or downplay the limitations of such management by international institutions (Gallarotti, 1991). Any attempt to understand the role of IOs in international environmental policy must balance both the positive and negative effects of the multilateral management of the global environment. Given the complexity of international environmental policy, what is needed is extensive use of theoretical assumptions and perspectives that can be integrated with related work because of some commonalities in definition and purpose. Global policy studies is one example of a still evolving framework that has potential to facilitate integration of much existing IO literature. In general, there is a need for research based on the policy process approach and meta-policy traditions (see Chapter 14).

Unlike analycentric policy analysis, with its studied indifference to the politics of policy selection, the policy process approach focuses attention on the decision-making processes and makes clear that policy selection can be understood only in the context of other stages of the policy process (Bührs and Bartlett, 1993). Much of the work in the present volume falls within this genre of policy research. What is largely missing in the international environmental policy arena and is sorely needed is meta-policy analysis.[10] Evaluating the existing theoretical frameworks within international relations that are currently used to analyze international environmental policy is a first step (see Chapter 14). There is clearly a need for a comprehensive policy framework that can provide the social, political, and economic contexts within which environmental policy may be situated.

A meta-policy perspective views policy change as a consequence more of "cumulative social enlightenment, rather than the direct adoption of the recommendation of a single study" (Bührs and Bartlett, 1993:30). Thus Caldwell (1990a, 1990b) describes and analyzes the emergence of a planetary polity. And in Le Prestre's analysis of the World Bank's capacity for environmental learning, we see such a grappling with a meta-policy perspective (see Chapter 6). In the same way, the assessment of the need for organizational and institutional transformation in order for long-term environmental protection to become a reality reveals a meta-policy perspective (see Chapter 2). But, clearly, very little exists at this level of policy analysis in international environmental policy research. More fundamental and wide ranging work is needed.

Significant meta-policy theorizing about IOs and international environmental policy might be made from a feminist standpoint, for example. A feminist reconstruction of policy design reconceptualizes the issues of context, power, and partisanship, recognizing their centrality to policy analysis and design (Rixecker, 1994). Thus, understanding how a mechanistic worldview sanctioned the exploitation of nature and created a socioeconomic order that subjugated women in the West (Merchant, 1980) could pave the way for a more egalitarian international environmental policy design. International organizations consequently need to frame policies that take into account the context in which policies will be applied and that will allow the participation of "target populations" (Ingram and Schneider, 1993) traditionally ignored in international policy processes. Indeed, women's participation as policy analysts and in the decision-making process can shape in distinct ways the policy process (Kathlene, 1989, 1990). Thus, a fundamental restructuring of international organizations to facilitate greater participation of women at all levels and to integrate feminist perspectives in environmental policymaking is critical for ecologically rational policymaking. Furthermore, the link between women and environment, based on their material reality (Agarwal, 1992), is of particular significance in international environmental policy, given the intrusive roles international organizations play, especially in the Third World, that have implications for the environment. Industrial and agricultural projects having profound impacts on the environment have been promoted by international funding agencies. Such projects have resulted in the marginalization of women and have increased their poverty, dependence, and alienation from the productive processes (Sen, 1985; Shiva, 1988). Thus, integrating a feminist perspective into international environmental policy analysis might significantly transform the way we conceptualize both the policy-making process and ecologically rational environmental policy.

CONCLUSION

Like ecologically irrational social structures, systems of thought also perpetuate themselves. In a world of already existing paradigms, new research and new agendas for theory and practice can flounder. Institutional and systemic barriers exist. But these aside, the practical difficulties posed by scarce funding for research on IOs cramp anything but the most modest of research agendas. To begin to understand the organizational complexities of even one international organization calls for a significant investment of funds. Whereas national agencies have been studied in depth because of their perceived importance to the domestic policy-making process, the same is not true for IOs. Furthermore, few people can straddle both worlds—of academia and the practitioner world of the IOs. Thus, the valuable experience of IO officials rarely finds translation into critical analyses of the functioning of the organizations.

But if politics and institutions must adapt and change to grapple better with the environmental problematique, research and practice must address the centrality of ecological rationality. A shift in values, politics, and institutions—a move away from the self-perpetuation of old paradigms—may indeed be a perilous process. Yet, "the sport, it seems . . . is worth the candle" (Stone, 1988:310). The aspiration for ecological rationality—indeed even sustainable development despite its many flaws—drives our policy vision of a greener, better world.

NOTES

We thank Lynton K. Caldwell and Stefanie Rixecker for helpful comments on earlier versions of this chapter.

1. Soroos defines problematique as "an interrelated group of problems that cannot be effectively addressed apart from one another" (1993:318). Ophuls and Boyan define it as "an ensemble of problems and their interactions" (1992: 43).

2. Diesing identifies three phases or aspects of rationality (1962:3-4). *Substantial rationality* applies to individual decisions: "A decision or action is substantially rational when it takes account of the possibilities and limitations of a given situation and reorganizes it so as to produce, or increase, or preserve, some good." *Functional rationality* is characteristic of organizations that are structured "to produce, or increase, or preserve, some good in a consistent, dependable fashion." *Principles of order* underlie all concepts of rationality: "Decisions are made according to principles, and organized structures embody principles of order."

3. For a thorough exploration of these five rationalities, see Diesing, 1962.

4. The international system is not, of course, the only commonality IOs share. Ernst Haas points out that all IOs are faced with "situational constants" such as the unequal

distribution of power and the varying types of decisions they make. In addition, all IOs are seen to share behavioral constants such as "volatile domain consensus," conflicts within and among coalitions, limits on the discretionary power of executive heads, and so on (1990:ch. 3).

5. Dryzek points out that an ecologically rational human-nature system is "one in which humans and natural components stand in a symbiotic relationship" (1987:46). Given the complexity, uncertainty, variability, nonreducibility, and collective nature of ecological problems, ecologically rational social choice mechanisms need to be characterized by negative feedback, i.e., "deviation-counteracting input within a system"; coordination among actors both within particular collective actions and across different collective actions; robustness or flexibility, i.e., to have the ability to perform well across different conditions and to adapt if need be; and finally, resilience to withstand ecological stress over a period of time (1987:47-54).

6. Whether the European Union is an international organization is perhaps open to debate. It may be seen also as a form of supranational government. As the European Community prior to 1993, it certainly was a special kind of international organization and it is as an IO that it is taken in this book.

7. Besides, as Caldwell points out, "[T]he permeability of national borders to invisible agents of disease has never been remedied by declarations of national sovereignty. Closed borders and quarantines offer limited protection against invasive pathogens, but require costly vigilance; they did not keep out unrecognized and undetected microorganisms such as viruses that destroyed native elms in North America and vineyards in Southern Europe" (1990a:129).

8. Dasmann describes what he terms as the "invader effect" seen in the devastating effect on the biota when humans occupy new and unfamiliar ecosystems (1988:278). This same effect can also come into play when people having an otherwise sustainable lifestyle take up new technologies, especially when they are brought in from the outside. For example, the introduction of the horse into the American Plains Indian culture brought in a potentially destructive relationship with the bison herds, which never came to the test with the decimation of both the Indians and the bison by another invader, the European.

9. UNEP, for example, has adopted a broad interpretation of the environment in developing its mandate. It is concerned not only with the protection of nature and the biosphere but also with desertification, human settlements, urbanization, and so on. Using such phrases as "spaceship earth" and "only one earth," the participants of the 1972 Stockholm conference sought to present a holistic view of the global ecosystem and the interrelatedness of local, national, and regional components.

10. In policy research generally, the meta-policy perspective may be seen in the work of Bobrow and Dryzek (1987) who offer analysis of five frames of reference that have dominated policy analysis: welfare economics, public choice, social structure, information processing, and political philosophy. Diesing (1982), similarly, evaluates eleven schools of policy science in terms of the standpoint and perspective of each on public policy inherent in each of them. Stone (1988) and Majone (1989) argue that language is central to both public policy and policy analysis. Argument and persuasion determine the nature of policies and are thus fundamental to the policy-making processes. Indeed, for both Stone and Majone, argument and persuasion are central in bringing about institutional transformation.

2

Necessity for Organizational Change: Implementing the Rio Agenda of 1992

Lynton K. Caldwell

Implementation of Agenda 21 adopted at Rio de Janeiro by the United Nations Conference on Environment and Development (UNCED) provides an opportunity to review the demands that preservation of the biosphere and its human infrastructure will place on international institutions of governance.[1] The effectiveness of an institutional response to challenging circumstances depends not only on commitment to Agenda 21 objectives, but also on the suitability of the organizational structure necessary for its undertaking. A difficulty in implementing environmental policy in a world of nations is that no set of organizing principles or guidelines has been provided. The conference in Rio is an aspect of what Alexander King and Bertrand Schneider (1991) have called "the first global revolution."[2] The emergence of a global economy has necessitated the development of a global environmental policy in a world of nations adhering to the legal doctrine of sovereignty. There is growing recognition of the obsolescence of this doctrine—at least in its 17th century form. The scope of sovereign power has been relatively diminished by the rise of powerful multinational corporations and by the growing influence of nongovernmental environmental and human rights organizations. A supra or extranational structure for international policies appears to be emerging, but no clear pattern has as yet appeared. Therefore, before turning to the Rio conference and its accomplishments, I will briefly review the relationship between organizational structure and the prospects for achieving the goals of policy.

ORGANIZATION AS AN INSTRUMENT OF POLICY

Although organizational structure and behavior have evolved historically out of circumstances in a society—including the biosocial tendencies of its people—institutional changes (organization and behavior) do not necessarily keep pace with circumstantial change. Indeed, institutional conservatism appears to have characterized human societies generally. Over time, social organization responds to environmental changes by adaptive response. But the response has often been retarded or misdirected, resulting in the inability of institutions to function effectively. The causes of failure in organizational effectiveness are found in the circumstances that led to or induced them, including time, place, intraorganizational personnel or structural deficiencies, or irresistible external challenges, and an inability of a society or a culture to agree upon response to change.

Adaptive organizational arrangements for international affairs are not new to experience with governance. An example is the Hanseatic League of commercial cities, formed in AD 1241 as an alliance for trade between western and eastern Europe and asserting political power with its own army and navy (Schildhauer, 1985). Other quasi-political organizations for trade and colonization have arisen over the years, but they have ultimately been displaced or absorbed in the expansion of the functions and domain of national states. The 17th century and the era of the economic-political doctrine of mercantilism saw the rise of more extensive quasi-governmental commercial organizations. For example, the East India Company of England and the London and Plymouth Companies, for colonizing America, were antecedents of the modern multilateral corporation with authority to manage their business affairs and also exercise powers of governance in their respective territories. In the perspective of national states, the territory and operations of these organizations might have been defined as extranational; they were clearly more than nongovernmental. By the end of the 20th century, international organizations operating autonomously or under international control have proliferated in number and variety beyond easy classification. For many of these having political powers of coordination and governance the descriptive term "regime" has been applied, and a body of theory has been developed to explain their status and functions (Young, 1989b).

This diversity of organizational structures developed in response to the perceived inadequacies of the conventional national state. For some needs of the present era the structure and centralized jurisdiction of national states are inappropriate. For some sub-national activities centralized national agencies are too inflexible and too remote. And increasingly in recent decades the historical jurisdictions and limitations of national states have become maladapted to dealing with transnational and global affairs. At the end of 500 years of evolution, the adaptive capabilities of the historical national state appear to be inadequate to respond to accelerating changes in world circumstances. After centuries of seldom questioned dominance, the state appears to be approaching a primes inter pares relationship to organizations for governance—its absolute sovereignty attenuated in many ways. The multinational business organization has already acquired a power in international decisionmaking on economic and related issues that even the greatest states must now take into account.

During the 20th century the national state became the ultimate form of political organization. Vestiges of feudal, tribal, or theocratic organization were either absorbed by national states, or subjected to their hegemony (as in colonies or protectorates), or were accorded de jure national status (e.g., Singapore, Vatican City, and Luxembourg). Near the end of the 20th century, however, the conventional national state began to show signs of obsolescence. Especially after 1945, its extraterritorial functions were progressively supplemented by international and regional organizations (e.g., the UN specialized agencies), some of which were nongovernmental or quasi-governmental. Following establishment of the United Nations many of these organizations assumed a global character.

Independent national states have been characterized by their autonomy, authority, and legitimacy (i.e., by their jurisdiction and sovereignty). But these states were never exclusive forms of organizations for collective social purposes. Beyond the national state was the organizational structure of the Roman Catholic Church and of multinational empires (e.g., Austria, Great Britain, France, Russia, and Turkey). By the end of the 20th century, all of these multinational regimes had been dismembered, and the authoritative power of the Catholic Church over national governments had been virtually eliminated.

The dominance of the national state concept and its concomitant doctrine of sovereignty have hitherto obstructed the development of terminology appropriate to identify or designate nonstate or extrastate organizations exercising some restricted or unconventional functions of governance. Nevertheless, these exceptional organizations, within their own domain, may exert notable power even though they lack the jurisdiction of general government. The Rio conference and its preparatory phases demonstrated the increasing influence of nongovernmental organizations (NGOs) and intergovernmental organizations (IGOs) in setting agendas. It remained for national governments to act on what was proposed. But a political moral imperative had been established which implied that governments should consider the objectives of Agenda 21 regardless of how they might react to them.

UNCED: PRODUCT AND PROCESS

After three years of preparation, UNCED concluded two weeks of deliberation at Rio de Janeiro in June 1992. Perhaps the principal implications of the Rio conference for political organization were that national and international environmental policies can no longer be compartmentalized and that new organizational arrangements will be necessary.

The principal official agreements achieved at the Conference were the Rio

Declaration on Environment and Development, a Statement on Forest Principles, and Agenda 21 (United Nations, 1992b, 1992c). The declaration was a statement of twenty-seven principles to govern the rights and responsibilities of nations toward the environment. The legally nonbinding authoritative Statement on Forest Principles did not obtain the degree of consensus necessary for a formal convention. Agenda 21 was an action plan consisting of forty chapters to guide environment-related policies of government from the present into the 21st century (in the news media, often called the Earth Charter).

The conference was also the occasion for the signature of two treaties of organizational significance: the Convention on Biological Diversity and the Framework Convention on Climate Change (United Nations, 1992a, 1992e). The substance of these treaties—notably the latter—had been separately negotiated for some months prior to the Rio conference. They were open for signature at Rio but were not strictly speaking products of the conference. The associated Global Forum at Rio of NGOs from 150 countries produced forty-six "alternate draft treaties and declarations," the future significance of which is conjectural (Padbry, 1993:193-99). But they document a growth in public concern since the 1972 UN Conference on the Human Environment, and a recognition of national responsibility for protection of the life-supporting systems of the human environment and the biosphere. They may presage greater political receptivity to future organizational change. Many of these NGOs are linked internationally and are more committed to biospheric ecological objectives than to the legal sovereignty of their national governments.

The UNCED process of preparation and negotiation was not unique. Similar procedures preceded the 1972 United Nations Conference on the Human Environment, and these procedures are now becoming an expected way of negotiating major global agreements. The expectations of openness and public participation in defining agendas and negotiating compromises are especially demanded by nongovernmental citizens organizations and the news media.

The so-called UNCED process, with its antecedents in the 1972 Stockholm Conference and in subsequent treaty negotiations, has involved large numbers of volunteer organizations and concerned individuals. One reason for the greater transparency of these international negotiations from Stockholm to Rio may be that at national levels government officials, who are the duly constituted lawmaking authorities, are more cautious in proposing international agreements than are conference delegates who represent nations but are not necessarily official policy makers. In addition, through their presence and participation, NGOs from developed countries have given widespread publicity to official proceedings. International agreements must be returned to national legal authorities for ratification and implementation. Governments must take account of conflicting national interests and capabilities but can hardly help being influenced by the active participation of their citizens in conferences such as UNCED.

Participation in agenda setting and policy formulation by unofficial representatives of public interests (NGOs) has not been common to the political processes and ethos of most countries. Only recently has this NGO participation in international affairs (as distinguished from lobbying) become conventional in North America and Western Europe. For example, its role has been documented in negotiations leading to the Canadian-United States Water Quality Agreements. It is not surprising that NGOs entered into the debate over the North American Free Trade Agreement (NAFTA). Environmentally concerned NGOs sought to balance the primarily economic emphasis of NAFTA with a proposal to create a parallel North American Environment Commission (NACE) (Hudson and Prudencio, 1993; Ferretti, 1993).

The concept of citizen initiative in governmental and international affairs appears to be contagious and has been spreading even into countries traditionally authoritarian in governance. But while the era of exclusive official diplomacy may be over, the influence of NGOs should not be overdrawn. Their role in the UNCED process, although significant, often fell short of their more expansive ambitions, but they nonetheless attained a legitimate and recognized role in the United Nations system.

The strength of the NGOs was primarily evident among delegates from the more economically and technologically advanced countries, wherein public opinion and citizen action influence decisions as to what is desirable and feasible in the international relations of government and business. And in a globalizing international political economy, even governments hitherto indifferent to environmental knowledge and values may have to accede to environmental policies that are gaining acceptance among informed people throughout the world. With this new view of human-biosphere relationships has come concomitant change in policy and organization. A broadening of the scope of environmental policy has been advanced by the participation of NGOs in the policy-making process. Government organization charts that omit the increasingly official role of NGOs fail fully to describe political reality. Organizational change has followed from change in perspective on the responsibilities of government. The IGOs and NGOs do not enact laws or ratify treaties, but they do develop the research, the agendas, and the proposals before the policy-determining bodies of the nations.[3]

FROM PERSPECTIVES TO POLICY

That an attitudinal change has been occurring is evidenced by the representation of an estimated 178 countries at UNCED and the personal attendance of 110 heads of state. Attendance by nongovernmental groups (an estimated 1,400) exceeded any previous UN conference, and news media coverage was possibly double that given to the 1972 conference held in

Stockholm. A member of the United States delegation, Senator (now Vice President) Albert Gore, had written a widely publicized book, *Earth in the Balance* (1992), which clearly and forcefully articulated the biospheric paradigm. For an active politician to author a book advocating an international "Marshall Plan" for environmental protection and development would seem indicative of changing attitudes and values. Even should this book prove to be largely rhetorical, noncommittal declarations by politically prominent persons have often been taken subsequently as serious political objectives.

This widespread concern for an environmentally sustainable future, which influenced the activities at UNCED, seems certain to affect future national policies. Perspectives on global issues, which were translated into the policy objectives expressed in Agenda 21, were also implicit in the two treaties. As to be expected in multinational sociopolitical developments, some inconsistencies prevailed at Rio, and a few important issues received what some observers regarded as insufficient attention (i.e., population and energy). How Agenda 21 could be translated into cooperative policy was addressed only marginally at Rio, primarily in the proposal for a UN Commission on Sustainable Development.

UNCED may thus be most realistically seen as a milestone in a policy process begun at least as early as the 1972 UN Conference in Stockholm—earlier perhaps in the Biosphere Conference held in Paris in 1968. The UNCED process is definitive in that it will be difficult for future international conferences to achieve political legitimacy unless provision is made for openness and for participation of all major parties affected. Closed-session deals by diplomats and expert advisers may have greater difficulty than heretofore in obtaining national ratification. The General Agreement on Tariffs and Trade (GATT) and NAFTA negotiations have encountered resistance to ratification partly because of a perceived absence of public input. This suggests a relative weakening of special interests and bureaucratic exclusiveness in decisions on policy and organization where NGOs are aroused and committed.

By keeping in mind the sociopolitical context of UNCED regarding (1) the scope of issues and of conference participation, (2) the factor of time in the environmental impact of human activities, and (3) the changing paradigm of humans' relationship with Earth, we may more fully comprehend its implications for political and organizational implementation. But implications are neither prognoses nor predictions. They represent real possibilities—even trends—but unforeseen factors may alter their prospects.

With regard to the transboundary, multilevel implications of Agenda 21, UNCED has accentuated and accelerated trends already discernible in international relations. More than ever, policymaking at every level must take account of interactions with other levels—national, regional, provincial, municipal, and international. International policies are usually initiated and must be confirmed at national levels, but in environmental issues the distinction between domestic and international considerations is rapidly becoming blurred.

The interconnectedness of various levels of governance on transnational issues implies change in the ways in which most public organizations have operated.

Agenda 21 depends for its implementation on national action, often affecting policies once regarded as wholly domestic (e.g., agriculture, forestry, indigenous people). Developed countries will be under growing pressure to assist capability building in developing countries (Agenda 21, chapter 37). Policies regarding foreign aid and international technical assistance will be under pressure to respond to existing realities rather than, as formerly, expressions of national, largely political, ideologies and abstract economic theories. Developing countries may be expected to resist conditional assistance that is not supported by demonstrable findings of environmental science. Some governments may reject conditional assistance even when it is supported by conclusive evidence. But NGOs are now more likely to oppose development projects by donor governments or intergovernmental agencies (e.g., the World Bank, the United Nations Development Programme, and regional development banks) that degrade the environment or disrupt the lives of people. They are also becoming aware that the organizational structure of these development agencies is not only intended to implement their original policies but also to perpetuate them even in the face of professed reform. Internal organization of the UN specialized agencies will doubtless need reexamination to obtain the coordinated action required by many of the provisions of the Rio objectives.

Local and regional components of governments (e.g., provinces, states, municipalities, river basin authorities) will need to take account of national treaty obligations when developing and administering their policies. This is already a necessity under the Constitution of the United States; international treaties may supersede conflicting statutory laws or ordinances. In time, the ubiquity of many environmental problems (e.g., atmospheric transport of pollutants, oil and chemical spills in boundary waters and international seas, and transport of hazardous materials) will tend to force a harmonization of relevant policies and laws among all levels of government; this will force organizational change.

The push toward common or comparable standards for environmental policies may be felt most directly by international business. But business interests also are among the promoters of uniformity in environmental laws and regulations—especially to prevent or to reduce trade restrictions. This effort usually has been directed toward modifying or removing environmental laws and regulations regarded as restrictive to international trade. But legalistic and bureaucratic complexities and jurisdictional conflict and inconsistencies at all levels—especially in international affairs—may pose even greater handicaps to national-global cooperative efforts than do laws and regulations per se.

Policy makers at national and intergovernmental levels are now facing conflicts generated by the simultaneous growth of the free trade and environmental movements. Conflict is prevalent between advocates of economic and trade priorities and those defending environmental and consumer protection, labor standards, public health, and preservation of biological species.   In principle, these conflicts need not be irreconcilable; in practice, they often are.

Indications of political problems that implementation of the Rio agreements may encounter is obtainable from experience with other environment-related treaties or agreements.   A case in point appeared in the *New York Times* on Monday, 14 April 1990.   A full-page appeal, entitled "SABOTAGE! of American's Health, Food Safety, and Environmental Laws—George Bush and the Secret Side of Free Trade," was endorsed by twenty-one nongovernmental civic action organizations including the Sierra Club, Greenpeace, the Humane Society of the United States, and the National Consumer League.[4]   As previously noted, the opposition was intended to arouse citizen concern to possible environmental and legal consequences of NAFTA and the Uruguay Round of GATT.   The NAFTA structure as originally designed addressed only economic objectives.   Environmentally concerned protesters insisted on an independent organizational arrangement within or paralleling NAFTA, such as a "balancing" NACE.

Perhaps the objectives and priorities of GATT and NAFTA can be reconciled with the goals and values implicit in UNCED.   Compromise rather than reconciliation or synthesis seems more likely because two different sets of assumptions and two dissimilar paradigms are in confrontation. The Declaration of Rio represents a broad, albeit sometimes indeterminate, public commitment. The trade agreements represent a much narrower but more explicit set of objectives advanced by interests having an "inside track" in the course of national policymaking.   The initial settlement of this controversy may not be its final resolution.

BALANCE OR SYNTHESIS?

The grand purpose of UNCED was to reconcile environmental and developmental (primarily but not exclusively economic) objectives in national and international policymaking.   In this effort the objective could be either balance or synthesis, but the organizational implications of the choice between the two are not the same.   Balance suggests compromise—so-called splitting the difference—with each side giving up something to reach an agreement that is in essence political.   Policy balance might be achieved—albeit often against resistance—within existing organizational arrangements.   But synthesis may require reorientation of entire organizations or the establishment of new organizations partially or completely displacing older structures.

The UNCED objectives in the Declaration of Rio, the associated treaties, and Agenda 21 are heavily influenced by scientific findings or hypotheses which neither easily yield to political or economic expediency nor facilitate the balancing of competing objectives.   This is notably true of Section 2 of Agenda

21, "Conservation and Management of Resources for Development." The implications for organization are both internal and external to the structure of the national state system.

The UNCED process of compromise was necessarily political and required the concurrence of national governments. The role of science was more implicit in the formulating of policies to achieve UNCED objectives than is explicit in the actual text of its documents. Given the diversity of nations, and their innate bureaucratic conservatism, agreement on principles or goals is more attainable than agreement on action to be taken. Not all UNCED objectives are supported by scientific evidence, yet in action to realize most of the substantive objectives some measure of scientific information is required. In the absence of science and science-based technologies, UNCED objectives that would alter established arrangements would not be readily attainable. Without persuasive scientific evidence, defensible operational strategies would be difficult to devise and the popular credibility needed to support organizational innovation would be difficult to obtain.

Governments everywhere are confronted by the perceived necessity for choice among trade, finance, and economic growth along with a multiplicity and variety of environmental problems. The outcome of policy choice cannot be predicted with assurance, but if the numbers of people affected and the pressures of organized citizen response prove to be politically decisive, trade agreements may not be sustainable unless modified to accommodate environmental, public health, demographic, and quality of life (e.g., cultural) considerations. Conversely, environmental policies may not be defensible if they are unnecessarily obstructive of generally beneficial and sustainable development processes.

As Agenda 21 is implemented by national governments and international organizations, institutional means to attain coordination and consistency among policies will be necessary. Establishment of the UN Commission on Sustainable Development (Agenda 21, chapter 38) and reform within the Global Environmental Facility (associated with the World Bank) indicate a trend toward institutional restructuring. The aphorism that "you can't solve problems through reorganization" may give way to a realization that complex, interrelating sets of problems will not be resolved by uncoordinated, unplanned action. In any case, public (and business) policymaking will increasingly be compelled to deal with the complexities and interrelatedness of the problems of the world. And if the risk of policy failure is to be reduced, the linear programming that has characterized domestic policies must give way to multiplex efforts.

Agenda 21 is probably as specific in its 40 chapters as any action plan could be when the action must take place in more than 170 different countries with different political, social, and environmental circumstances. Beyond inevitable compromises, the concept of a holistic future-oriented global perspective was implicit in the documents presented to the delegates at Rio. The prime minister of Japan, Kiichi Miyazawa, put the results of Rio in perspective when he declared, "The joint endeavor to protect the global environment has only just begun." In an opinion editorial for the *Earth Summit Times*, he wrote,

> The Rio Declaration and other policymaking agreements reached at the Conference on international cooperation in the field of the environment and development constitute an important first step in the effort to attain sustainable development. Even more important, however, is how effectively we translate the political will demonstrated in Rio into action to save our planet. This, I believe, must be the yardstick by which the success of the Conference is to be measured. (Miyazawa, 1992)

To conjecture how each of the forty chapters of Agenda 21, or the treaties on global climate change and biodiversity, will specifically affect policy and organization would be impractical. The Agenda 21 action plan is nonbinding and may be implemented in different ways in different countries toward a common objective. The treaties signed at Rio are legally binding under international law but will doubtless require protocols in the course of their implementation. Much depends on the course of change in popular attitudes. Policies may also be influenced by scientific assessments of probability and risk yet to be made.

Some generalizations are feasible, however, regarding the orientation of policymaking insofar as national and international organizations undertake to implement Rio commitments. The growing influence of NGOs over environment, consumer, and health policies suggests that it will not be easy for governments to satisfy their constituents with only rhetoric. In addition, the environmental trends and problems that shaped the substance of the Rio conference will not disappear, and science will seldom offer arguments that would support inaction. Yet action may be slow in coming, and uneven in degree among nations. Issues more immediately pressing may be expected to receive higher political priorities—especially those involving economics and ethnic conflict.

From the Rio provisions one may deduce two sets of propositions regarding the legitimate options of policymakers in the future. Although seldom expressed in explicit guidelines, the Rio provisions provide, in principle, a conference consensus regarding what governments ought to do and ought not to do. If put into practice, the obligations implied at Rio would represent a significant reinterpretation of the traditional sovereign right of a nation to do as it pleases with its own natural resources and economic assets. Although the Rio Declaration asserted a state's sovereign right to exploit its own resources in accordance with its own policies without harming the environment elsewhere (Principle 2), the assertion contained a significant qualification. Many acts of government, both of commission and of omission, do harm the environment of other states or of areas beyond the limits of national jurisdiction.

The principle of international law that a nation should not use its territory to harm its neighbors has been given an enlarged relevance as science documents the migration of pollutants throughout the biosphere, the effects of massive deforestation, and the consequences of desertification. The principle of sovereignty is now paralleled by the principle of a nation's responsibility for the custody and care of its environment and for the effects of its actions on the biosphere.

Under international law, as it stands today, a nation may not lawfully permit environmentally damaging activities or events within its territorial jurisdiction to override international boundaries to the harm of other nations. Accidents within one state, such as the nuclear event at Chernobyl, are matters of international concern and have led to treaties to cope with such circumstances. Less dramatic but chronic transboundary pollution has also resulted in international agreements at different jurisdictional levels—in some cases, modifying existing organizational arrangements. International protective measures (e.g., inspection and quarantine) have long been used (with uncertain effectiveness) to prevent the transboundary transmission of plant and animal diseases.

In these measures the national sovereignty principle has been tacitly modified for common advantage—that is, participating nations have merged their sovereignties. A no less critical but more sensitive concern is the massive transboundary migration of people seeking relief from economic deprivation or politically motivated genocide. The transboundary migration of humans en masse may have environmental implications no less disturbing than the transboundary movements of other living organisms and pollutants. Many people may regard this observation as irrelevant and inappropriate, but such reaction more than likely reflects a perception of human life and the environment that places humankind outside of nature—a belief sometimes called "exceptionalism." That humans and their numbers, actions, and pathologies (social and physical) are everywhere relevant to the environment because they are an integral and dynamic part of it is a conclusion uncomprehended by a large part—probably much the greater part—of humanity. As of today, the doctrine of national sovereignty, although no longer in fact absolute, is still dominant in political ideologies everywhere. People may have a "sovereign right" to impoverish their own environment, but do they have a sovereign right to seek refuge in other countries having brought their own to socioecological bankruptcy?

Because protective measures are often expressed as positive obligations, the distinction between *do* and *do not* is often a matter of the way that an issue is presented. The more effective use of impact analysis—environmental, economic, and social—is likely to reveal hitherto unrecognized or unadmitted causes of environmental degradation and to clarify linkages and relationships among environmental, economic, and social issues.

Among the preventive measures expressed in Agenda 21 are assessments of impacts upon the environment and the monitoring of environmental effects and changes. These obligations were clearly set out in Chapter 35, "Science for Sustainable Development," and in Chapter 4, "Information for Decision Making." Endorsement of the adoption and improvement of environmental impact assessment and the advancement and dissemination of scientific information appear directly or by implication throughout Agenda 21.

Techniques of information gathering and analysis were repeatedly recognized as necessary to the formulation of rational and realizable policies for environmentally and economically sustainable development. More than ever, open communication and adequately informed judgment will be regarded as requisite for acceptable legislative and administrative decision making. This expectation has implications for the education, appointment, and promotion of public officials, for the staff support required, and for relationships among legislative committees, administrative agencies, and the worldwide scientific community.

Obligations to protect the life support of the planet—atmospheric, terrestrial, and marine—and to conserve biodiversity were major themes of the UNCED documents. They have been implicit in many prior treaties and declarations, and especially in the report of the World Commission on Environment and Development (Brundtland Commission), *Our Common Future* (1987). Responsibility for the conditions of human life was emphasized notably in the Rio Declaration and was also prominent in draft treaties prepared by NGOs. A notable departure from the historic practices of governments was a declared obligation in Agenda 21 to respect and protect indigenous peoples (Chapter 26). But can this resolve be implemented if abuse, even genocide, of people under national jurisdiction continues to be viewed as an internal national affair in which external international interference is impermissible?

There was little new that governments (as distinguished from nations) were obligated by UNCED documents to refrain from doing. The historic principle of international law, *pacta sunt servanda* (treaties should be obeyed), was, however, given more than moral obligation in provisions to discourage noncompliance or negligence in treaty obligations. Agenda 21, Chapter 38, "International Institutional Arrangements," and Chapter 39, "International Legal Instruments and Arrangements," dealt particularly with issues of monitoring, reporting, compliance, and dispute prevention. The Commission on Sustainable Development was established by the UN General Assembly in December 1992 to monitor and report on progress by governments and international organizations toward the goals of Agenda 21 (Centre for Our Common Future, 1992b). Reporting and publicity can be effective means for obtaining compliance with declared commitments. Public officials everywhere try to avoid embarrassing disclosures. For flagrant violations by intransigent regimes, however, rhetorical measures may not be enough.

Even before Rio the $1.3 billion Global Environmental Facility was established in 1990 to help finance environmental prospects in developing countries. Jointly managed by the World Bank, the United Nations Environment Programme, and the United Nations Development Programme, it is a new intergovernmental institutional facility which may play an important role in implementing Agenda 21 (World Bank, 1990b).[5] A possibly more significant development planned for 1994 under the leadership of the United Nations Fund for Population Activities (UNFPA) was the United Nations International Conference on Population and Development (ICPD) (Centre for Our Common Future, 1992c). This conference is certain to involve many NGOs and UN specialized agencies. It is premature to speculate on what organizational changes, if any, it is likely to generate at the international level. Changes at the national level are more probable. In the Global Climate Change and Biodiversity treaties, action by governments would be necessary to guide or prevent behaviors that will be harmful to the environment and the biosphere.

In the Rio documents, as often happens in international agreements, controversies were frequently avoided or obscured by ambiguous or innocuous word choices. Ambiguity and the choice of words or phrases that could be read in more than one way without offending sensibilities were sometimes the price for obtaining agreement. In many cases, as in the Convention on Global Climate Change, the objectives were strongly worded, whereas the obligations to act and the timetables for action were deliberately left vague. On some issues representatives from developing countries insisted on the "right rhetoric" even though modified or contradicted by obligatory commitments. An example of euphemistic substitution was the use in Agenda 21, Chapter 5, of the term "demographic dynamics" instead of "population trends." In time, follow-up regional conferences may lead national governments to more explicit national and international policies for interrelating aspects of population, environment, quality of life, and economic development.

In brief, despite some national sensitivities, the UNCED agreements moved forward the conditions and processes of policymaking toward increased reliance on scientific information and analytic methods. Greater involvement of popular representation in decisionmaking, and much broader consideration of the consequences of policies and decisions, suggests a movement toward forms of organization more appropriate to objectives. Greater and more use of environmental impact assessment recommended by Agenda 21 may be anticipated. Environmental impact analysis has already been adopted in some form by eighty-seven different countries. But moving *toward* is not being there *now*. In an opening address to the conference, Secretary-General of the Conference Maurice F. Strong declared,

The Earth Summit is not an end in itself, but a new beginning. The measures you agree on here will be but first steps on a new pathway to our common future. Thus, the results of this Conference will ultimately depend on the credibility and effectiveness of its follow-up. (United Nations, 1993)

POLICY-DRIVEN ORGANIZATIONAL CHANGE

Organization is always an agent of policy. Yet organizational structure does not always reflect its declared purpose. Ulterior motives in government and international affairs have sometimes resulted in organizations designed for ineffectuality. This may happen when governments, for whatever reason, are obliged to adopt policies that they oppose or fear may harm their interests. Multilateral agreements requiring organizational implementation almost always require compromise among the parties. Organizational change may be driven by sub rosa policies protective of bureaucratic or nationalistic reasons having little or nothing to do with the substance of the agreement per se. But where there is recognition that national needs and interests can be served only by multinational cooperation, nationalistic introversion has given way to a transfer of some part of traditional sovereignty to transnational authority.

Most organizational changes needed to implement Agenda 21 do not involve a major departure from multilateral organizations already in place. Regional organizations internal and external to national states are functioning with varying degrees of effectiveness. Multinational river basin authorities and coordinative organizations for transnational enclosed and coastal seas have been established by bordering states and have also been initiated by the United Nations Environment Programme. Policies for the protection and preservation of plant and animal species and of natural ecosystems almost invariably require some form of regional organization. The distribution of species and ecosystems seldom corresponds to the boundaries of political jurisdiction. Where multinational regional environments are studied and monitored for ecological conditions and trends, some form of international organizational arrangement is necessary. The United Nations Educational, Scientific, and Cultural Organization (UNESCO) program of biosphere reserves exemplifies an organizational response to a policy based on scientific evidence.

In summation, UNCED and Agenda 21 continue and extend international organizational trends that have been in effect for several decades and that have precedents as far back in time as the emergence of the national state itself. International organizations will almost certainly increase in numbers and diversity. Some policies once regarded by nations as domestic or internal affairs will be shared with other states or international organizations. Some areas of policy may be ceded altogether to international organizations. Nuclear energy may become an international responsibility beyond those aspects already internationalized. It is more likely that existing international programs will be strengthened and extended than that unprecedented forms of multilateral cooperation will be established, although innovations not now foreseen may become necessary—Antarctica and the outer space environment are possible candidates.

The national state is unlikely to "wither away," but its status and jurisdiction will continue to be modified. Regime theory and bioregionalism will gain practical significance as efforts are undertaken to implement Agenda 21. To describe the political geography of the future, a series of transparent overlay maps will be necessary. Transnational structures for nongovernmental scientific and technical functions will have international political implications, as they already do. Questions of funding, programming, allocation of responsibilities, and personnel policies will arise and must receive answers that people and their governments will regard as authoritative.

Ascertaining national compliance with treaty commitments has always been uncertain. Hitherto, official international organizations felt obliged to accept at face value whatever national governments reported. But some NGOs undertook their own unofficial investigations (e.g., Greenpeace) and publicized violations of treaty obligations. There has been wide recognition that some system of monitoring and reporting of national performance is necessary to achieve the purposes of international agreements. Access to "on the ground" observation and freedom from censorship or from denial of access are essential to the effectiveness of any monitoring system. Currently NGOs may be the most reliable source of monitored information. Several years ago a legal system for monitoring performance of treaty obligations was proposed to the judicial committee of the intergovernmental Organization of American States (OAS). Monitoring is now anticipated to be a function of the UN Commission on Sustainable Development.

Obstacles to these efforts persist in the doctrine of national sovereignty when invoked by governments to avoid exposure of their own dereliction. Observation by satellite is a powerful technical means of preliminary monitoring and greatly assists IGOs and NGOs in estimating a large number of transboundary and global environmental trends—for example, in desertification, deforestation, pollution of air and water, weather phenomena, urbanization, and changes in land use. International and nongovernmental organizations seem destined to play important roles in monitoring and reporting on the health of the planet.

Will "world society" in the 21st century construct a sociotechnological polity the complexity of which exceeds the ability of humans to administrate? For example, what kinds of popular sovereignty or democracy will be possible to guide and hold accountable organizations whose functions few people understand? How much time and attention can citizens give to a system of governance of unprecedented complexity and technicality? And because organizations for various purposes will inevitably overlay mosaics of cultural diversity, how can ethnic differences be reconciled to obtain consensus sufficient to achieve common policy objectives?

Governance at any political level is more than a legal or technical process. This reality is today widely acknowledged in the so-called private sector, and organizational changes are being introduced to allow for sociological, psychological, and biological factors that were largely unrecognized or discounted in the past. Government generally has been slower to respond to the maladaptations of contemporary society and to a growing though insufficient understanding of social behavior.

Organizational structure obviously makes a difference. The skeletal structure of the human body permits erect posture and hands that can manipulate. Organization charts describe the formal structure—the skeleton of an agency or a government. But they no more describe the way an organization operates than does the articulated bony structure of the human body tell us how the human individual functions. Organizations, unlike organisms, may be restructured to better meet new challenges. New organizations may be invented by rational choice free from the relatively slow and random selectivity of organic evolution. But conflicting rationalities may compete in organizational change. Psychosocial factors, such as power, prestige, wealth, individualism, and the values of independence add to a normal human aversion to altering familiar arrangements and relationships.

The multiple city-states of Renaissance Italy may be in many ways seen as a microcosm of the present world of nation-states. The failure of the Italians to devise appropriate institutions for governance resulted in social and political failures for which their high achievements in the arts and humanities and even in economics (e.g., in banking) were unable to compensate. Observing this state of affairs and its disastrous consequences for Italy moved Niccolo Machiavelli—the founder of modern political science—to write:

> The ruin of states is caused . . . because they do not modify their institutions to suit the changes of the times. And such changes are more difficult and tardy in republics; for necessarily circumstances will occur that will unsettle the whole state. (Machiavelli, 1518)

NOTES

1. Among the readily comprehensive guides to and accessible assessments of UNCED are: *Environment* (1992); *Environmental Policy and Law* (1992); *IUCN-World Conservation Union Bulletin* (1992); United Nations (1992d); Robinson, Hassan, and

Burhenne-Guilmin (1992); Yost (1992); and *Colorado Journal of International Law and Policy* (1993).

2. King and Schneider call attention to the "rising role and effectiveness of national and international NGOs in various fields" (1991: 15).

3. See, for example, Woods (1993); Centre for Our Common Future (1992a); Finger (1991); Manno (1992); and *Environment* (1992). For a more general view of institutional complexity, see French (1992).

4. See full-page appeal against GATT and NAFTA in the *New York Times* (1992) and the *New York Times* (1993). See also United States Congress (1991) and United States Congress (1992).

5. See also bulletins issued by the Global Environment Facility.

3

Environmental Policy and the European Union

John McCormick

Because many environmental problems are transnational by nature, they cannot be addressed effectively by individual countries acting alone. Recognition of this reality has led in the last twenty years to notable progress in international responses to such problems as acid pollution, whaling, and the management of shared rivers, lakes, and seas. But agreement on environmental policy at the international level continues to suffer at least two basic handicaps.

First, most governments have so far proved unwilling to give significant powers or support to international environmental organizations. The many problems (constitutional, financial, and otherwise) experienced by the United Nations Environment Programme come readily to mind in this regard (McCormick, 1989b:109-14). Second, governments are inclined to put the short-term interests of their domestic electorates and economies above the long-term interests of the global environment. And because the costs of environmental regulation are often seen to compromise comparative economic advantage, few governments are willing to take unilateral action.

Against this background, one productive channel for the resolution of international environmental problems may lie in regional economic integration. As nations become more dependent upon international trade and foreign investment, and reach the compromises that allow them to be more closely tied into regional and global economic systems, so parochial concerns about loss of comparative economic advantage may diminish. At the same time, the trade distortions created by differing environmental standards will become more obvious, and national governments may be more inclined to take collective action and come to agreement on common policies. In the case of the European Union (EU), formerly the European Community (EC), this has already happened.

Originally created to help rebuild Western European economies after World War II and to promote common security, the influence and authority of the EU has broadened in recent decades to affect a growing number of policy areas within the fifteen member states.[1] The problems experienced in achieving ratification of the Maastricht Treaty on European Union has blinded many to the fact that the Eu has made remarkable strides in the past decade, moving well beyond the Europessimism and Eurosclerosis that prevailed in the early 1980s. It is now widely recognized that Europe was "relaunched" with the Single European Act of 1986 (SEA), which led to the creation of a single internal market on 1 January 1993. In order to abolish the barriers to the movement of goods, capital, people, and services that finally made this possible, nearly 300 new pieces of legislation were agreed to, EC institutions were given new powers over policymaking, and the jurisdiction of the EC was extended to new policy areas that were not anticipated by the authors of the founding treaties.

Among those new areas was environmental protection. On the basis that different environmental standards would pose a barrier to the achievement of the single market, the SEA made environmental policy an explicit constitutional interest of the EC (Vandermeersch, 1987; Sbragia, 1991). Despite the fact that EU action is restricted to problems and issues better addressed at the EU level than at the member state level, the EU has since encouraged member states to strengthen environmental standards where domestic pressures may otherwise have failed. Not only has the SEA hastened progress toward the development of a more cohesive European Union environmental policy, but it has even been suggested that the work of the EU may pave the way toward the development of pan-European environmental policies common to the EU *and* non-EU European states (Schultz and Crockett, 1991:301-19).

I argue that, given the overall goals of European integration, policy on environmental issues that directly affect competition and that transcend national frontiers is better made at the EU level than at the level of the member states. The gradual transfer of authority over environmental policy from the member states to the EU has thus been inevitable. The EC is developing a record as one of the most effective international organizations in the field of environmental policymaking and implementation. Given the logic of neofunctionalism, regional economic integration may be a promising channel for the resolution of transnational environmental problems in other parts of the world.[2]

NEOFUNCTIONALISM AND THE ENVIRONMENT

As Stephen George notes, neofunctionalism dominated studies of the EC in the 1950s and 1960s, was abandoned in the 1970s, and has not yet been replaced as a predictive theory of integration (George, 1985:16-17). Robert Keohane and Stanley Hoffmann (1991:75) suggest that the standing of neofunctional theory is related to the standing of the EC or EU in the eyes of Europeans; neofunctionalism went out of favor when the EC stagnated in the 1970s and came back into favor with the "relaunching" of Europe in the mid-1980s.

Writing during World War II, David Mitrany (1943) argued that world peace could be promoted by creating a series of specialized international agencies with responsibilities for specific technical functions; if governments would hand over responsibility for these functions, they would gradually enmesh themselves in a web of international agencies and regulations, reducing the likelihood of conflict. These ideas were developed by Leon Lindberg, Ernst Haas, and others in the 1950s and 1960s as neofunctionalism (Lindberg, 1963; E. Haas, 1964, 1968). In the absence of any subsequent and stronger theories of integration, neofunctionalism has recently undergone a revival. Two particular aspects of neofunctionalism are of interest for present purposes: functional spillover and supranational institutionalism.

Functional spillover implies that if states integrate one sector of their economies, technical pressures will lead to the integration of other sectors (George, 1985:21). Joseph Nye defines spillover as a situation in which "imbalances created by the functional interdependence or inherent linkages of tasks can press political actors to redefine their common tasks" (1971:200). In the case of economic integration, the integration of one sector (say agriculture) will work only if other sectors (say transport and agricultural support services) are integrated, thereby leading to spillover.

In his study of the European Coal and Steel Community (ECSC), Ernst Haas noted the "expansive logic of integration" inherent in the ECSC (1968:283). The ECSC was created in 1952 partly for short-term goals (such as a desire to encourage Franco-German rapprochement), but its founders—Robert Schuman and Jean Monnet—explicitly saw it as the first step in a process that would lead to European political integration (Urwin, 1991:44-46). Supporting the notion of spillover, Urwin observes that the sectoral approach of the ECSC proved problematic because it "was still trying to integrate only one part of complex industrial economies, and could not possibly pursue its aims in isolation from other economic segments" (1991:76). Hence it was only six years after the creation of the ECSC that agreement was reached among its members to achieve broader economic integration when the European Economic Community came into being in 1958.

Article 100 of the 1957 Treaty of Rome provided for the harmonization of member state laws in the interests of promoting a common market. During the 1960s and 1970s, most notably through mechanisms such as the Common Agricultural Policy, the reach of integration—and of EC authority—expanded. Harmonization and spillover were given their biggest boost with the SEA, which extended EC authority to a number of new areas, including the environment. A 1980 decision by the European Court of Justice had already noted that competition could be "appreciably distorted" without harmonization of environmental regulations (Case 91/79, *Commission vs. Italy* [1980] ECR 1099, 1106). Applied to the SEA, the implication was that the single market could not be fully achieved without such harmonization.

Another form of spillover that neofunctionalist theory does not address relates to the effects of integration on raising standards. In what might be termed technical spillover, disparities in standards can lead the member states of the EU to rise (or sink) to the level of the state with the tightest (or loosest) regulations. Although poorer EU countries in an earlier stage of economic development (such as Greece and Portugal) may argue that environmental controls amount to a handicap, making it more difficult for them to catch up with their wealthier partners, the decision-making process in the EU nevertheless leads countries with the strongest environmental laws (such as Germany and the Netherlands) to accelerate the adoption of tighter controls by the poorer states. The SEA allows member states to adopt environmental protection measures that are stronger than those of the EU, provided they do not interfere with trade.

The second aspect of neofunctionalism that is of interest is supranational institutionalism, a concept which suggests that international institutions and transnational interest groups play a vital and increasing role as integration proceeds (Keohane and Hoffmann, 1991:75). The example of the environment meets the terms of Ernst Haas's description of supranational integration as including a "demonstration by a resourceful supranational executive that ends already agreed to cannot be attained without further united steps" (1968:xiii-xiv). The European Commission has long made such an argument, hence agreement was reached, for example, to give environmental policy constitutional status with the SEA. In the case of the environment, national interest groups have played an important role in drawing the requirements of EU law to the attention of member governments, and links between them have strengthened as they have increasingly appreciated the importance of working at the EU level.

THE EUROPEAN UNION AND THE ENVIRONMENT

Since World War II, politics and economics have both taken on an international flavor of unprecedented and probably irreversible proportions. Many domestic policy decisions are now being taken not by national governments working in isolation, but as a result of international negotiation and compromise. Many of these decisions come as a result of international economic trends, bilateral or multilateral negotiation, or discussion through intergovernmental organizations (such as the UN system and the General Agreement on Tariffs and Trade [GATT]). With the European Union, West Europeans have gone farther by creating a (so far) unique form of supranational government, submitting themselves to a new level of international legal authority.

The EU is the only international organization in the world with the power to adopt policies binding on its members. Since the mid-1970s, it has been at the heart of the most concerted program being undertaken anywhere in the world to replace national environmental controls with international regulation: to date, more than 250 environmental controls have been adopted by the EU (Crockett and Schultz, 1991:301-19). These cover issues as diverse as lead in fuel (1978 and 1985), sulfur dioxide and suspended particulates (1980), lead in air (1982), emission of pollutants from industrial plants (1984), nitrogen dioxide (1985), pollution from large combustion plants (1988), environmental impact assessment (1988), and vehicle exhaust emissions (1989). Of the EU directives that have been adopted or proposed in the last decade, twelve relate to water pollution, fourteen to energy conservation, twenty-one to waste management, and twenty-four to air pollution.[3] This level of activity is all the more surprising considering that the environment was a relative latecomer to the EU policy agenda.

The environment was not mentioned in the 1957 Treaty of Rome which founded the European Economic Community. In fact, the EC did not formally agree to the need for a community environmental policy until the October 1972 Paris summit of heads of state and government (held shortly after the landmark UN Conference on the Human Environment in Stockholm). In 1973 the European Commission adopted its first Environmental Action Programme, and it has since adopted a new program every five years; the fifth was published in 1993. The goal of these programs was initially remedial and a call for the harmonization of policies; more recently, the emphasis has been on prevention and the creation of new policies (Vandermeersch, 1987). EU policy is now driven by a belief that environmental protection is a precondition for sustainable economic development and by a desire to remove trade distortions (Commission of the European Communities, 1990a:20).

Article 130 of the Single European Act spelled out the goals and principles of EC (and subsequently EU) environmental policy, pointing out that action is subject to the principle of subsidiarity. In other words, the EC would take action on the environment where the objectives could be "attained better at the Community level than at the level of the individual Member States." Article 130 stipulated that community action should be based "on the principles that preventive action should be taken, that environmental damage should as a priority be rectified at source, and that the polluter should pay." Article 130T notes that EC measures would not prevent member states from taking more stringent measures of their own, provided only that they do not amount to discrimination or a disguised restriction on trade. The SEA also outlined the need to integrate environmental standards with other community policies. As preparations for the single market accelerated in the late 1980s, so did the program of harmonizing environmental policies, and the body of EC environmental legislation grew.

A further boost was given to EC environmental activity in the late 1980s with the strengthening of public support for environmental protection. A

Eurobarometer poll in 1988 found that EC citizens ranked the environment above finance, defense, or employment as an issue of EC concern, and a 1989 European Commission poll revealed that 75 percent of EC citizens felt that pollution was an "urgent and immediate problem" (quoted by Crockett and Schultz, 1991:169-91). A June 1989 Eurobarometer poll showed that 77 percent of EC citizens felt that environmental protection was a policy area better addressed jointly by EC states than by member states alone (Commission of the European Communities, 1990a:21). Meanwhile, Green parties won growing support in most member states; thirty Green members were returned from seven EC countries in the 1989 European parliamentary elections, when British Greens won a remarkable 15 percent share of the vote (but, thanks to the math of winner-take-all, no seats) (Mackie, 1990:21). By 1995 Green members sat in the national legislatures of ten EU member states (McCormick, 1995).[4]

In May 1990, the European Council agreed in principle to create a European Environment Agency (EEA) and a European Environment Monitoring and Information Network (Westbrook, 1991:257-73). The EEA was not to be a regulatory agency along the lines of the U.S. Environmental Protection Agency (EPA), but rather was to gather data in order to provide the European Commission and the member states with the means to take effective environmental protection measures (Council Regulation (EEC) no. 1210/90 of May 7, 1990). It would have no direct power to compel any member state to take any kind of action on the environment (Westbrook, 1991:257-73). Although the structure of the EEA was decided immediately, a decision was not made on the precise relationship between the EEA and either the member states or the other EC institutions.

Ironically, while the EC member states disagreed over what powers to give the EEA, and even over how much support the Agency deserved, the EEA concept won considerable support outside the EC. Apparently following neofunctionalist logic, former German foreign minister Hans-Dietrich Genscher argued in 1990 that a pan-European environmental agency could be a valuable part of the process of building the Conference on Security and Cooperation in Europe, while several East European states and members of the European Free Trade Association expressed an interest in taking part in the work of the EEA (Westbrook, 1991:257-73). The EC responded by offering EEA membership to non-EC states, and made environmental protection part of the mandate of the European Bank for Reconstruction and Development (Schultz and Crockett, 1991:169-91).

Although joint environmental policymaking has made great progress, the record with implementation is less heartening. Despite the large number of environmental laws adopted by the EU, many have not yet been implemented by the member states. A 1989 report revealed that Spain was the worst transgressor, having implemented only 79 percent of EC directives; Denmark had the best record, having implemented more than 98 percent of the directives

(Commission of the European Communities, 1990b). Crockett and Schultz explain the poor implementation record in terms of differences between northern and southern states (i.e., richer and poorer states), variations in the types of environmental problems from one state to another, and "philosophical and functional" differences in the regulatory programs and systems of member states (1991:301-19).

Liberatore explains the record in terms of a lack of financial and technical resources, and organizational problems within EU institutions (1991:281-305). She notes the problems created by two "implementation gaps": between the passage of EU law and its incorporation into the national law of member states, and between incorporation and implementation at the national level. One such implementation gap relates to the failure of countries to implement EU laws by particular dates, which Haigh et al. (1986) argue can be blamed on the failure of the negotiators of directives to appreciate the difficulties of fulfilling the obligations they are undertaking.

Further explanations for the poor record on implementation lie in the fact that most EU legislation has to date focused on developing policies rather than on developing the means for implementation and enforcement. EU law also seems to leave the power of implementation solely with member states (although, given apparent contradictions in EU law, this issue is still actively debated) (Crockett and Schultz, 1991:301-19). Furthermore, given that the EU is still evolving and that debates continue to rage about its real nature and about the powers that member states are prepared to accede to the EU, the uncertainty over its environmental powers is hardly surprising.

EFFECTS OF EU ENVIRONMENTAL POLICIES ON MEMBER STATES

Despite the fact that not all EU regulations and directives have been equally applied in the member states, several commentators have argued that the environment has proved to be one of the more successful of the policy areas in which the EU has been engaged (see, for example, Freestone, 1991:135-54). Even British Eurosceptics agree; speaking in 1992, the then commissioner for the environment, Carlo Ripa di Meana, observed that "the only EC policy that has won much sympathy in Britain is environmental policy" (*The Economist*, April 25, 1992:60). There is evidence to suggest that EU policies have brought changes where they might not otherwise have come, and that—along neofunctionalist lines—the agreement of common policies has led to spillover and to the strengthening of pan-EU institutions and decision-making processes. The effects of EU policy are particularly notable in three areas: harmonization of environmental standards, harmonization of policy-making processes, and changes in the relationship among the EU, national governments, and environmental interest groups.

Harmonization of Standards

The creation of a European common market has always ultimately depended on the agreement of common standards among EU countries. The process of environmental harmonization in particular was given a notable boost with the creation of the internal market in 1993. In order to prevent distortions in trade flows, unfair competition, and barriers to the free movement of goods, capital, people, and services, common standards have been adopted, for example, on the quality of drinking water, bathing water, and water for freshwater fish; levels of various pollutants in water; toxic waste disposal; levels of air pollutants such as smoke and sulfur dioxide; lead in gasoline; pesticides; and noise pollution.

Technical spillover has come where standards have been set sufficiently high in one country that they have obliged other member states to adopt stronger standards than they might otherwise have done. This is well illustrated by the issue of acid pollution, where policy changes in (West) Germany encouraged the EC as a whole to adopt more stringent policies, which in turn obliged Britain (previously unwilling to take action) to reduce its pollutive emissions.

In 1982 the West German government, in the wake of new evidence of growing acid pollution damage to West German forests, and in the light of the growing popularity of the Green party (McCormick, 1989a), abandoned its long-held opposition to controls on sulfur dioxide (SO_2) and nitrogen oxides (NO_x), the primary components in acid pollution. Concerned that its unilateral action would compromise the competitiveness of German industry by imposing upon it the burden of the cost of pollution control, West Germany also began lobbying through the EC for community-wide SO_2 reductions. The European Commission produced a series of proposals on pollution control, aimed at developing a comprehensive program of community legislation on air pollution.

Meanwhile, the Thatcher administration refused to acknowledge that acid pollution was a problem in Britain, or that action should be taken to bring it under control. Rather, it argued that there was a need for more research and greater scientific certainty. This decision was taken despite reports published during 1984 by the Royal Commission on Environmental Pollution, the Environment Committee of the House of Commons, and the House of Lords European Communities Committee. All subjected the policies of the Thatcher administration to close scrutiny and to criticism. The Commons and Lords reports argued that enough was known to justify the development and application of pollution control technology (Royal Commission on Environmental Pollution, 1984).

In 1988 the EC agreed upon a directive on large combustion plants, thereby committing all member states to major reductions in emissions of SO_2 and NOx. While this change of heart can be ascribed in part to worsening British relations with Norway and Sweden (recipients of much British pollution), the growing weight of scientific evidence, visible damage to British forests, and pressure from parliamentarians and interest groups, the decisive event was undoubtedly the adoption of the EC directive and the obligation imposed on Britain to meet its terms.

Changes in the Policy-Making Process

The second major consequence of EU membership has been to harmonize the environmental policy-making process in the twelve member states. Britain again provides a good example.

Unlike the United States and Germany, which rely on enforceable air quality and emission standards, Britain has relied on flexibility, consensus, consultation, and tailoring standards to meet the particular circumstances of specific polluters and the local environment. Arguing that government should interfere as little as possible with industry, while at the same time trying to placate public opinion, it long relied on the use of the "best practicable environmental option" to prevent pollution (Ashby and Anderson, 1981). It also relied on the principle of voluntary compliance, whereby pollution control agencies saw themselves as being in a partnership with industry, and relied on the "good public sense" of industries to implement control measures, rather than forcing them using the threat of prosecution (Elsom, 1987). Meanwhile, in order to make voluntary compliance and the partnership between industry and regulators work, pollution control arrangements were shrouded in secrecy.

The combined effect of these approaches to pollution control was to restrict pollution issues to private rather than public negotiation and to limit public debate about air and water pollution. Although British environmental interest groups were active in countryside conservation issues, few paid much attention to pollution or felt any need to change the system; Vogel noted that there was "no significant domestic pressure to change the way British pollution-control policy is either made or enforced" (1986:101).

EU membership has had a notable effect on how British pollution policy has been debated, designed, and implemented. First, the harmonization of environmental standards throughout the union has led to the establishment in Britain for the first time of uniform air and water quality standards and the standardization of pollution control procedures; thus Britain has had to comply increasingly with the standard-setting policies of its EU partners. Second, the need to comply with EU law has made pollution control a public issue, and for the first time has drawn widespread public attention to the parlous condition of Britain's water. Third, as pollution policy has become a public issue, so the traditions of secrecy, negotiation, and voluntary compliance have been diminished.

The EU and Environmental Interest Groups

In the absence of effective government responses to environmental problems, interest groups have often provided not only the pressure for change, but also the scientific data upon which change is based and many of the ideas upon which policy is based. This has been as true in most Western European countries as in the United States, and is becoming increasingly true of the EU. The second half of the 1980s saw new offices being opened in Brussels by groups such as Friends of the Earth, Greenpeace, and the World Wide Fund for Nature—all interest groups with international interests. (Other groups have employed full-time lobbyists rather than open full-time offices in Brussels.) George argued that, "with the exception of agriculture, there has been no marked tendency for pressure groups to operate at the Community level rather than at the national level" (1985:27). This was explained, he argued, by the fact that different national interests did not find it easy to agree on what was in the interests of their particular sector, and by the fact that the commission had not emerged as the major actor in the EC decision-making process.

The situation today is very different. Not only are national environmental groups in Western Europe broadly agreed on their collective interests, but the commission (especially under the presidency of Jacques Delors) has achieved a new dynamism and prominence. This fits with neofunctionalist ideas of a central institution that can "assert itself in such a way as to cause strong positive or negative expectations" (E. Haas, 1968:xiii-xiv). Additional developments have encouraged environmental groups to play a central role in the policy-making process.

First, given its preference for dealing with European-wide organizations, the commission has actively encouraged interest group formation at the union level (Daltrop, 1986:189). At the planning stage of new legislation, the commission solicits the help of interested groups in drafting proposals. It asks the groups for factual and statistical information, and seeks their opinion on potential support for—or opposition to—its proposals. Daltrop argues that this process has developed to the point where consultation has become an integral part of the legislative process (1986:185). Interested groups are given the opportunity to comment on draft legislation at almost every stage in the process. This may slow down the process of decisionmaking, but it also encourages active lobbying.

Groups also fulfil an active role at the implementation stage, monitoring the compliance records of member states and informing the European Commission of transgressions. In 1984 the European Commission received only eleven complaints from interest groups, local authorities, members of the European Parliament, and private individuals; by 1990, the number had grown to 450 per year (Commission of the European Communities, 1990a:31).

Second, union membership has given environmental groups new outlets for lobbying, mainly in the form of the European Commission, the European Parliament, and the European Court of Justice. The commission is the key point of access for the lobbyist, so interest groups try to win representation on commission consultative committees and to establish long-term contacts with commission departments (Daltrop, 1986). Particularly since the institution of direct elections, the European Parliament in Strasbourg has become an increasingly important point of access, mainly because of its powers to amend or delay commission proposals. In the case of countries lacking a constitutional court system—such as Britain—union membership has given interest groups access to a weapon they did not have before: judicial review. By appealing through the European legal system to the European Court of Justice, groups can bring more pressure to bear on national governments to implement EU environmental laws.

The utility of the EU differs according to the extent to which environmental policies have been strengthened in each member state. For groups in Britain, where the national government has made relatively few concessions on domestic environmental issues until recently (McCormick, 1991), Brussels is increasingly seen as a "court of redress" and a means of outmaneuvering the government (Baldock, 1989). Baldock suggests that groups in most continental countries are more ideological, more concerned with trying to "win hearts and minds," and less concerned with being involved in the mechanics of individual projects. German environmental groups, he argues, "prefer writing radical pamphlets, and not dirtying their hands dealing with official bureaucracies. They don't tend to know what goes on in Brussels, and actually see the Commission as a threat to good environmental practice in (West) Germany" (Baldock, 1989).

Third, among the environmental groups that have turned their attention to the EU, there has been an increasingly systematic approach to Eurolobbying, and a clear trend toward seeing domestic environmental problems as part of union-wide problems. This has in turn encouraged domestic groups to work more closely together and to form transnational coalitions. One study of U.S. interest groups concludes that coalition building is often necessitated by the complexity of an issue being addressed, and that coalitions can play a central role in influencing how much public attention is given to an issue. Cooperation may take place at different stages in the policy process and will often be determined by the nature of the issue being addressed (Schlozman and Tierney, 1986). Given the breadth and complexity of international environmental issues, the motives for coalescing have been compelling.

One such European coalition is the European Environmental Bureau (EEB), an umbrella body for national interest groups operating in the fifteen EU countries. The EEB was founded in 1974 with the active encouragement of the European Commission (Daltrop, 1986:111) as a conduit for the representation of environmental interest groups to the community, particularly the European Commission. By 1991 the EEB represented 120 national environmental groups with a combined membership of 20 million (Hagland, 1991). While it enjoys much support among groups, it has suffered consistently from financial problems. Haigh (1990) notes the difficulties emerging from an internal debate about the functions of the EEB: whether it should serve the needs of its members or carry out independent lobbying.

Partly because of the limited utility of the EEB, and partly because of the new realization of the importance of the union as a policy-making institution, environmental groups have opened new offices in Brussels, which has in turn tended to undermine the ability of the EEB to speak on behalf of union environmental groups. Despite this, the bureau is still important as an umbrella group, and Baldock (1989) and Lowe (1989-90) see a long-term tendency toward the creation of more European networks of organizations, at both the voluntary and statutory levels.

CONCLUSIONS

At a time when Eurosceptics point to the problems that the European Union is facing in adopting common economic and foreign policies, it is often forgotten that the European Union has successfully proceeded with policy integration in a number of areas. Among the most successful of these has been the environment. Membership in the EU has had a substantial effect on how environmental policy is made and implemented in the fifteen member states and has led to a significant improvement in the breadth and depth of environmental regulation.

The changes to domestic policy in the member states come at a time when it is increasingly recognized by policymakers that economic development and environmental protection are not mutually exclusive, but rather mutually supportive. The drive toward economic integration and the single market in the EU has given a new prominence to the importance of rational environmental policies and has shown how the removal of trade barriers between countries can happen only if environmental standards are harmonized.

By reducing the disparities between "lead and lag" nations, economic and political integration has brought about improvements in environmental management and quality more quickly than might otherwise have been the case, and has compelled EU member states to agree to common environmental regulations. The drive to integrate economic and agricultural policies has raised the need to harmonize environmental regulations in order to reduce the technical barriers to integration; this has been a clear example of functional and technical spillover at work.

At the same time, there has been a clear trend in the EU toward member states steadily giving up authority over environmental regulation to EU institutions, a trend that has wide public support. The need to remove technical barriers to integration has encouraged the development of supranational institutions, again much as predicted by neofunctional theory.

Neofunctionalism suggests that regional cooperation among countries promises a quicker and more effective resolution of transnational environmental problems than any other approach, at least among countries with similar political systems and similar levels of economic development. Isolated national approaches may be handicapped by fears of a loss of competitive advantage; bilateral or multilateral approaches have proven to be effective only if limited to selected issues of mutual concern, such as the management of shared rivers, lakes or oceans; broader global approaches are handicapped by the increased likelihood of disagreement and deadlock and by the lack of competent authorities with the powers to promote and enforce regulation. Given the extent to which the causes and effects of environmental problems do not respect national frontiers, the EU model may provide the only effective response to such problems.

NOTES

1. The Treaty on European Union, which came into effect in November 1993, created a new European Union, of which the European Community was a part. This chapter uses the term "European Community" in describing specific events before November 1993, but otherwise uses the term "European Union." After January 1995 the fifteen member states of the EU were Austria, Belgium, Denmark, Finland, France, Germany, Greece, Ireland, Italy, Luxembourg, the Netherlands, Portugal, Spain, Sweden, and the United Kingdom.

2. Other experiments in integration include the North American Free Trade Area (three members), the Andean Group (five members), the Latin American Integration Association (eleven members), the Central American Common Market (five members), the Caribbean Community and Common Market (ten members), the Arab Common Market (four members), the Economic Community of West African States (sixteen members), and the Preferential Trade Area for East and Southern Africa (fifteen members).

3. Regulations and directives are the two strongest legislative tools available to the EU; the former are binding in terms of their goals and the methods of achieving those goals, whereas the latter are binding in terms of the goals but not the methods.

4. Greens from Belgium, France, Germany, Italy, the Netherlands, Portugal, and Spain won seats in the European Parliament in 1989. Green representatives sit in the national legislatures of Austria, Belgium, Finland, Germany, Greece, Ireland, Italy, Luxembourg, Portugal, and Sweden.

4

Policymaking in International Organizations: The European Union and Ozone Protection

M. Leann Brown

The policy foci and priorities of international organizations are perpetually in transition in response to changing global conditions and problems arising among and within constituent units. New manifestations and interpretations of perennial policy concerns require policy innovation. Old issues are replaced by new policy concerns. For example, the United Nations (UN), the World Bank, the International Monetary Fund, the Organization for Economic Cooperation and Development, and the European Union (EU) have now incorporated environmental priorities among their more traditional objectives.

How do new issues reach the agendas of international organizations? How are policy alternatives delineated? What processes within international organizations characterize issue selection, policy alternative identification, and decisionmaking? These questions acquire greater import as increased global interdependence and the end of the Cold War have led to a proliferation of problems requiring the attention of international organizations.

Although theoretical understanding of policy formulation and innovation in international organizations is rudimentary, recent efforts have focused on issue areas, regimes, collective goods problems, and organizational learning. A significant literature has emerged relevant to these processes in the context of pluralistic government in the United States. Synthesizing theories include Hofferbert's open-systems framework (1974), Ostrom's rational actors within institutions approach (1986), Kingdon's policy streams framework (1984), and Sabatier's advocacy coalition framework (1988).

Among these perspectives, two interpretations stand out: those that focus on the importance of *values, beliefs, knowledge,* and *learning* and those that assign primacy to *power interests* and *political interactions* as sources of policy. To emphasize either to the exclusion of the other, however, is to forfeit understanding of important aspects of policymaking. If policymaking is conceptualized as the interaction of actors within and outside of formal organizational structures for solving problems and allocating resources, all tangible and intangible assets brought by participants to the process may affect policy outcomes. "Power" assets, such as organizationally conferred authority and legitimacy and economic and military resources, are most commonly associated with political interactions. Yet, less tangible factors, such as problem solving and ambiguity amelioration capabilities, ideas, information, and the ability to persuade, associated with organizational "learning," are also important assets in policy-making processes.

I hypothesize that agenda setting, policy alternative delineation, and decisionmaking in international organizations derive from an issue-specific amalgam of learning and other more overtly "political" interactions. European Community (EC) policymaking between 1974 and 1990 to end the production and consumption of chlorofluorocarbons (CFCs) is examined as a "best case" of learning dynamics at work within international policy-making processes because of the prominence of scientific information and experts in the deliberations. Paul Sabatier's model, which conceptualizes policy output as a consequence of advocacy coalitions' learning and other political interactions, will be employed to structure the data. Learning and other political dynamics figure in EC agenda setting, policy alternative delineation, and decisionmaking to affect ozone protection. Policy experts—the epistemic community—are a source of learning within advocacy coalitions. The activities of the EC commission and members acting in the capacity of council president offer a test of Sabatier's hypotheses regarding the importance of policy brokers in policymaking.

The evidence suggests that, in this case, EC agenda setting and policy formulation were initiated and catalyzed by information and pressures generated by the scientific community, non-EC governments, other intergovernmental organizations, and the public within nongovernmental organizations (NGOs) in response to these data. But, individual member-state (hereafter member) interests—primarily a reflection of the influence of industry and domestic politics—and intracommunity political dynamics determined the pace of EC action and the ultimate substance of the decisions.

LEARNING AND POLITICS WITHIN COALITIONS AS SOURCES OF POLICY

The primary proposition of Sabatier's model is that policy decisions derive from the evolution of beliefs and preferences through gradual enlightenment and political interaction among competing advocacy coalitions. An advocacy coalition is "a time-limited organization in which there is a convergence of interest on the part of a number of. . . individuals and organizations, and an interaction around furthering these common interests" (Dluhy, 1990:10). Coalitions are distinguished by their policy beliefs, resources, and the strategies they advocate. They compete to translate their beliefs into policy through mobilizing political resources, including ideas, information, and analysis. They may challenge the opposing coalition's beliefs, data, and policy proposals. When confronted with opposing perspectives, a coalition will vigorously defend its fundamental policy beliefs. Secondary beliefs, such as those about cause-and-effect relationships or policy prescriptions, are more easily compromised (Jenkins-Smith, 1991:162-63). Policy innovation is likely to require coalitional interaction over substantial periods of time (Stewart, 1991:172).

"Policy brokers" are also posited as essential actors in Sabatier's policy-making model. These individuals or groups may hold views approximating those of the coalitions, but they also facilitate negotiation, identify compromises, and coordinate the selection of policy options. Brokers may be as concerned with system maintenance as with achieving particular policy goals. Brokers within and between organizations are a likely source of policy options. They may have special intellectual and communication skills that allow them to learn even as coalitions talk past each other. Thus, brokers are able to identify compromise policy positions and play pivotal roles in arranging policy compromises (Organ, 1971). Policy decisions ultimately derive from the interaction of the coalitions' policy beliefs, strategies, and resources and the role of brokers in the process. A modified version of Sabatier's model is depicted below (Sabatier, 1991:154).

Policy Subsystem

Coalition A	Policy Brokers	Coalition B
a. Policy beliefs		a. Policy beliefs
b. Resources		b. Resources
c. Policy prescriptions		c. Policy prescriptions

Policy Decisions

Although Sabatier's model does not incorporate these distinctions, separating policymaking into stages facilitates understanding of the process. Different combinations of learning and other political interactions characterize agenda setting, policy alternative identification, and decisionmaking. One might also expect coalition actors to exert varying levels of influence during successive stages. For example, technical experts and the entire policy community are usually involved in setting the organization's agenda and in generating policy alternatives whereas only political leaders possess the authority to make decisions (Kingdon, 1984:4).

A further augmentation to Sabatier's model will be an explication of the role of policy experts as members of advocacy coalitions. Recent literature focusing on learning in international organizations has identified the "epistemic community" that exists both within and outside of formal organizational structures as an important actor in policy-making processes. Epistemic communities are "network(s) of professionals with recognized expertise and competence in a particular domain and an authoritative claim to policy-relevant knowledge within that domain or issue-area." Community members may be scientists or academics, interest-group analysts, governmental or intergovernmental personnel. They have

> shared causal beliefs, which . . . serve as the basis for elucidating the multiple linkages between possible policy actions and desired outcomes; . . . shared notions of validity--that is, intersubjective, internally defined criteria for weighing and validating knowledge in the domain of their expertise; and . . . a common policy enterprise--that is, a set of common practices associated with a set of problems. (Haas, 1992b:3)

Epistemic community members interact with each other in the domestic and international context; policy alternatives circulate among them. They test their ideas by presenting papers, publishing articles, holding conferences, consulting, and drafting and promoting legislative proposals. A highly cohesive community possesses common ways of thinking and communicating that are powerful resources in policy advocacy. Members of the policy community may or may not agree on a single proposal; more likely they will produce a short list of alternatives worthy of serious consideration. After some diffusion, there is a take-off point after which many people discuss a given proposal. Consensus spreads throughout the community and the proposal becomes orthodox thinking (Kingdon, 1984:122-24, 146-48).

Epistemic communities play an increasingly important role in policy formulation on national and international levels because decisionmakers need technical information to deal with complex issues and the uncertainty they generate. In addition to information, community members provide an interpretive framework of cause-and-effect relationships that may alter decisionmakers' views of their national interests. In the long term, the epistemic community's perspective may be institutionalized by members' appointment to official or advisory positions or having their policy beliefs and proposals incorporated into organizations' legal and operational frameworks.

This study posits that some combination of learning and other political processes characterizes the stages of policymaking. A conception of policymaking that incorporates the importance of working with ideas to solve problems is more accurate than viewing policy solely as a consequence of nations' power interests, political leaderships' mobilization of relevant publics, or interest groups' influence. Keohane critiques purely power-oriented, rationalistic theories of international organizations:

> [R]ationalistic theories seem only to deal with one dimension of a multidimensional reality: they are incomplete, since they ignore changes taking place in consciousness. They do not enable us to understand how interests change as a result of changes in belief systems. They obscure rather than illuminate the sources of states' policy preferences. (1988:391)

The concept of learning may be fruitfully employed to analyze several processes in policymaking: simple trial and error-induced adaptation; the institutionalization of new actors and, thus, their ideas; or the application of more sophisticated patterns of reasoning to policy issues. Early literature on learning processes within organizations conceptualized policy as "the residue of learning from accidents of past experience, and pragmatic inventions of necessity" (Cohen, March, and Olsen, 1972:1). A more sophisticated level of learning may be discerned when organizations embrace new policy beliefs. When a new epistemic community becomes entrenched in national and international bureaucracies, the organizations "learn" as the community's beliefs and policy prescriptions are incorporated into personnel, policies, and operational and legal structures.

A third, more complex level of organizational learning may also occur. Etheredge defines learning as "increased intelligence and sophistication of thought, and of increased effectiveness of behavior" (1979:4). Deutsch discusses learning in the context of political systems as "the ability of any political decision system to invent and carry out fundamentally new policies to meet new conditions . . . related to its ability to combine items of information into new patterns" (1966:163). Obviously, the adoption of more sophisticated patterns of reasoning and enhanced understanding of increasingly complex interrelationships among multiple factors may result from the epistemic community's becoming entrenched within the organization's apparatus as well as policymakers' embracing the community's beliefs, frame of reference, and policy prescriptions. As the consensus of the epistemic community is embraced by decisionmakers, however, and as the nature of the problem is redefined in broader and more interlinked terms, the need for more comprehensive patterns of policy coordination may also be recognized (P. Haas, 1990:30, 59).

An indicator that learning has taken place appears when actors identify new or reorder the priority of existing national interests as a consequence of coalitional interaction. Referring to the influence of the epistemic community in policymaking associated with the United Nations Environment Programme (UNEP) Plan for the Mediterranean, Peter Haas writes,

> These new actors led governments to recognize and follow new interests in environmental protection, so that they were willing to resist systemic forces that would push them to pursue more constrained and transitory arrangements. International environmental cooperation is generated by the influence wielded by specialists with common beliefs, contrary to conventional approaches which stress the role of interstate powers. (1990: xxii)

In the international setting where analysts have traditionally conceptualized policymaking as deriving from state-centric prioritization of interests, the exercise of hegemonic leadership, or problems associated with the provision of collective goods, a new element is introduced if it can be demonstrated that actors learn new interests.

Beliefs, interpretive frameworks, and learning are, however, only part of the policy process. There is rarely complete congruity even within the epistemic community regarding policy beliefs, frameworks, and data interpretation. Experts' policy perspectives may conflict with other actors' perspectives defined by differing philosophical, political, economic, or even personal interests. Policymakers may disagree on the priority of agenda items, on the most effective policy alternative to address the problem, and on the timing or resources to be devoted to policy implementation. Political leaders negotiate, bargain, influence, pressure, accommodate, and compromise in response to interests within and without the issue area. When issues concern problem recognition, research, or monitoring, the processes and agents of learning will be involved. When the issues pertain to distributing costs and benefits, however, political processes and actors predominate (Ruggie, 1975:558). The dynamic interaction of cognitive and political processes suggested in Sabatier's coalition model will be analyzed in the following case study of EC policymaking to protect the ozone layer.

EC POLICYMAKING TO PROTECT THE OZONE LAYER

Without ozone to block the sun's ultraviolet light, radiation can induce skin cancers and adversely affect the immune response system in humans, lower crop yields, and kill tiny organisms in the food chain. Studies by the U.S. National Academy of Sciences also indicate that continued release of CFCs could affect an average warming of the earth's surface by a few tenths of one degree Celsius before the middle of the 21st century (Caldwell, 1990b:262). Members of the scientific community, the United States, UNEP, and Dutch government officials were responsible for placing CFC restrictions on the agenda of the European Community. The finding that CFCs might be damaging to the ozone layer was first publicized by University of California-Irvine scientists, Frank Rowland and Mario Molina, at a 1974 American Chemical Society conference. In response, the U.S. Environmental Protection Agency (EPA) prohibited the use of CFCs as aerosol propellants in nonessential applications by 1978 and urged the EC to follow suit. But the Council, the EC's supreme decision-making body, did not embrace the United States' sense of urgency regarding the matter.

In 1975 UNEP funded a technical conference that yielded the first international scientific statement of concern about the effects of CFCs. In January 1976 it released a plan calling for a review of existing scientific research on the issue, outlining areas requiring further investigation, creating a program to monitor ozone, and examining the need for controls on ozone-depleting substances. In March, in Washington, D.C., EC delegates joined scientists and representatives from thirty-two countries in adopting the World Plan of Action on the Ozone Layer, the first intergovernmental agreement on the issue. Its twenty-one point research program mirrored the foci of the January plan. The plan formalized UNEP's coordinating role in international deliberations on ozone depletion by mandating the establishment of a Coordinating Committee on the Ozone Layer. Under its auspices, scientists from national governments, specialized UN agencies, environmental agencies, research institutions, and CFC industries met to exchange scientific, economic, and technical information.

The first intergovernmental meeting held to consider regulation of ozone-depleting substances was convened by UNEP and hosted by the United States in April 1977. This established a precedent of intergovernmental meetings following scientific conferences. At this meeting, participants discussed practicable national programs and agreed on the importance of exchanging scientific and other information, but failed to reach a consensus that international regulation was necessary (see Chapter 12).

Europe's largest producer of CFCs was Britain's Imperial Chemical Industries (ICI); Atochem was the primary French producer. EC firms supplied 40 percent of the world's demand for CFCs and were principal exporters to the developing world. As scientific and public concern about CFC use was still relatively undefined during this stage of agenda setting, these companies exerted significant influence on the position of their national governments in EC Council deliberations on CFC reductions. In 1977 the EC Council rejected a Dutch proposal to require labeling of spray cans containing CFCs. In 1978 the Council adopted a relatively benign resolution advocating preventive measures against CFC emissions (European Communities, 1978:1).

At a UNEP conference on CFCs held in Munich later that year, EC members and other participating countries agreed to work for substantial reductions in emissions of CFCs (Johnson and Corcelle, 1989:150), but they could not agree on coordinating voluntary CFC reductions. A call by the West German Bundestag in 1979 for a Community-wide CFC aerosol ban was rejected. That same year, the Committee on the Environment, Public Health, and Consumer Protection of the European Parliament proposed a 50 percent reduction in CFC aerosols by 1981 and a total ban by 1983. After heated debate, the European Parliament rejected the committee's recommendations and endorsed a weaker EC Commission plan (Benedick, 1991b:24). (As the community's executive and civil service, the commission drafts and administers legislation.) In 1980, under this plan, the Council stipulated an immediate freeze on production *capacity* (rather than actual production) of CFC-11 and -12 and a 30 percent reduction (compared to 1976 levels) in CFC-11 and -12 use in aerosols by 31 December 1981 (European Communities, 1980:45). This level had already been achieved mainly through West German efforts. According to Haigh: "There is reason to believe that the figure of 30 percent was chosen because it was known that it could be achieved without creating too much difficulty for the industry" (1989:268). The EC subsequently defined "production capacity" as twenty-four-hour continuous plant operation, which allowed output to increase by more than 60 percent from current levels. Therefore, this capacity restriction would not begin to affect EC production until the end of the century (Benedick, 1991:25). In 1982 the council adopted a decision reconfirming its 1980 position and calling for a 1982 production capacity freeze on CFC-11 and -12 at 480,000 metric tons (European Communities, 1982: 29). With existing voluntary limits on aerosols, this capacity freeze built in a surplus capacity of 30 percent for European producers.

At this stage of policymaking, those scientists subscribing to the Rowland-Molina hypothesis, the U.S. government, UNEP, the Dutch government, the West German Bundestag, and the Environmental Committee of the European Parliament made up the coalition advocating limitation of CFC production and use. The policy options ranged from a Community-wide CFC aerosol ban to the Dutch government's suggestion that spray cans containing CFCs be labeled. The chief European industrial producers of CFCs and their government representatives constituted the opposing coalition. The commission-formulated policy options adopted by the council in 1980 and 1982 imposed little hardship on industrial producers.

Despite the council's resolutions to limit the use of CFCs, it was unwilling to grant the commission a broad mandate to negotiate CFC reductions on a global basis at UNEP-sponsored talks held in Vienna in 1982. The Council preferred that discussions of substance-specific protocols be postponed and that Vienna negotiators draw up a framework agreement on scientific and technical cooperation, information exchange, pollution monitoring, and research. Because its mandate from the Council clearly proscribed signing a reduction convention, the commission possessed no maneuvering room at the Vienna negotiations.

The commission was eager to enhance its policy initiator and broker roles as well as to reduce CFC levels. In 1981 and 1982, it struggled to acquire authorization to represent EC members at the Vienna meetings. The commission preferred that the EC be a party to the convention without its members being obligated to sign individually. The commission reasoned that, if it succeeded in this goal, it would gain greater competence over internal as well as external environmental affairs. It could claim the right to propose EC legislation to implement ozone protection and other environmental conventions. In 1985 the European Environmental Bureau (EEB) accused the commission of endangering the adoption of the Vienna Convention because it was more concerned with its organizational prerogatives than protecting the ozone layer (Jachtenfuchs, 1990).

In line with the 1982 decision, the commission presented a communication to the council in 1983 assessing scientific knowledge and economic data relating to CFCs. Basing its comments on UNEP studies, the commission stressed that the ozone layer may have been reduced by 3 to 5 percent due to CFC-11 and -12 emissions, whereas previous estimates had suggested 5 to 10 percent. The commission noted that, by 1982, the use of aerosols containing CFCs had been reduced throughout the community an average of 37 percent compared to 1976 levels, exceeding the requirements of the council's 1980 decision. Codes of good practice restricting the emissions of CFCs in sectors of refrigeration, plastic foam, and solvents had been drawn up.

At the Vienna negotiations held in 1985, the United States and Toronto Group members (Canada, Finland, Norway, and Sweden) argued for consumption controls on different CFC uses, an immediate freeze in production, and a 30 percent reduction from 1976 use levels of CFC-11 and -12, to be implemented within two years of the treaty's entry into force. EC members favored freezing production capacity for CFCs at current levels. Since EC firms had a 30 percent surplus capacity, such a freeze would permit them to increase output to 1.5 times its present levels. This would have allowed EC companies to expand their global markets while others were being limited. With this polarization of positions, the coalitions' differences could not be resolved (P. Haas, 1992a:202).

The resulting Vienna Convention for the Protection of the Ozone Layer, signed on 22 March 1985, called for research cooperation and developing means to control activities that might modify the ozone layer. A resolution called for further negotiations to effect a protocol on CFC reductions; a number of workshops were to precede resumption of negotiations. A participatory clause was drafted, in accordance with commission preferences, which provided a new model for EC participation in global international agreements. The EC was party to the "mixed" international agreement without individual members being obligated to sign (Jachtenfuchs, 1990:263-64).

Meanwhile, U.S. scientists' analyses were gradually being confirmed by computer simulation and even more dramatically in 1985 by a British team, led by Joseph C. Farman, which detected a "hole" in the ozone layer above Antarctica (Kevles, 1992:31). Policymakers in the EC countries joined the anti-CFC coalition as soon as communication was established between individual members of the epistemic community and their national administrations. In West Germany, a new environmental ministry was created and became an outspoken supporter of CFC controls (Haas, 1992a:215). In April 1986, Danish and German experts publicly attacked their British and French counterparts for not taking ozone protection far enough in Vienna.

NGOs maintained public pressure and media attention on the ozone question as national and regional leaders deliberated. In June, the EEB organized a symposium in Brussels on scientific and political aspects of ozone protection under the theme "The Sky Is the Limit." The symposium was well attended by European and U.S. NGOs and personnel from Directorate-General XI (Environment and Nuclear Safety, DGXI), which represented the commission in ozone negotiations. The European Parliament's Environment Committee called for an 85 percent reduction in CFC production and consumption within ten years.

In July, a report was released summarizing the state of knowledge about ozone based on a two-year study coordinated by the U.S. National Aeronautics and Space Administration (NASA). Funding for the project was provided by the EC, the German Federal Ministry for Research and Technology, UNEP, the World Meteorological Organization, the U.S. National Oceanic and Atmospheric Administration, the U.S. Federal Aviation Administration, and NASA. The report concluded that the threat to the ozone layer was serious and that CFCs were a possible source of the danger (Haas, 1992a:203).

The UK presidency of the council in the second half of 1986 was largely responsible for the failure to reach a compromise within the council during this period. The French and Germans also continued to oppose a wider negotiating mandate for the commission (Jachtenfuchs, 1990:265). In November, the commission sent the council a third communication examining control measures for CFCs. It summed up the economic tendencies regarding production and use of different CFCs and assessed the scientific and technical situation. The council authorized commission participation in the Montreal Protocol negotiations (Johnson and Corcelle, 1989:151-52).

Negotiations on CFC reduction began again in Geneva in December on a semibilateral basis between the EC (led by the United Kingdom and France, with Japan and the Soviet Union) and the United States (with Canada, Denmark, Finland, the Netherlands, New Zealand, Norway, and Sweden). The United States wished to control five CFCs and two halons which were thought to have the greatest ozone-depleting potential. The EC wished only to control CFC-11 and -12 on which it had already set capacity limits. The United States favored consumption controls in contrast to the EC's preference for a production capacity freeze. In response to EC inclinations, the United States proposed a production capacity freeze within one year, a 20 percent cut two years later, and another 30 percent cut after six to eight years. European producers argued that they were ten to fifteen years behind U.S. firms in researching CFC substitutes. The EC was interested only in a freeze after a three-year wait with no subsequent cuts.

Gradually weakening EC opposition to U.S. proposals can be traced to changes in the chairmanship of the council and the attitude of the German government. Britain, which had been hostile to CFC controls, was council president from July through December of 1986, until Belgium, more sympathetic to strong controls, assumed leadership in January 1987. In March, the council approved freezing production of CFCs-11 and -12 at 1986 levels and phasing out production by 20 percent within five to seven years subject to scientific confirmation that it was necessary. The Green party made a strong showing in the 1987 West German federal elections and pressured the government to endorse a ban on aerosols and the eventual elimination of CFCs. The head of the West German Ministry of the Environment took the position that EC reduction proposals were too low and called for 40 to 50 percent reductions. But France's environmental minister denied any definite link between CFCs and ozone depletion. And Britain, basing its position on pre-1985 data, maintained that any possible ozone depletion was inconsequential.

UNEP's Coordinating Committee on the Ozone Layer met eight times between 1977 and 1986. Scientists tested models of the future effects of alternative regulatory strategies that incorporated varying combinations of controlled substances and reduction schedules. Between December 1986 and February 1987, the U.S. promoted its position worldwide through scientific exchanges. The chief U.S. negotiator, Richard Benedick, and NASA scientists discussed the issue with experts, policymakers, and journalists in ten European capitals via interactive satellite transmissions. Scientists, convened by UNEP in April 1987 in Wurzburg, West Germany, and coordinated by NASA's Robert Watson, were asked to compare models and assessments of ozone depletion. They discussed the consequences of no change, an immediate freeze, and a midpoint of 50 percent cuts, crafting the policy alternatives to be considered at the ongoing negotiations. They reached a consensus that a 50 percent reduction in CFC emissions would still result in a 5 to 20 percent depletion of ozone, and that CFCs -11, -12, and -113, -114, and -115 and halons 1211 and 1301 should be covered in the protocol. In addition, a standard for determining the "ozone-depleting potential" of compounds was approved.

UNEP Executive Director Mostafa Tolba immediately transmitted this information to the negotiators with the statement that since "consensus among the scientific community has been confirmed by the major ozone modelers, it was...no longer possible to oppose action to regulate CFC releases on the grounds of scientific dissent" (P. Haas, 1992a:211). The results of this meeting had a decisive impact on the ongoing negotiations. Whereas in the past the scientific community had provided data and analysis supporting the link between CFC emissions and ozone depletion, it now formulated specific policy options. Scientific consensus made a number of EC and Japanese arguments based on questions of the accuracy of the models now impossible to sustain (Haas, 1992c:211-12). Benedick acknowledged that CFC regulation "couldn't have occurred without modern science, without atmospheric chemistry, computer models, and projections. It couldn't have happened as recently as 1982" (Haas, 1992c:196).

At the Geneva negotiations held in April, the EC indicated its willingness to adopt a freeze and move toward 20 percent cuts in the production of CFC-11 and -12 by 1993 or 1994. In May, after the German Environmental Minister argued that the April negotiating session did not go far enough, the EC reconsidered its position. In June, during its final days as council president, Belgium held informal meetings with the U.S., Japan and the Soviet Union to discuss outstanding issues. In July EC environmental ministers finally supported a second 30 percent cut. The EC position, formulated under the leadership of Belgium, Denmark, and West Germany, and the policy preferences of the U.S.-led coalition were now sufficiently proximate to permit compromise.

The Conference of Plenipotentiaries convened in Montreal in September. Some issues were not resolved until the last day of the meeting when the heads of the U.S. EPA and the EC delegation "horse-traded through the early hours of the morning" (P. Haas, 1992a:207). Even when U.S. leadership or pressure led to cooperation as power-based explanations would predict, the substantive content of the cooperation was determined by the epistemic community which directed U.S. policy toward strong CFC controls and set the parameters within which the political negotiations took place. The final Montreal Protocol on Substances that Deplete the Ozone Layer, signed on 16 September 1987 by twenty-eight countries, provided for a 50 percent reduction on production and consumption of CFCs from 1986 levels by 1998. EC "rationalization" plans were accommodated in the protocol by a special provision that, when its members ratified the treaty, the community would be treated as a single entity. This allowed companies to distribute production among plants in member countries to achieve the most efficient production levels (Haas, 1992a:206-12).

On 16 September Germany and Denmark went on record as believing the Montreal Protocol insufficient. Following the signing of the Montreal Protocol, regional environmental groups became more active participants in the anti-CFC coalition. They began a campaign to push the EC toward stricter standards than provided by the protocol. The EEB and the European Bureau of Consumers' Unions (BEUC) advocated an 85 percent reduction in CFC use. They called upon industry to undertake voluntary reductions in CFC production; failing that, they threatened to organize product boycotts. The EEB and BEUC also attempted to carry out direct negotiations with the European Federation of

Chemical Industries and the organization of European aerosol producers.

Industry argued that it needed time to develop safe and inexpensive substitutes for CFCs. British firms, in particular, attempted to gain time by concluding voluntary agreements to undertake research into substitutes and to eliminate CFCs in aerosols. The willingness of British firms to go beyond Montreal Protocol provisions led to a slow erosion of the UK position in the council. A change in the position of the British government was discernible, however, only after ICI lifted its opposition to further reductions.

In 1987 the commission transformed the Montreal Protocol into EC legislation without alteration. The legislation assumed the form of a regulation rather than a directive to avoid trade distortions from nonsimultaneous application and to underscore the urgency of the issue. After consulting government experts, industrialists, and environmentalists, Directorate General XI decided not to press for standards exceeding the Montreal Protocol partly because it believed that stricter measures had no chance of receiving the required unanimous council approval. Critics charged that DGXI's position was the result of long and close cooperation with industry. The commission's reluctance to propose tougher standards may also be explained by the influence of Directorate-General III (Internal Market and Industrial Affairs, DGIII) which contended that the Montreal Protocol already imposed heavy costs on industry.

In 1987 public statements by and informal contacts with parliament members strengthened the environmental coalition which included DGXI, the EEB, and the BEUC. In 1988 the Parliament Committee for the Environment joined with environmental organizations to criticize industry's reluctance to develop marketable substitutes for CFCs. It supported the EEB's and BEUC's demand for an 85 percent decrease in CFC emissions within ten years, the inclusion of all full-halogenated carbons in protocol provisions, and an immediate ban on the use of CFCs as propellants. The Economic and Social Committee decided unanimously that the Montreal Protocol was inadequate and should be renegotiated. A majority of the parliament approved amendments urging the Council to adopt stricter CFC standards (Jachtenfuchs, 1990:267-69).

At its June 1988 meeting, the council agreed to a decision concluding and implementing the Vienna Convention and Montreal Protocol and a regulation laying down common rules applicable to certain ozone-depleting products. To enable the two international agreements to enter into force on 1 January 1989, the decision required EC members to ratify the convention by 1 October 1988 and the protocol by the end of the year.

It should be noted that the scientific community still did not unanimously subscribe to the Rowland-Molina hypothesis. Skepticism was most pronounced in Britain and France. Prime Minister Margaret Thatcher, preferring to rely on the opinion of British scientists, appointed her own commission, the Stratospheric Ozone Review Group (SORG), to investigate ozone depletion. In its first report in August 1987, SORG downplayed the threat to the ozone layer and the role of CFCs. When a March 1988 report by the Ozone Trends Panel presented evidence that chlorine gas in the stratosphere was present during periods of high ozone depletion over Antarctica and that CFC emissions were related to Antarctic and global ozone depletion, Thatcher suspected bias toward U.S. interests because of NASA's strong involvement in the deliberations. She turned to SORG for further advice. SORG membership was mostly independent of U.S. ties, although it included Joseph Farman who had discovered the ozone hole in 1985. Farman had publicly dismissed the earlier SORG findings, arguing that they were based on outdated evidence.

In June 1988, SORG published an executive summary which supported the findings of the Ozone Trends Panel. In July Britain's House of Lords Select Committee on the EC announced its acceptance that CFCs were responsible for ozone depletion and recommended an extension of the Montreal Protocol to cut CFC use by 85 percent. The real turnaround came in September when, in a speech to the Royal Society, Thatcher called for immediate action to safeguard the ozone layer and fight acid rain and global warming. Immediately before the speech, Crispin Tickell, the UK ambassador to the UN and a long-time confidant of the prime minister, had forwarded documents to her warning of the danger of global warming. Britain's economy was in trouble at the time, and Thatcher's privatization program was particularly unpopular. The speech came a week before the Labour Party Congress. At the time, public opinion polls showed rising proenvironmentalist sentiments and support for the Green party. (In fact, 15 percent of British voters cast ballots for Green Party candidates in European Parliament elections the following year.)

Thatcher convened a conference on "Saving the Ozone Layer" in association with UNEP in London in March 1989. At this conference, she called for an 85 percent cut in CFC use and announced that Britain would double its annual monetary commitment to UNEP to three million pounds and would restore and slightly increase British Antarctic Survey funding.

French officials stood firm in their opposition to stricter CFC standards. French scientists did little ozone research, and environment and industry officials paid scant attention to scientific findings. The Industry Ministry, biased toward the interests of Atochem, successfully dominated policy-making processes (Haas, 1992a:216-18). In October 1988, France blocked an EC resolution going beyond the Montreal provisions and calling for voluntary reductions in CFC production (European Communities, 1988a, 1988b, 1988c). It appeared that France would not change its position as long as Atochem was unwilling to reduce CFC production. In November the commission presented a communication on the greenhouse effect and called for a renegotiation of the Montreal Protocol to eliminate CFCs as rapidly as possible (Commission of the European Communities, 1988). Greece (serving as council president), Denmark, and Germany called for a reduction of CFCs beyond the 50 percent limit set by the Montreal Protocol. France demanded that revisions be delayed until the protocol came into force. It argued that ozone depletion was a global problem and should be addressed on that level to avoid advantaging U.S. companies.

In early 1989, evidence from the most recent Antarctic expedition demonstrated that the ozone layer was being depleted more rapidly than had been predicted originally. In March, Spain, acting as president of the council, called for an 85 percent reduction of CFCs. With an eye to its upcoming ozone conference, the British allied themselves with the 85 percent reduction forces. The council suddenly decided to completely eliminate CFCs by the year 2000, accepting a complete ban over the "pragmatic 95 percent" proposal of Germany and the Netherlands, which would have allowed some essential uses of CFCs. The 100 percent position was designed to improve the EC's image with regard to environmental protection. This unexpected outcome was a consequence of external pressures on the French and partly a result of negotiating dynamics within the Council.

The French volte-face occurred when the government of President François Mitterand decided to put its own political interests above the economic interests of its national CFC producers. A week after the council meeting, Mitterand was slated as coorganizer for a meeting at the Hague to launch an initiative to protect the atmosphere. To remain intransigent on the 85 percent reduction issue in the council would have been politically embarrassing for Mitterand at the Hague (Jachtenfuchs, 1990:270-71).

At the first governmental review of the Montreal Protocol held in Finland in May 1989, representatives from eighty-one countries adopted the Helsinki Declaration on the Protection of the Ozone Layer calling for a total phase out of production and consumption of CFCs by the year 2000. In January 1990, the commission proposed to the council a new regulation providing for 100 percent reduction of a wide range of ozone-depleting substances by the end of 1997.

ANALYSIS

This case study of European Community environmental decisionmaking confirms the thesis that policymaking in international organizations is an issue-specific consequence of learning and other political dynamics. As scientific understanding evolved between 1974 and 1990, all coalition participants learned that CFCs presented a threat to the ozone layer and that emissions restrictions were required to redress the problem. Much of this learning derived from European Community participation in multilateral, particularly UNEP-orchestrated, research teams. There is evidence that the learning was more sophisticated in nature than simple trial-and-error adaptation. Coalition members learned new factual information and accepted the validity of the proposition that CFC emissions and ozone depletion are causally linked.

Government representatives came to identify ozone protection as a new national interest. The priorities of existing national interests were reordered as protection of the ozone layer took precedence over promoting the immediate economic interests of national CFC producers.

Concurrently, there is little doubt that political interests aside from learning played a significant role in shaping EC members' council voting on restricting CFCs. Industrial producers' reluctance to develop substitutes made Britain, France, and Germany early opponents of wholehearted EC participation in multilateral negotiations. But EC members were not of a single mind on the subject. The Netherlands was consistently numbered among those favoring stronger controls over CFC emissions. Germany, whose Greens emerged as a national political force in the early 1980s, was the first to defect to the emissions reduction coalition. Although Thatcher's initial position reflected ICI interests, her conversion reflected a combination of learning and other political influences. France's stance on the CFC question seemed most driven by industrial interests. There was never sufficient epistemic activity within the French government to affect a reversal on the question, yet the French eventually went along for political reasons.

The process whereby ozone depletion came to the attention of European Community decisionmakers is distinct from the processes that ultimately shaped policy directives. Evidence of the wide-ranging effects of ozone depletion was so persuasive that the scientific community, the U.S., and UNEP began campaigning vigorously for multilateral redressment of the problem. When, however, European Community deliberations began on reducing CFCs, the authoritative decisionmakers were individual members within the council. Their positions were influenced by the political, industrial, and environmental players of their respective countries. They also were subject to the influence of other community actors: the council presidency, the commission, and, to a lesser extent, the parliament.

The juxtaposed coalitions were distinct in terms of policy assumptions and prescriptions, resources, and strategies. Coalition membership transcended formal organizational boundaries and included actors from several levels: nongovernmental, national, regional, and international. Scientific experts, industry, NGOs, intergovernmental organizations, the public, and other countries such as the United States commonly influenced decisionmakers. A fascinating feature of the policy-making process is that the preponderance of learning and political interactions took place outside of the European Community itself. Although significant political interaction took place within the context of council deliberations and in response to commission-initiated proposals, domestic political factors ultimately determined members' council voting. International protocols, negotiated outside of the formal EC structure, were adopted verbatim as EC legislation, which underscores the significance of coalition actors external to the EC apparatus.

The epistemic community, armed with a growing body of evidence regarding the threat to the ozone layer, was an active member of the anti-CFC coalition at every stage of policy formulation. It is clear that scientists were uniquely influential in this case because policymakers were dependent upon their input to identify the problem, to assess the severity of the threat, to specify the chemical substances responsible for ozone depletion, and to delineate the policy instruments necessary to address the problem. Scientific investigation of ozone depletion proceeded on both national and multilateral levels. The work of the British Antarctic team and NASA was highly influential in the policy-making process while the UNEP-orchestrated working sessions of experts were instrumental in generating actual policy alternatives for political consideration. Members of the epistemic community brought their perspectives to the Montreal Treaty talks as members of the European Community and national negotiating teams. Within the commission itself, DGXI personnel shared common beliefs and policy prescriptions with their colleagues in the scientific and NGO community.

Interest groups were prominent members of the advocacy coalitions. The major CFC producing industries, ICI and Atochem, were immediate natural opponents of policies that would limit their productive capabilities and markets. Because of their economic significance for the national economies and long established ties with national and regional makers of industrial policy, their interests were automatically represented in Community Council deliberations. Although they enjoyed an early advantage in policy-making circles, industry lobbying was not particularly successful in discrediting the growing tide of scientific evidence in favor of limiting CFC emissions. Instead, CFC industries succeeded in focusing community policy on capacity freezes and providing time for research and development of CFC alternatives.

Beginning in the early 1970s, environmental interest groups were active within the political parties and governmental agencies of individual EC member-states. By the mid-1980s, regional interest groups were prominent members of the advocacy coalitions. In 1986 the EEB allied with the BEUC to support DGXI and parliamentary calls for strong restrictions on CFC use. NGOs kept the focus of media and public opinion on the issue as the council deliberated in the wake of the Vienna meetings. Symposia and conferences gained media and public attention and exerted pressure on policymakers to move ahead in CFC restrictions.

The record of the commission and council presidencies is mixed when compared to the broker's functions described in the literature. The commission was in conflict with EC members for years over the prerogative to represent their interests in multilateral environmental negotiations. This conflict progressed to the degree that the EEB accused the commission of pursuing its power interests to the detriment of environmental objectives. Commission efforts to link the CFC issue with enhancement of its legal and administrative authority conforms to the broker's role of system maintenance or augmentation of organizational power; yet this activity limited the commission's ability to identify and negotiate policy alternatives. The commission was not monolithic in its approach to these issues. DGIII differed with DGXI over how far commission advocacy should go in pressing for environmental protection over the interests of industry. In the end, despite internal debate, the commission was ahead of the more recalcitrant members of the council in advocating CFC limitations.

The record of council presidencies as policy brokers was also clearly mixed. Each member, serving a six-month term as president of the council, sought success in terms of its policy priorities in addition to system maintenance. Progress toward negotiation of reductions in CFC production was stymied while Britain held the council presidency. By contrast, the Belgium presidency called informal meetings with the United States, Japan, and the Soviet Union to facilitate CFC discussions in June 1987. This demonstrates that council presidents may serve as policy brokers or deter policy-making processes. The conflicting evidence on the role of the commission and council presidencies as brokers in international organizations suggests that further research is required to validate theoretical propositions concerning the importance of brokers in policymaking in international organizations.

This case of EC policymaking to limit ozone depletion provides evidence that policy formulation within international organizations is an issue-specific amalgam of learning and other political processes. CFC-related ozone depletion provided an extraordinary need for input from the scientific community at all stages of the policy-making process. Further in-depth analysis of environmental and nonenvironmental decisionmaking within the European Community and other international organizations will be required to elucidate the extent to which learning affects policymaking in the international context.

5

The World Meteorological Organization as a Purveyor of Global Public Goods

Marvin S. Soroos and Elena N. Nikitina

Weather has always been a concern of human civilizations, whose survival and prosperity have depended upon their ability to adapt to the prevailing climate where they resided. Numerous civilizations have declined and disappeared through the ages because they were unable to adjust to climate changes, including some they unwittingly brought upon themselves by their land use practices (Hughes, 1975). Traditional civilizations improvised mythologies to explain the vicissitudes of the weather, in particular the more extreme events such as storms and droughts. The scientific study of weather can be traced to the fourth century BC, when Aristotle and his pupil Theophrastus sought to explain weather by replacing fantasy with observation and reason (Davies, 1990:1).

International cooperation on monitoring weather and climate was among the first subjects to be addressed by international organizations. The World Meteorological Organization (WMO), a critical actor in contemporary international environmental policy, carries on many of the traditions and functions of the International Meteorological Organization (IMO), which dates back to 1873. Since it came into being in 1950, WMO has greatly expanded its monitoring and research activities aimed at improving weather forecasts and understanding the physical processes of the atmosphere that determine weather and climate. The past fifteen years have brought significant new challenges for the organization, as scientific evidence mounts that the world's human population is altering the chemistry of the atmosphere in ways that could trigger other massive environmental changes with profound implications for human communities worldwide.

WMO has been regarded both by itself and by outside observers as one of the most effective specialized agencies in the United Nations (UN) system, one that offers a model for facilitating international cooperation on scientific matters (e.g., WMO, 1990:2; Cain, 1983:97). The mission of WMO has evolved in response to changing perceptions of weather, climate, and the atmosphere. The array of WMO's programs has grown as have the organization's contributions to international environmental policy. Why the organization has been so successful in fulfilling its missions can be explained with reference both to practical operational factors and, in a more theoretical sense, to the type of functions it performs, namely the providing of international collective goods.

WEATHER, CLIMATE, AND THE ATMOSPHERE AS POLICY PROBLEMS

The expanding mission of WMO over four decades reflects an evolution in perceptions about the atmosphere and climate, which are partly a result of scientific knowledge generated by the projects of the organization. When WMO was established, weather was still generally viewed as a force of nature to which human beings could only react; they could neither influence it, nor interfere with it in a substantial way. Thus, the original primary task for WMO, as it had been for IMO since the 19th century, was a passive one: to anticipate weather and learn about its causal dynamics. These objectives continue to be central to the mission of WMO.

Interest began to grow during the 1950s in the possibility of modifying weather by human design, such as by enhancing precipitation, dispersing fogs, suppressing hail, and lessening the intensity of hurricanes. Weather modification research and experimentation was motivated by economic objectives, such as increasing stream flow for agriculture and urban water systems, as well as by hostile purposes, for example, cloud seeding over Vietnam and Cambodia by the United States to increase rainfall that would make jungle trails muddy and impassable for enemy supply convoys (Westing, 1976, 1984). Weather modification has not proven to be as adaptable for peaceful purposes as had been hoped earlier, but it continues to be a secondary interest of WMO. Manipulating weather for military or other hostile purposes was banned by an international treaty adopted in 1977.

A revolution in perceptions of climate took hold during the 1970s. While it was known previously that substantial long-term variations in climate occurred naturally, as was apparent from the evidence of periodic ice ages, it was assumed that these changes were too slow and gradual to be of consequence for contemporary civilizations. Persistent drought in the African Sahel, combined with unusual and adverse weather conditions in other regions during the early 1970s, prompted a reexamination of presumptions about the stability of the global climate. Even more ominous were warnings from scientists that increasing concentrations of carbon dioxide (CO_2) and other "greenhouse gases" could be altering the heat-absorbing and retention qualities of the atmosphere in ways that would greatly accelerate global climate changes. These changes, within a few decades, could have immense consequences for the natural environment and subsequently for human communities (Malone, 1986; McKay and Hengeveld, 1990).

The new thinking on climate change poses several new challenges for international public policy pertaining to the atmosphere and, accordingly, for WMO as the international institution primarily responsible for research on weather, climate, and the condition of the atmosphere. One task is to improve the scientific capacity to detect and project climate changes and to determine the extent to which they are being driven by human activities. Achieving these objectives requires not only more extensive monitoring of weather and the condition of the atmosphere, including levels of anthropogenic pollutants, but also a better basic understanding of climate dynamics. A second is the need to anticipate the impacts of climate change on the natural environment and accordingly the ramifications these natural changes will have for human societies. The ultimate imperative is to use an expanding body of knowledge on climate change and its consequences to inform efforts to formulate and implement international policies, policies that will limit climate change by regulating the human activities that are contributing to it (Stern, Young, and Druckman, 1992).

Awareness of the threat of human-induced climate change has been accompanied by a deepening consciousness that weather is an extremely complex phenomenon that is not governed exclusively by atmospheric factors, but is also affected by processes involving the oceans, landmasses, glaciers, and biological systems. The periodic *El Niño* effect in the Pacific Ocean testifies to the integral relationship between oceans and atmosphere. Thus, anticipating the impact of climate change must take into account an even broader range of natural and social processes. Accordingly, climate change and its impact cannot be exclusively the domain of atmospheric scientists and meteorologists, the predominant creators and developers of WMO, but must be an enterprise that is both interdisciplinary and multidisciplinary involving such fields as hydrology, agriculture, oceanography, glaciology, forestry, and ecology. Thus, it has been essential for WMO to draw together scientists from these diverse fields and to form partnerships with governmental and nongovernmental organizations (NGOs) having responsibilities with other environmental domains that have an impact on weather, or are affected by it (Davies, 1990:140-50).

EVOLUTION OF WMO AND ITS PROGRAMS

The origins of WMO can be traced to the First International Meteorological Conference in Brussels in 1853, at which delegates from eight European countries and the United States agreed to use uniform procedures for making and reporting meteorological observations from ships plying the world's oceans.

IMO was established twenty years later at the First International Meteorological Congress, which was held in Vienna and attended by directors of national meteorological services. The original task of IMO was to incorporate the weather stations operated by national meteorological and hydrological services into an international network that would collect weather and ocean data using uniform standards and procedures.

Even before the outbreak of the World War II, the membership of IMO began to realize that its mission could be pursued more effectively if it were transformed from an NGO to an intergovernmental organization (IGO). In 1950 IMO was recast as the intergovernmental World Meteorological Organization (WMO), which had an original membership of forty-six states and twenty territories. A year later the UN General Assembly approved a resolution designating WMO as a specialized agency in the United Nations system. WMO maintained much of the organizational structure of the IMO, and the delegates to the First Congress of WMO in 1951 included many who had represented their countries in meetings of the IMO (Davies, 1990:11-16).

WMO is a functionally specific, international agency of the type that Mitrany (1946) argued could bind the world together in peaceful cooperation, thereby avoiding future world wars. In pursuing its relatively narrow mission of improved weather forecasts and a deeper understanding of atmosphere and climate, WMO has undertaken an extensive array of projects, many in partnership with other international governmental organizations, national governmental agencies, and nongovernmental associations. Most of these projects were designed either to facilitate the collection and dissemination of weather data or to further scientific research on the determinants of climate.

Monitoring Programs

The value of systematic weather observations has long been recognized. In some regions of China, weather records date back 5,000 years. In 1653 Ferdinand II of Tuscany organized the first known weather reporting network, which included seven stations scattered around northern Italy and neighboring countries (Davies, 1990:1-2). As an NGO, IMO sought to improve weather forecasting by coordinating national weather services through standardized meteorological instruments and methods of observation, common symbols for climatological tables and charts, and a global network of observation stations. IMO concentrated observations of weather and ocean conditions along the major sea routes to be of use to its primary constituencies, merchant and military navigators (Davies, 1990:1-9). Three-quarters of a century later, a substantially expanded and refined network for collecting and disseminating meteorological information was transferred to WMO.

The General Assembly adopted a resolution in 1961 challenging WMO to take advantage of the technological opportunities offered by satellites to improve weather forecasting and to advance atmospheric science. In the realm of weather monitoring, WMO responded by launching the World Weather Watch in 1963, which has become one of the principal components of the Global Environmental Monitoring System (GEMS) coordinated by the United Nations Environment Programme (UNEP). The World Weather Watch is generally regarded as a highly successful project that can be a prototype for other international monitoring programs.

The World Weather Watch is an institutional mechanism for coordinating the weather reporting networks of the meteorological and hydrological services of more than 160 states. Its Global Observing System is a network of 9,500 synoptic land-based stations that is supplemented by a vast array of other facilities for collecting meteorological data from sea, air, and outer space. Balloons, aircraft, ships, satellites in solar and geostationary orbits, moored and drifting buoys, and ice stations are used to achieve global coverage. The Global Data-processing System, a second component of the World Weather Watch, comprises three World Meteorological Centers, located in Melbourne, Moscow, and Washington, D.C., and a network of eighteen Regional Centers, which collect, compile, and analyze the data generated by the monitoring system as well as issue forecasts that are available to national weather services. The third part of the World Weather Watch, the Global Telecommunications System, rapidly transmits data, reports, and forecasts between weather stations and the various global, regional, and national meteorological centers (WMO, 1990:13-20).

An appreciation of the critical interrelationships between the atmosphere and oceans led WMO to collaborate with the United Nations Educational, Scientific, and Cultural Organization's (UNESCO) International Oceanographic Commission to establish in 1977 the Integrated Global Ocean Services System (IGOSS) to collect and disseminate data on the oceans, such as surface and upper layer temperatures, salinity, and currents at various depths. The program, which parallels the World Weather Watch and uses many of the same automated buoys as observation stations, has been used to monitor the *El Niño* phenomenon in the Pacific Ocean and will provide information for forecasting and assessing the impact of climate change on the oceans, including the amount of sea level rise (Davies, 1990:39-44).

WMO has undertaken several more specialized monitoring projects, including one that focuses on tropical storms. Typhoons and hurricanes, which are similar meteorological phenomena that originate in the tropical regions of the Pacific, Indian, and Atlantic oceans, have long been a bane of seafarers and the cause of immense loss of life and destruction due to storm surges, gale force winds, heavy rainfall, and floods when they reach landfall in any of fifty countries that are vulnerable to them. An unusually active typhoon season in 1970, including a fierce storm that killed 200,000 people in low-lying areas of Bangladesh, led

WMO to work with the Economic and Social Commission for Asia and the Far East (formerly the Economic Commission for Asia and the Far East) to create the Tropical Cyclone Project (later upgraded and renamed the Tropical Cyclone Programme). The program, which was initiated in 1971, provides timely warnings of the presence and course of these intense storms, as well as the threat of related phenomena such as storm surges and flooding (Davies, 1990:33-38).

Growing speculation that changes in the chemistry of the atmosphere will have significant implications for climate led WMO to undertake projects that monitor the atmosphere's chemical composition, including concentrations of a variety of human pollutants. The Background Air Pollution Monitoring System (BAPMoN) was established by WMO in 1969 in partnership with two U.S. agencies, the National Oceanic and Atmospheric Administration and the Environmental Protection Agency. BAPMoN later became a key part of UNEP's GEMS program along with a companion network operated by the World Health Organization (WHO) that monitors air pollution in urban and industrial areas. WMO also monitors the deposition of pollutants into the oceans through its participation in the Group of Experts on the Scientific Aspects of Marine Pollution (GESAMP) and the Pollution Monitoring and Research Programme of the Mediterranean Action Plan.

BAPMoN has grown to a network of more than 200 stations in sixty countries that monitors the composition of air at locations remote from urban areas and sources of air pollutants. Monitoring CO_2 levels in the atmosphere takes place at twenty-three BAPMoN stations. Approximately 100 BAPMoN stations in twenty European countries are part of the Cooperative Program for the Monitoring and Evaluation of the Long-Range Transmission of Air Pollutants in Europe (known as EMEP). EMEP is operated jointly by WMO, UNEP, and the United Nations Economic Commission for Europe to provide data on the transboundary flows of air pollutants that are the precursors of acid deposition (Köhler, 1988).

In response to mounting concern about human-induced global change during the 1980s, WMO launched the Global Atmospheric Watch to expand substantially its capacity for monitoring the chemical and physical dynamics of the atmosphere. One of its objectives is to provide early warnings of any significant changes in the composition of the atmosphere that could have consequences for climate and other earth systems. Two of the principal networks coming under the umbrella of the Global Atmospheric Watch are BAPMoN and the Global Ozone Observing System (GO_3OS), which was set up in 1976 by WMO to coordinate observations of the stratospheric ozone layer (Davies, 1990:95-96).

Research Programs

There is also a long tradition of international research on the physical dynamics of the atmosphere as a means of improving weather forecasting. The IMO sponsored two International Polar Years held in 1882-1883 and 1932-1933, which sought to learn about meteorological conditions in the polar regions and their impact on global weather patterns. WMO was one of the sponsors of the International Geophysical Year in 1957-1958, an ambitious project designed to coordinate worldwide research on the atmosphere and the other physical systems of the planet. This project was also billed as an experiment in East-West cooperation designed to lessen Cold War tensions (Atwood, 1956, 1959).

WMO's response to the General Assembly resolution included not only the World Weather Watch, but also a major research effort called the Global Atmospheric Research Program (GARP), which was conducted between 1967 and 1982. GARP was notable for being a partnership between WMO and the International Council of Scientific Unions (ICSU), which brought together operational meteorologists and academic scientists. The enterprise was designed to learn more about the dynamics of the global atmosphere in order to extend the period for useful weather forecasts. The principal GARP projects were two "global experiments," which entailed an intensive collection of meteorological data over designated periods and a subsequent analysis of the data. The first was the Atlantic Tropical Experiment in which seventy countries participated in collecting data from June to September 1974 to study the role of the tropics in global atmospheric circulation patterns. The second was the Global Weather Experiment, which was conducted over a twelve-month period beginning in December 1978 and involved more than 9,000 surface stations and 7,000 ships, in addition to numerous aircraft and ocean buoys and several geostationary and polar orbiting satellites. This elaborate undertaking provided data for the general circulation models used in the 1980s to project future climate changes (Davies, 1990:77-84).

In the aftermath of the first World Climate Conference held in 1979, WMO shifted much of its research effort to climate change. The successor to GARP is the World Climate Research Program (WCRP), one of the four components of the multifaceted World Climate Program that was launched in 1980 and involves several other specialized agencies. WCRP is investigating the relationship among the four Earth systems that contribute to climate—the atmosphere, the oceans, the cryosphere (glaciers, ice, and snow), and land surfaces—to improve forecasting capabilities for time spans ranging from seasons, to decades, and even to centuries. The WCRP complements ICSU's International Geosphere-Biosphere Program which was launched in 1984 to investigate global change and the extent to which it is being caused by human activities.

Three of WCRP's principal projects are the Tropical Ocean and Global

Atmosphere Program, which among other things has been investigating the *El Niño* phenomenon; the World Circulation Experiment (1990-1995), which seeks to map ocean circulation in a way that parallels the general circulation models of atmospheric scientists; and the Global Energy and Water Cycle Experiment (planned for 2000-2005), which will investigate energy transfers involving the atmosphere, evaporation, rainfall, water vapor, and clouds (Bruce, 1991; Morel, 1991).

WMO AND INTERNATIONAL ENVIRONMENTAL POLICY

Before assessing WMO's contributions to international environmental policy, it should be noted that atmospheric policy is not well developed relative to other domains, such as the marine environment. Existing treaties prohibit testing of nuclear devices in the atmosphere and the use of weather modification as a tactic of war. The 1979 Convention on Long Range Transboundary Air Pollution and subsequent protocols are a partial response to acidification in Europe and North America. The outstanding policy-making success in this domain is the series of agreements reached between 1985 and 1990 to preserve the ozone layer, which provide for a virtually complete phasing out of the production of chlorofluorocarbons (CFCs) and other ozone-destroying chemicals by 2000. Thus far, the climate change problem is addressed by nothing more than a framework agreement adopted at the 1992 Earth Summit, which imposes no limits on emission of greenhouse gases (Soroos, 1991:209-12).

WMO's involvement in international environmental policy reflects, and is circumscribed by, its scientific and technological character. WMO was created, developed, and operated by professional meteorologists to facilitate and coordinate the collecting, compiling, and disseminating of weather-related data. In recent decades, WMO has assumed increasing responsibility for conducting atmospheric research projects and assessing the state of scientific knowledge on environmental matters. Given the scope of its mission and capacities, WMO's contribution to international environmental policy has been largely to provide scientific information and advice as needed in the policy process. Thus far, WMO's contributions to policies on the global atmosphere have been primarily in two early stages of the policy-making process: problem identification and problem investigation.

Problem identification involves the early recognition of circumstances that may need to be addressed and calling them to the attention of the international policy-making community. Atmospheric changes that could have immense consequences can be detected only by means of a systematic monitoring with highly sensitive instruments scattered over large geographical areas. If these consequences are to be avoided, international policies regulating human activities that trigger atmospheric changes must anticipate the emerging problem decades before its manifestations are readily apparent.

Through its monitoring programs, WMO has contributed to the early discovery of previously unknown environmental risks involving the atmosphere. In the case of the stratospheric ozone layer, WMO developed a network of ozone-observing stations during the 1950s in conjunction with the International Geophysical Year. The stations began feeding their observations to the World Ozone Data Centre, which was set up in Toronto and operated by the Canadian government. In the aftermath of the Molina and Rowland (1974) revelations about the threat CFCs posed to the ozone layer, WMO established in 1976 the Global Ozone Research and Monitoring Project, which has grown to 140 ground stations in sixty countries. In the case of climate change, WMO has played a similar role in detecting the steady buildup of greenhouse gases over recent decades through its BAPMoN network (Köhler, 1988:262).

Problem investigation entails further study and assessment of the problem to understand more fully both its nature and severity. An agreement on international regulations is unlikely if significant scientific questions remain unanswered and there is substantial disagreement among scientists about the severity, and even the reality, of the problem. Thus, a growing part of WMO's mission is to investigate problems through its monitoring and research programs and to participate in assessments of the state of scientific knowledge on certain questions. For example, during the early 1970s, WMO investigated the hypothesis that exhaust from supersonic aircraft posed a serious threat to the ozone layer, concluding that it was not borne out by scientific evidence (Davies, 1990:88). The World Climate Programme, of which WMO is a principal partner, is a major international effort to understand more fully the climate change phenomenon and its consequences (Bierly, 1988).

WMO has been a key participant in several major assessments of scientific knowledge undertaken to inform international negotiations on atmospheric problems. Two such reports documenting the strength of scientific evidence on the depletion of the ozone layer led to substantive international agreements. Warnings of a significant global ozone loss contained in a lengthy report of WMO, in collaboration with UNEP and several national agencies (WMO et al., 1986), gave strong impetus to negotiations that led to adoption of the Montreal Protocol in 1987, which mandated a 50 percent reduction in CFC production and use by 1998. WMO was also a partner with the National Aeronautics and Space Administration and several other international institutions, in the Ozone Trends Panel, which issued a report in 1988 that authoritatively linked the Antarctic "ozone hole" to CFCs (Kerr, 1988). The report triggered another series of negotiations that culminated in the 1990 London Amendments to the Montreal Protocol which mandate a phasing out of most of the chemicals known to be causing the phenomenon by the turn of the century (Benedick, 1991b).

WMO joined with UNEP and ICSU to sponsor a scientific conference in Villach, Austria, in October 1985, which issued an influential report calling attention to the mounting evidence of the prospects for global warming due to the buildup of CO_2 and other greenhouse gases in the atmosphere (UNEP/WMO/ICSU, 1985). A few years later, WMO and UNEP cosponsored the Intergovernmental Panel on Climate Change (IPCC), which assessed the scientific evidence of global warming and its likely impacts and issued a report in 1990 prior to the Second World Climate Conference and the beginning of negotiations on a climate change treaty (IPCC, 1990).

WMO's principal forays in policymaking and implementing have involved standards and procedures for the uniform collection of meteorological data, tasks that the organization and its predecessor have performed very well. In contrast to the International Telecommunications Union, another technically oriented UN specialized agency that manages use of airwaves and slots in the geostationary orbit, WMO is decidedly not a regulatory agency with a mandate for adopting rules on the activities of countries that impinge on the environment. In the words of its Executive Council, WMO's responsibility goes as far as to "actively support and encourage the development of environmentally sound policies by the international community to respond to climate change, and encourage its 160 members in cooperative efforts and appropriate programs within their own countries" (Davies, 1990:108).

WMO and UNEP have developed a complex partnership in the atmospheric policy process that takes advantage of their complementary capacities. UNEP is better equipped to take on the political challenges associated with formulating and implementing international environmental law and policy. The most common procedure is for UNEP's Environmental Law Unit to prepare drafts of international agreements, which are reviewed and revised by an ad hoc working group of legal and technical experts. If it is to be a legally binding document, UNEP seeks to secure its adoption at a specially convened diplomatic conference (Petsonk, 1990:356). UNEP sponsored the series of negotiating sessions on protecting the ozone layer, and it was largely through the persistence and diplomatic skills of its executive director Mostafa Tolba that the landmark agreements were concluded (see Chapter 10 and Chapter 11). UNEP also provides the secretariat for the agreements. The climate change negotiations were not assigned to UNEP, but to the Intergovernmental Negotiating Committee that was specially constituted by the General Assembly for this purpose.

Although WMO does not assume responsibility for making international environmental policy, in particular the more political tasks of overseeing negotiations, its monitoring systems and the scientific expertise it can marshall will play an increasingly important role in the formulation and analysis of policy options and in the implementation and review of policies once they are adopted. For example, technical questions arose in negotiations on the 1990 London Amendments to the Montreal Protocol on ozone depletion, especially in establishing maximum permissible atmospheric chlorine loadings and in calculating the impact of various policy options on chlorine concentrations (Benedick, 1991b:129-47). As international regulations on air pollution come into force, WMO will be called upon to assist in developing techniques for monitoring compliance, as it has already been doing for the protocols of the Convention on Long Range Transboundary Air Pollution through the EMEP system. WMO will also be involved in assessing the impact of the regulations on addressing atmospheric problems, as it has been doing for the ozone-depletion accords.

EXPLANATIONS OF WMO'S EFFECTIVENESS

WMO is often commended for being a highly successful example of how international governmental organizations can facilitate international cooperation on both scientific research and the assessment of scientific findings. The organization prides itself on being a "temple of rationality" in a world in which sovereign states all too often act upon petty national interests rather than work for the common good (Izrael, 1991). The historical assessments of WMO, prepared for its fortieth anniversary in 1990, recount a remarkable array of achievements in atmospheric monitoring and research. Among the tangible fruits of its meteorological programs is the extension of usable short-term weather forecasts from approximately two days in the early 1960s to five or more days today.

Several explanations can be offered for WMO's accomplishments. The triumph of rationality stems in large part from the organization being run by professional meteorologists, including a series of farsighted presidents and secretaries-general, who have generally provided constructive, forward-thinking leadership (Malone, 1992). Furthermore, the delegates to the congresses and other decision-making bodies, normally the directors of national meteorological and hydrological services, are in most cases chosen for technical expertise rather than for political credentials. This type of representation accounts in part for the virtual absence of the political conflicts between Eastern and Western blocs and between developed and less developed countries that have hamstrung other international organizations, the International Labour Organization and UNESCO in particular. Even during the height of the Cold War, the United States and the Soviet Union maintained a cordial and cooperative working relationship within WMO (Cain, 1983:92; Izrael, 1991).

Several other ingredients are part of WMO's formula for success. One is a long tradition, inherited from IMO, of taking advantage of new technologies, including the telegraph, aircraft, computers, automated instruments, and satellites, to improve its capacity for fulfilling its mission. Another has been the receptiveness of the operational meteorologists involved in WMO's networks to work with academic scientists in major research projects jointly sponsored with

NGOs, in particular ICSU and its relevant committees and unions (Cain, 1983:97). Finally, WMO has come to terms with the complex nature of weather and its consequences and applications by actively entering into partnerships with other international agencies and organizations with complementary functions and capabilities (Davies, 1990:139-50).

WMO AS A PURVEYOR OF PUBLIC GOODS

At another level of analysis, the accomplishments of WMO can be explained by the compelling nature of its basic mission, which is to facilitate the collection and dissemination of information about weather, climate, and the atmosphere that enhances weather forecasting capacities (Malone, 1992). Anticipation of weather conditions is important to numerous industries, such as marine transport and fishing, aviation, and agriculture, as well as to societies in general. Weather monitoring and climate research are natural subjects for international cooperation because the atmosphere circulates without regard to national boundaries. No state can adequately forecast its weather or understand its climate without information collected from vast areas beyond its boundaries (White, 1979).

A strong rationale for collective action among interest-seeking actors does not ensure, however, that cooperation will take place. Numerous cases in which states have not acted cooperatively to achieve a more beneficial outcome have been explained by the payoff matrix of the prisoner's dilemma game. The reasons for WMO's successes in facilitating international cooperation can be better understood in reference to the theory of collective goods (Olson, 1965).

WMO's services are examples of a "public good." In its purest form, a public good is distinguished by two characteristics: jointness of supply and impossibility of exclusion. *Jointness of supply* means that one party's consumption of a good does not reduce the extent to which it is available to others. Thus there is no rivalry between consumers for the enjoyment of a public good (Hardin, 1982:17). Weather data, forecasts, and scientific reports fully satisfy this condition in that the availability and value of meteorological information to any given user is not diminished by its accessibility to any number of other users.

Impossibility of exclusion implies that it is not feasible to restrict access to the good to a designated group of parties (Hardin, 1982:17). Fulfillment of this condition is less clear-cut in the case of WMO because the daily flow of some types of meteorological information can be limited to certain subscribers. Access cannot be denied, however, to published and generally circulated publications of WMO and to publicly issued weather forecasts based on data from WMO networks. Reports on scientific research and assessments relevant to problems such as ozone depletion and climate change are in the public domain, and it is in the interests of their creators to have them disseminated and publicized as widely as possible.

As a purveyor of international public goods, what distinguishes WMO from other organizations that have not been as successful? A problem commonly encountered by organizations established to facilitate collective action is an unwillingness of the membership to pay the cost of providing public goods. If the public goods can be used by all regardless of whether they contribute to their creation, users may be tempted to become "free riders" benefiting from the good that is provided by others. Under some circumstances, what a free rider saves by not paying its share for a public good may give it a competitive advantage over the parties that do (Ophuls and Boyan, 1992:196-97).

There are several reasons why WMO programs have not been hampered by free riders. First, WMO's public goods do not require significant additional sacrifices by its members. Collecting weather data is not a major expense, especially in view of the availability of technologies for automated weather stations, and this is something that modern states would be doing anyway. For most states, the cost of making meteorological observations according to internationally specified standards and procedures is marginal. For states lacking the instruments and the expertise to be full partners in generating weather data, WMO has established technical assistance and education and training programs, which also make possible more effective use of its various meteorological services (Davies, 1990:111-31).

Second, the advanced members with highly developed meteorological services have been willing to provide a disproportionate share of the resources necessary for WMO's public goods. They have done this not only because they have a strong stake in anticipating weather throughout much of the world, but also because of the desire of their large scientific communities to learn about the global dynamics of climate and the atmosphere. Thus, expanding the breadth of geographical coverage of weather stations around the world has been a high enough priority for them to be willing to absorb much of the cost of upgrading the meteorological capacities of poorer states that would not otherwise be able to participate in WMO monitoring networks. For the same reasons, the technologically advanced states have been willing to take the lead and provide the lion's share of the resources needed for WMO's research programs.

CONCLUSIONS

WMO is widely recognized as a highly effective international organization within the domain of its relatively narrow scientific mission of monitoring and conducting research on weather, climate, and the atmosphere. The foreboding prospects of depletion of the ozone layer and global warming due to the impact of human pollutants on atmospheric chemistry have added much to the demands being placed upon WMO as the United Nations agency primarily responsible for providing scientific information on the physical processes of the atmosphere. In view of the complex interrelationship between the atmosphere and the other earth systems, WMO has been drawn increasingly into partnerships with other governmental and nongovernmental organizations with complementary expertise.

WMO's considerable accomplishments over the past forty years derive largely from the nature of its mission. The organization provides an informational public good at relatively little cost to its members and one that is important enough to the more meteorologically advanced states that they are willing to shoulder a disproportionate share of the cost. WMO has not been the organizational forum for negotiations on policies that address the atmospheric problems it identifies and investigates. Assigning responsibility for preserving the ozone layer and minimizing climate change, which could also be categorized as public goods, is intrinsically a much more contentious task, for which WMO is not well equipped nor is it inclined to assume such a task.

WMO is probably well advised to limit its participation in the international public policy processes on the atmosphere to its traditional roles of providing scientific information and expertise that are policy neutral. Were it to inject itself more forcefully into the making of regulatory policy, the organization could lose much of the credibility on scientific matters it has earned over many decades. Furthermore, the experiences of UNESCO are reason for concern that WMO might jeopardize the political and financial support of major contributing states if it calls upon them to shoulder what they consider to be an excessive and unfair share of the cost of preserving the atmosphere.

6

Environmental Learning at the World Bank

Philippe G. Le Prestre

How and what organizations learn or fail to learn are central to the promotion of environmentally sensitive international policies. In the 1980s, nongovernmental organizations (NGOs) and a few governments chastised international financial institutions for their inability to integrate environmental values into the definition and implementation of their tasks. They attacked the World Bank for first adopting weak environmental guidelines and then for ignoring them, and then they accused it of supporting ecological disasters. The organization appeared unwilling or unable to correct its errors. Convinced that it could never learn, some called for its downsizing or even for its elimination (e.g., Korten, 1991; McCully, 1992).

Yet the World Bank has also demonstrated leadership and was encouraged to exert it. The 1989 G-7 Summit exhorted it to integrate the environment into its development activities and to promote sustainable development. Industrialized countries have asked the World Bank to undertake a major role in the formation of a policy consensus and in the management of environmental issues in the developing world. Although NGOs condemned it at the 1992 Rio Summit, governments reaffirmed its central role through their support for the Global Environment Facility (GEF) and additional financial resources. After reviewing the performance of major international organizations, Ernst Haas (1990) has argued that the World Bank was perhaps the only organization that had been able to change its development policy, ideology, and behavior in the face of evolving systemic conditions—that is, to demonstrate learning.

This chapter explores efforts made by the World Bank to correct past errors and implement a new environmental policy adopted in 1987. The organization itself talks constantly about lessons from experience and uses them to justify its positions. Has the World Bank shown sufficient capacity to learn in order to play the role now assigned to it? What type of learning has taken place, and with what impact on organizational performance? What explains either the inertia or the changes observed? If learning has occurred, it ought to be evident in the definition and implementation of two central features of the reform: environmental assessments and public participation. The characteristics of three factors—consensual knowledge, stable dominant coalitions, and leadership—have influenced learning, but learning has also given rise to new dilemmas.

ORGANIZATIONAL LEARNING

"The purpose of learning," according to Katona, "is to improve performance and to master the environment" (Hedberg, 1981:5), a statement that applies to individuals and organizations alike.   Rather than individual psychosocial processes and belief changes, however, what concerns us is whether and how an organization alters its behavior in light of changing conditions. Learning is informed by the political interests of the organization and by its routines and internal divisions. From an open systems perspective, organizational learning means securing access to resources, prestige and autonomy.

Ernst Haas tried to clear the confusion surrounding the concept of learning by distinguishing it from adaptation. An organization can adapt in three ways: (1) through incremental growth where new tasks are added to older ones without any change in organizational decisionmaking; (2) through "turbulent non-growth" where there are major changes in the decision-making process but increasing difficulties in reconciling ends, and where internal consensus disappears; and (3) through the development of new consensual knowledge that leads to changes in decisionmaking and the adoption of new values, new interests, and new problem definitions (Haas, 1990:4, 23). Only the last would constitute true learning.

This distinction, however, may induce confusion since learning is itself a form of positive adaptation, a meaning that is not intrinsic to Haas's definition. Learning, for him, appears closer to evolution. The organization that has "learned" has become a different organization rather than one that has just learned to do its job better. Further, Haas often mixes learning as process and learning as outcome.   Here I focus largely on an organization's attempt to integrate environmental parameters into development policy, rather than on the question of whether its projects have effectively mitigated or avoided environmental destruction.

Four forms of learning become adaptive goals: (1) error correction, or how to improve the organization's performance in light of its objectives; (2) change in the norms built into theory in use, accompanied by a change in the organization's model of the world (Haas, 1990; Schön, 1983:119-20); (3) the capacity to integrate new knowledge into its operations or to respond more quickly to new demands and to new information (Hedberg, 1981), which becomes crucial as the policy environment becomes more uncertain; and (4) transformation of the organization's environment in order to improve the organization's access to key resources.

Adaptation involves choices (adapt to which set of demands?) and risks (alienate whom? endanger which other organizational task? create what other vulnerability?). The early record of the World Bank reflects specific attitudes toward risks and constraints on choice.

THE EARLY POLICY AND THE 1987 REFORM

The Failure of the Bank's Environmental Policy before 1987

The World Bank was the first multilateral development agency to recognize the importance of environmental parameters in development lending and to include environmental criteria in project evaluation (Le Prestre, 1989; Goodland, 1992). Having recruited an environmental adviser in 1969, it set up an Office of Environmental Affairs in 1971 that was to review projects for their potential environmental impact, and sensitize the organization and the developing countries to these issues. The desire to reconcile the different perspectives of its members led the World Bank to promote a definition of the problem that would include resource use, the modification of ecosystems, and the quality of life of the people. Since the 1970s, its rhetoric has rested on the twin imperatives of poverty reduction and economic growth.

In spite of this development perspective, the environmental policy of the World Bank developed slowly. The first policy directive was adopted in 1984 (excluding policies on indigenous resettlements in 1980 and on tribal peoples in 1982 that were based mainly upon human rights considerations). A skeleton staff reviewed projects after appraisal. Quantification difficulties, the extremist character of the initial environmental discourse, the suspicions of developing countries, and internal doubts complicated the adoption of a progressive and sustained policy. Different sectors of the organization perceived the environmental dimension differently. Operational checklists put out by the environment office were considered optional. This attitude persisted even when policies were formally adopted (Morse and Berger, 1992; Goodland, 1992). Short-term economic justifications predominated over long-term impacts, and American-style environmental impact statements were opposed by borrowers and rejected in the context of poor countries. Environmental hazards were justified as long as they were "balanced" by economic benefits and did not endanger the immediate financial success of the project.

The policy stumbled mainly on the implementation of the mitigation measures, although these were specific to the project and negotiated with the borrower. The World Bank overestimated the capacity and willingness of local administrations to follow provisions and schedules formally agreed upon, as in Brazil's Polonoroeste case. A review of the Sardar Sarovar project in India charged that the Bank did not follow its own procedures on resettlement and did not enforce the negotiated agreements (Morse and Berger, 1992:xv). Finally, the fate of mitigating provisions remained precarious once the project was completed and the loan fully disbursed.

Ignorance of the sociological, political or natural context of projects also led to many project failures, especially dams, rangelands development, and forestry. Several became *causes célèbres*. The Trans-Juba cattle project in the Sudan failed because its design did not consider grazing rights, cattle movements, sociological constraints on production, land use patterns, the needs of populations, or the infrastructure needed. Polonoroeste accelerated colonization of the state of Rondonia in Brazil, triggering massive deforestation and violation of Indian rights. Indonesia's Transmigration Project had similar consequences. The operational units of the Bank and the Indian government were persuaded that the importance of the Sardar Sarovar projects overrode design shortcomings.

Under these conditions, the Bank often kept on lending even though recipients repeatedly ignored its environmental conditions. It argued that continuous involvement at least might help mitigate some abuse and allow it to monitor implementation. Various organizational incentives—the need to maintain close links with and support from its constituency, the need to increase both the volume of lending and the number of loans, the lack of expertise in resource economics in the environmental office, and a reluctance to complicate one's work—conspired to create much inertia.

Yet it became increasingly clear that the Bank's basic development goals were threatened; too many projects failed for environmental reasons. Controversies led to political crises that translated into financial and managerial ones. Both the Third World Left and the Reagan Right used the environment to pursue their ideological critiques, condemn the organization, and endanger its growth. These actions decreased its legitimacy and autonomy. The lack of consultation in project design sometimes led local populations supported by activists to oppose projects, presenting significant obstacles to successful implementation.

Evolving human rights values—regarding the resettlement of peoples for example—and successful coalition building among environmental activists, anthropologists, and supporters of new development thinking threatened the organization's access to key resources. By fostering mobilization and channeling antigovernmental opposition, environmental controversies also undermined the political stability of the recipients and, consequently, the organization's relationship with its borrowers and creditors.

The 1987 Reform

Learning, then, first entailed error correction: how to prevent future environmental problems that would delay the implementation of a project or endanger its economic viability; how to ensure respect for agreed-upon guidelines; and how to modify or stop failing projects. It implied weakening the alliance of environmental NGOs with right-wing critics of the Bank in the U.S. Congress and government, which harmed its prestige and jeopardized its access to financing and projects. It meant reducing the uncertainty attached to the success of its projects and to the survival and growth of an organization dependent on the support of both its clients and its creditors.

A general reorganization of the World Bank activities in 1987 sought to reinforce the organization's links with its members by decentralizing its operations, increasing the transparency of its activities, and improving its relations with its borrowers. With respect to its environmental record, Barber Conable, president of the World Bank, admitted that the organization had "stumbled" and that environmental degradation could lead to new economic and social difficulties (Conable, 1987). The Bank's Development Committee, composed of the finance ministers of member countries, discussed the environment for the first time in 1987 and encouraged the Bank to become more active in this field in subsequent meetings.

From then on, the environmental action of the Bank would take place on two levels: project and policy. At the project level, environmental considerations would be incorporated early into all lending decisions through environmental assessments, and an environmental lending sector would be developed. But the Bank had also recognized since 1982 that the project level was insufficient to help change national policies. The 1987 Development Committee report stressed that environmental questions should be approached within the framework of national economic policies rather than at the project level. Thus policy level action developed steadily in conformity with the general evolution of the Bank in the 1980s that saw increased emphasis on sectoral and structural adjustment lending—up to a high of 34.6 percent of Bank commitments in fiscal year 1991 (World Bank, 1991a:13).

A new Environment Department—which, together with the environmental staff of the regional and country units, accounted for close to 200 professionals in 1993, compared to five in 1985—became responsible for internal coordination, research and planning, staff support and training, data bases development and external relations. Environmental units were set up in the technical department of the five regional divisions in order to supervise environmental assessments and help develop national policies. Following another reorganization in 1993, which saw the creation of a new vice presidency for Environmentally Sustainable Development, several regional environmental units were merged into larger divisions, and the environmental capacity of country departments was strengthened (World Bank, 1993a).

The Bank identified five priorities: destruction of natural habitats, soil degradation, depletion of freshwater resources, pollution, and global environmental issues (World Bank, 1990a:13). Country environmental issue papers, drafted for each recipient, were intended to guide staff, coordinate unit work, and raise the consciousness of the clientele. Important issues could then be raised during the dialogue with the borrower and be included in national strategies, sectoral activities, loans, and national environmental action plans (NEAPs).

THE IMPLEMENTATION OF THE 1987 REFORM

The new structure evolved slowly. Technical units developed at different rates, more gradually in the Latin America region than in the Asia or Africa regions. The number of environmental projects went from two in 1989 to twenty-three in 1993—compared to three in 1975 or 1980. In 1993, two billion dollars—three times the 1991 amount—was allocated to "free-standing" environmental projects wherein environmental costs and benefits exceeded 50 percent of total costs and benefits. This increase, although still modest relative to the roughly $24 billion lent that same year, is noteworthy since a large proportion of previous environmental lending in fact went toward disaster relief—accounting for one-third of the 1991 total. In 1993, about two-thirds of the $2 billion committed was for pollution control and the urban environment, one-fourth for natural resources and the rural environment, and about 8 percent for institution building (World Bank, 1993a). Actual lending thus differed from the priorities identified a few years earlier. The Bank also claims that half the loans approved since 1990 contained environmental components—wherein over 10 percent of project costs or benefits are environmental—mostly in the agricultural sector. The figures were 38 percent in 1989 and only 7 percent in 1980. But the definition of what is an environmental component—or an environmental project for that matter—can vary greatly. Certain forestry, land reclamation, and water supply projects are now included. Lifting price controls on liquified petroleum gas in Bangladesh has been classified as an environmental component, presumably because price control encourages overconsumption whereas energy substitution is considered inherently positive. Since the Bank draws more and more positive linkages between the environment and its other activities, these figures can only increase in the future.

The World Bank has recognized the principle that environmental protection is an integral part of the development process and has adopted important initiatives on assessments, action plans, settlements, dams, and forests. Through the Global Environment Facility, it plays a major role in shaping the global agenda on environmental issues. Still, the capstone of the Bank's action, and of its capacity to learn, lies with environmental assessments (EAs), "an umbrella policy which fosters compliance with all the others" (Goodland, 1992:12).

Environmental Assessments and National Plans

Assessment of projects with major environmental impacts was made official policy in 1984 and tightened into a formal requirement through an operational directive (OD) issued in October 1989 (OD 4.00) and amended two years later (OD 4.01). The Bank now requires environmental assessments for every project likely to have a significant impact on the environment.

EAs help address unfulfilled expectations, develop new performance criteria, and defuse political opposition. Yet, in the 1970s and 1980s, the Bank had rejected the idea of mandating impact statements for fear they would be too costly, overtax staff resources, delay project preparation and appraisal, and lack meaning in countries with few legal, scientific, and administrative capacities. Impact studies were performed on an ad hoc basis and for specific aspects of the project. Proponents within the Bank were few; and few outside, apart from NGOs, favored this approach. What changed?

Changes in the political environment of the Bank and in the environmental capacities of its borrowers accounted for much of this evolution. The U.S., Canadian, and Scandinavian executive directors actively encouraged it. The U.S. Agency for International Development (USAID) and its Canadian counterpart had already adopted this requirement. In 1988, for example, Canada asked the World Bank to prepare and publish impact studies and annual reports, to inform and involve NGOs in these studies, to develop criteria for the exploitation and conservation of natural resources in collaboration with borrowers, and to explore new ways of financing conservation projects. At the same time, more and more engineers within and outside the Bank have turned to environmental management as a means of improving their professional status.

EAs aim to ensure that environmental impacts are recognized and taken into account early in project design. Ecologists wished to prevent the engineers' faits accomplis and resisted acting only as environmental fire brigades. Instead of being performed after basic decisions had been made, EAs are to help decide among several options, including non-lending. Accordingly, the policy requires that environmental screening take place at the time of project identification. Members of the Environment Department join the feasibility study team and draft a separate report made available before financial evaluation. Negotiations with the borrower cannot proceed without the green light from the regional environmental units (REDs).

Task managers classify projects according to their potential environmental impact into three categories (A, B, C), with full-fledged assessments to be conducted for category A projects, and limited ones for category B. EAs are a flexible procedure, the borrower's responsibility, and vary in breadth, depth and type of analysis. The policy encourages borrowers to involve affected groups and local NGOs and seeks to strengthen national environmental capabilities.

This development raised new issues about the initial classification of projects, the monitoring of sector lending, and the quality of the actual studies, since criteria should take local circumstances into account. Well-known for bowing to borrowers' wishes, the Bank, it was feared, would not enforce its provisions. Meanwhile, the earlier arguments against such guidelines remained.

In fact, the Bank claims that a typical study amounts to 5 to 10 percent of preparation costs and to about 1 percent of the total cost of the project, which is within an acceptable range. Borrowers can request financial help from the Bank as an advance on the loan or apply for a grant from a technical assistance fund set up in 1989. Further, the Consultant Trust Fund for the Environment provides direct funding to the Bank for EA grants and environmental activities.

The World Bank approaches EAs by their primary function of building up local capacity, which makes them more acceptable to the borrowers who undertake and pay for the study. The Environment Department has a special unit made up of EA specialists, and each RED either has assigned the task of supervision to specific individuals or has divided it among staff. In any case, since EAs are not required for all projects, the volume, although increasing, has not been quite as high as expected. Projections indicated that about 8 percent of all projects funded by the end of fiscal year 1992 required a full assessment (category A), 39 percent more limited studies (category B), and 42 percent none (Goodland, 1990:7). In 1993 the figures were 9 percent for category A, and 43 percent for category B (World Bank, 1993a). In contrast, the Bank had estimated in the 1970s that two-thirds of its projects required no particular precaution. Most full assessments concern the energy and agriculture sectors. EAs are required for all sectoral projects but not for structural adjustment projects.

The real worry among Operations was that delays would be unavoidable. The duration of EAs—between six and eighteen months—works against the desire of the organization to accelerate the preparatory phase of projects. For several Asian countries, for example, EAs that provide exhaustive environmental baseline data but little guidance on mitigatory measures are costly extras, delaying projects without improving them significantly. Thus, there is a danger that incomplete data will be used. The requirement that EAs start during project preparation and be tied to regional environmental plans, monitoring, and enforcement may help lessen that risk. In addition, the Bank decided to monitor the implementation of the policy carefully within the organization. Units were to share "best practice" experience gained in one place or project with others facing similar tasks. The EA Directive was also quickly reviewed and strengthened in 1991 in the light of early experience.

A comparison of the 1989 and 1991 directives identifies issues that arose during implementation of OD 4.00 and hints at the capacity of the Bank to correct potential errors, assimilate incoming information, and change behavior accordingly. Although the purpose and structure of the procedures remain the same, noteworthy changes include reduction in the number of categories from four to three—the old category D environmental projects could also have environmental impacts—and strengthening the requirement that affected groups and NGOs be consulted during design and implementation. Other changes stipulated that global issues be taken into account where feasible, that Operations keep the Environment Department informed of the EA process, that the classification of projects by the task manager be approved by RED, that EAs also assess impacts "in the area of influence of a project," and that the environmental impact of *all* options be considered.

The efficiency of the EA process depends on its acceptance within and outside the organization, on the growth of scientific knowledge, and on the capacity of the borrowers to prepare EAs. Internally, the EA directives complicated the work of task managers, although the acceptance of the procedure was helped by the rapid issuance of a detailed sourcebook. A new Economic Development Institute training program addressed the lack of expertise. It was partly designed to change existing beliefs about cause-effect relationships among senior managers and policy advisers regarding the interlinkages among environment, development, and social livelihoods.

Externally, especially in sub-Saharan Africa, EAs raised particular problems linked to the weakness of environmental institutions, the lack of national policies, and the prevalence of lending for policy and small-scale projects. Consequently, the Bank has promoted NEAPs and, in 1991, called for their urgent implementation (Jaycox, 1992: 7). The regional environmental division for Africa was instrumental in the creation of the Dublin Club in December 1990 intended to support the NEAP process through training, information sharing, network building, evaluation, and monitoring. Madagascar, Mauritius, and Lesotho were the first to initiate such plans, starting in 1987-1988; Bank borrowers had completed twenty-eight by mid-1993 (World Bank, 1993a:19). It is really after the completion of these plans that EAs can be most effective.

More and more projects address the importance of the legislative and policy environment and of land tenure security for effective resources conservation and sustainable development (Falloux, 1989:13, 14). EAs and NEAPs are less environmental than political instruments: they involve and depend upon the participation of many groups with different interests. The process then becomes more important than the product. It serves to mold a consensus behind the problem and acceptable solutions. Moreover, NEAPs later help identify new projects and lending areas, thus overcoming a key resource limitation. The Technical Assistance Facility will grant funds on the basis of environmental priorities so established.

EAs, NEAPs, and country environmental profiles provide ammunition for the future promotion of environmental concerns. They help keep the environmental scientific community and local consulting firms mobilized and their skills up to date. Yet the policy also tries to reconcile the different goals of the organization, of which the minimization of environmental damages is but one. EAs are tools for decisionmaking and consensus building, not blueprints for protection. Their primary functions are to reduce political and economic liabilities and to build local constituencies. Their technical merits are secondary to these functions.

Public Participation

The World Bank insists that EAs and NEAPs consider the needs of local peoples. Natural resources conservation will not be effective unless local populations profit from it and projects address local social conditions. This approach allows the Bank to deflect some NGO critiques but also clashes with traditional procedures. The organization is used to dealing with central authorities whose personnel often has a limited understanding of local field conditions.

In 1982 a Bank-NGO Committee was set up to encourage dialogue on broad issues of development policy. NGOs were mostly involved in implementation—for example, in the management of small-scale irrigation systems delegated to water users' associations. They were mostly present in the agriculture, population, and health sectors. Their role has since increased under their own pressure, with the encouragement of some governments, and because borrowers have shown more openness. In 1988 the Bank adopted policy guidelines governing its collaboration with NGOs. It has entered into a policy dialogue with them and has agreed to limited NGO involvement in project preparation and implementation. It conceded that indigenous groups should participate in the design and execution of Bank-assisted projects that affect their welfare, but it has encouraged them to develop a direct dialogue with their respective governments.

NGOs are increasingly involved in project design, and the Bank supports their role in strengthening local participation in development planning. They played an important role, for example, in the planning process of Madagascar's NEAP. On 11 March 1992 Mohammed El-Ashry, director of the Environment Department and former vice president of the World Resources Institute, said that NGOs' participation in project planning and implementation "gives a voice to the marginalized poor whose lives are impacted by the development process . . . . NGOs help to organize underrepresented people and facilitate their participation in the planning of their own development" (World Bank, 1992a). According to the 1991 operational directive (OD 4.01), the borrower must allow public participation as soon as a project is assigned to the A category. If it does not, or will not distribute information on the project, the Bank may refuse to lend money. Participation can also take place before completion of screening. Finally, the Pelosi amendment, adopted by the U.S. Congress in 1991, will facilitate the mobilization and involvement of local groups by ensuring that the American public and affected people in developing countries have access to environmental information about proposed projects.[1]

NGOs and affected communities can raise issues during the EA process through the government agency responsible for the project, the borrower's executive director (ED), the Bank's country representative, international NGOs, or directly through the Bank's Washington staff. Projects that require full EAs allow NGO and community participation during the entire project cycle. There is no formal public participation role in category B environmental analysis, although the public can ask the Bank for a change of classification.

Involving local peoples has two functions. First, it reduces the risks of failures by identifying potential financial and ecological problems. Participation allows the Bank to keep track of its funds and to maximize the probability of successful implementation by fostering the transparency of procedures, the accountability of government officials, the predictability of institutional actions, and the openness of the flow of information. Second, participation deflects attempts by ideological critics of the Bank to use environmental controversies as a means of questioning the legitimacy and existence of the organization.

Although the Bank needs NGOs for information gathering and implementation, participation can appear destabilizing and threaten the state. Governments, particularly in Latin America, recoil at empowering local groups or allowing direct intervention by, and contact with, outside institutions. Consequently, the meaning of consultation has remained vague. Several industrialized and industrializing countries argue that government representatives also represent local groups. Most countries view the participation of affected groups in planning, conducting, and reviewing EAs as a radical and unsettling departure from present practice. Units of the Bank relay specific misgivings in accordance with their clienteles' preferences. A 1993 review of EA concluded that, in many cases, "consultation with affected populations and local NGOs had been limited at best" (World Bank, 1993a:61).

Constraints on Performance

The implementation of the Bank's environmental strategy cannot take place overnight. For example, the implementation process of the environmental assessments directive was expected to take five years. Furthermore, this procedure does not guarantee that the environmental concerns and objectives so identified will be addressed during implementation. Indeed, constraints remain.

The blind transfer of foreign scientific models, techniques, and criteria has led to project designs unsuited to local conditions. Resource management models often rest on assumptions that are specific to northern conditions. For example, attempts to transfer soil conservation techniques appropriate for large holdings of more temperate climates to Asian countries characterized by small holdings, diverse cultivation techniques, extreme climatic ranges, financial constraints and shortage of expertise have been disappointing (Magrath and Doolette, 1990:9). This situation refers to the more general problem of supply-driven rather than need-driven policies (Falloux, 1989:12). In order to reach its scientific and commercial goals, the Bank has traditionally looked for projects and problems to which existing techniques and tools could be applied, rather than first identifying local, regional, or national needs and the technical, institutional, economic, or political obstacles to their fulfillment. The Bank hopes that NEAPs will remedy this situation since the countries themselves manage the process with the participation of the public.

Bureaucratic constraints also survive. Lending volume, speed of preparation, and number of projects all matter to task managers and to member governments. Environmental reforms add new disincentives to the translation of learning into policy, such as the sheer complexity of the diversity of new policies.

Further, past error corrections can impede other forms of learning if the organization has accumulated objectives in response to the demands of its milieu. The Bank must promote growth, reduce poverty, transfer capital and technology, strengthen private enterprise, increase investment in human resources and agricultural production, reduce population growth, foster public participation and the role of women in development, ensure environmentally sustainable development, address global environmental problems, help steer Eastern Europe toward growth, and manage structural adjustment plans and lending. Although the Bank often claims these goals are not only compatible but synergistic, they often do conflict. High fees needed to maintain costly antipollution devices hurt the poor. Rural colonization may increase the standard of living of the poorest at the cost of massive deforestation. Epidemiological concerns and the need for land justify draining swamps. How these different goals can be integrated into benefit-cost analyses, which have favored the social value attached to regional development, food security, and access to land, is unclear.

On the other hand, environmental issues can also serve more traditional goals. Indeed, this instrumental function shapes what the organization learns. The multiplicity of objectives the Bank has defined for itself frames and gives shape to its environmental policy. For example, the Bank has made natural resources sustainability an institutional priority in the context of the protection of agricultural lands (Jaycox, 1992:25, 31). The mobilization potential of socioenvironmental issues will increase the tendency to use them to further other aims. Food security, market liberalization, economic growth, the participation of women, poverty reduction, and structural adjustments can all have positive environmental values. The adoption of a homocentric definition of the problem, however, can contradict ecological imperatives. Environmental measures whose social and economic rate of return are nil or negative will hardly be supported.

Moreover, environmental protection legitimizes orthodox political and economic conditions imposed on the borrowers. Since state subsidies, price controls, and inequitable fiscal policies encourage wasteful uses of resources, they should be removed under structural adjustment. Right-wing critics of the Bank have charged that reliance on governmental institutions "often means strengthening the very agencies that hold back development" (Bandow, 1989:81). Birth control and promoting the role of women in development would also benefit the environment. Finally, the environment allows the Bank access to new financial resources and projects. These various links among the Bank's diverse goals may help advance its environmental policy, but they also may become catalysts for the emergence of new opposition if environmental concerns are perceived to cloak other interests. Such perceptions will seem justified by the organization's belief that, as the deputy director of the Environment Department declared in 1991, "While liberalization of markets is a necessary condition for environmental improvement, . . . it needs to be matched by political liberalization in which those adversely affected by environmental degradation can freely express their concerns."[2]

Misgivings also follow a growing consensus among donors and NGOs that blames national policies for the destruction of natural resources. For example, it ascribes a crucial role in deforestation and soil degradation to property and income distribution and to population growth (Spears, 1988; Foy and Daly, 1989; Leonard, 1989). Although these factors may be more important than bad national budgets, the Bank often feels more comfortable with less politically touchy budgetary questions, which happen to correspond with the expertise of its economists. National administrative capacities and unfavorable power distribution among governmental units have also been identified as important limiting factors.

Few governments are ready to adopt drastic conservation measures unless the impact of environmental destruction compromises their political survival or the country's short-range development prospects. Environmental issues provide many states with the means to expand state power and compensate for a reduction of aid transfers. Borrowers will favor environmental projects that increase employment, hold visible and immediate benefits within the national boundaries, and reinforce the authority of the state. Moreover, many developing countries question the international environmental agenda and the focus on conservation of natural resources or climatic issues. They would prefer more people-oriented projects with more visible political and human impacts.

DETERMINANTS OF LEARNING

Ernst Haas has identified two necessary conditions for learning: (1) the presence of consensual knowledge (nested in a new epistemic community) that provides the rationale for the new approach and (2) the existence of a stable dominant coalition within the organization (1990:164). In addition, the works of Cox and Jacobson (1973), Young (1989b), and Schechter (1990) suggest that top decisionmakers play an additional crucial role: learning must start at the top if change is to follow.

Project Failures and Consensual Knowledge

The Bank claims that the speed with which it has issued new policies in the past decade is rooted in the desire to improve task performance following "mounting evidence that continued environmental degradation threatens the attainment of the Bank's objectives: reducing poverty and promoting sustainable development" (World Bank, 1991c:2). A 1992 internal report stated that the share of problem projects in the portfolio had increased from an average of 10 percent between 1979 and 1981 to 17 percent in 1989-1991, the highest recorded rate of failure in the Bank's history (Wapenhans, 1992). The share of financially unsuccessful projects has increased over the same period from an average of 13.1 percent to a three-year average of 35 percent.

While many different causes can be invoked—Bank economists are likely to blame the economic environment of the countries themselves—neglect of environmental and social conditions were increasingly linked to project failures. Projects that were a success from a narrow economic viewpoint would end up social and political failures, with negative impacts on the Bank's political standing. Many projects could succeed locally in the short run and have disastrous regional impacts or entail additional expenses later. Further, as the focus of the Bank has shifted toward poverty, so have criteria of success and the importance of socioenvironmental impacts.

Successful adaptation implies that the organization will facilitate, impose, or promote a common definition of the problem and of the criteria used to evaluate its performance. Much of the Bank's strategy revolves around internal and external consensus-building, for it is political conflict even more than environmental failures that threatens the organization's access to key resources. This situation is not unprecedented; the evolution of development economics has repeatedly forced the organization to improve its intellectual fitness.

On the one hand, the breakdown of consensus enables change to take place; on the other hand, consensus-building becomes the overriding goal of the organization as it tries to reconcile the diverse interests of its internal feudalities and external clienteles. It is political consensus rather than scientific consensus that matters; the organization first looks for common ground, not new paradigms. The environmental assessment and planning processes, as well as the *1992 World Development Report* on Environment and Development, play a crucial role in this search for consensual knowledge around the notion of sustainable development. Regarding tropical forests, the vice president for the Africa region declared in November 1990 that the main lending criterion would be ecological sustainability rather than rates of return, thus pointing away from traditional forestry concerns (Serageldin, 1991:32). This shift might be facilitated by the recognition that rates of return have increasingly become meaningless evaluation criteria, or were misused as a result of "a systematic and growing bias in favour of optimistic rate of return expectations at appraisal" (Wapenhans, 1992:1).

Although the environment as a development variable has been largely accepted, divisions exist between economists and engineers; between Keynesian and liberal economists; among classical economics, sustainable development and resource conservation; and between two visions of a sustainable world: interrelated, self-reliant, local systems versus global sustainability (see Korten, 1991:184). Sustainable development has a variety of meanings: sustainable growth, fruitful investments, resource conservation, exploitation for maximum yield, or the maximization of long-term benefits—which can include converting a resource into wealth that will benefit the largest number of people (Ascher and Healy, 1990:5). The World Bank has strongly endorsed the Brundtland definition of sustainable development but insists that "[w]hat matters is that the overall productivity of the accumulated capital—including its impact on human health and aesthetic pleasure, as well as on incomes—more than compensates for any loss from depletion of natural capital" (World Bank, 1992b:8). A comparison of benefits and costs—technically uncertain—should form the basis for decision. In that sense, the organization reshapes its discourse without switching perspectives.

An iconoclastic internal memorandum sent in late 1991 by Lawrence Summers—then chief economist and vice president of development economics, and later a member of the Clinton administration—illustrates the lack of consensus. In an exercise in reasoning from pure neoclassical economics principles, Summers argued that the Bank should encourage more migration of dirty industries to developing countries—a practice that some countries actually supported in the 1970s—based on narrow benefit-cost calculations.[3] This note also raised issues that the Bank prefers to assume away, notably potential trade-offs between poverty and environmental protection. It caused outrage inside and outside the Bank, hurting the careful public relations that the organization had been building for the past five years. Several negative reactions suggested that not only economic but moral arguments mattered.

Haas (1990) regards learning as a process whereby one type of knowledge is substituted for another. Hedberg has noted that both understanding changing environments and effective learning require abandoning obsolete mental maps and old behaviors, in addition to learning new ones (1981:4). The focus of education as a teaching strategy rests on this assumption. Yet if one has paradigm change in mind, how new knowledge can help build a new consensus is unclear. Ad hoc theorizing takes place, and the knowledge under siege strains to accommodate new concerns and data. It may be more useful to approach consensus as the indicator of a political and social process: the replacement of a dominant coalition by another. What drove the 1987 reforms was as much the nature of the external criticisms and the political impact of controversies upon the Bank's well-being and autonomy, as any "new" knowledge that in fact had been around for years. The organization "learns" not because its individuals switched paradigms, but because a new coalition has been able to impose its preferred definitions and solutions. This is done more through attrition and evolving political dynamics than through conversion. Likewise, at the local level, the strategy is not so much to change values as to empower new groups and reconcile economic and political interests with environmental welfare.

It is easy to overemphasize the importance of knowledge by presenting it as both a necessary and sufficient condition of learning. Yet in the short run, behavior matters more than beliefs. The need to maintain access to resources and bureaucratic incentives to change are crucial determinants of evolution. What passes for intellectual opposition and evidence of rival epistemic communities often only reflects traditional bureaucratic concerns with predictability, career, and simplicity. Incentives can be changed to emphasize success rate, as President Preston promised to do. Many country officers complain that too many policies complicate their jobs. Big projects become less desirable not because of a changing consensus, but because they are too complex and open to unsettling controversies.

Stable Dominant Coalitions

Member countries and actors working through them heavily influence the Bank. For example, U.S. environmental NGOs have successfully pressured the Bank through Congress to pay more attention to the human impact of its projects. The continuing existence of a dominant coalition certainly helped the Bank evolve. When donors started yielding to public pressure, the organization not only had to respond but knew that any reform would benefit from external political reinforcements. For example, instead of undermining the Bank, bilateral agencies would spread a similar message revolving around EAs, institution building, and participation. The World Bank looked seriously into its support for the Sardar Sarovar project only after the Japanese government cancelled its participation. These concerns became legitimate; if borrowers could accept it, so could Operations.

Donors have been paying increasing attention to the long-term management of natural resources, a crucial aspect of development planning. The United Nations Conference on Environment and Development encouraged symbolic initiatives, political debates, and action. In 1988 the Group of Seven recognized the environment as a genuine and important policy domain. These heads of states and governments supported a rapid implementation of the Tropical Forestry Action Plan and the sustainable management of forest resources. The World Bank was asked to play a leading role in the search for a global political consensus on environmental and developmental concerns. In 1993 the representatives of donor countries to the negotiations for the tenth replenishment of the International Development Association insisted that all countries eligible for this fund prepare NEAPs.

Often, however, there is only the appearance of stability. Industrialized countries were divided over conditionality, the role of NGOs, and the Global Environment Facility. Bilateral aid agencies have differed over the wisdom of imposing the NEAP process. Further, stability can also work both ways. Haas considers as positive the very existence of a stable coalition because he regards learning as originating within the organization: stable coalitions enable internal reform. But if learning is externally triggered, stable coalitions can become obstacles when they do not share the organization's priorities. Preoccupation with the debt crisis starting in the late 1970s delayed environmental reforms until the 1987 general reorganization (Goodland, 1992:10). Reforestation and energy savings became less urgent when the oil crisis eased.

Internal Leadership

Although all individuals within the organization can initiate the organizational learning process, organizational learning itself is enabled by senior management. The experience of other organizations has shown that active support of the executive head is vital to overcoming internal resistance, improving the coherence of operational priorities, and influencing borrowers' attitudes. When Robert McNamara decided to lend for education, he ordered economists to ignore the rates of return, which until then had been used to justify opposition to this sector.

The top decisionmakers do not have to belong to a new epistemic community, but they have to support the groups or coalitions that try to impose their preferred definitions and solutions. They influence the way task managers in charge of a project see their role. Any change in career incentives will demand leadership from senior management. In times of task uncertainty, reassurance from the leadership is essential. Leadership also implies support for the decisions of the Environment Department and the RED by insisting that policies—such as public participation—are mandatory and not optional recommendations. Top management has also increasingly used the bully pulpit to persuade both the institution and the borrowers that environmentally unsustainable development is uneconomical, even immoral.

CONCLUSION: LEARNING AS A POLITICAL PROCESS

Learning addressed two requirements: rebuilding favorable political coalitions and improving performance. The Bank approached both tasks first through error correction, which took different forms depending on the political dynamics at work. The EA directives enabled REDs to stop projects in their tracks. In some cases, the Bank took dramatic action as when it suspended disbursements for the first time in 1985 for environmental reasons or cancelled a loan on similar grounds for the first time in 1989. This procedure remains rare, however. Only after years of controversy, pressures from donors and NGOs, and the release of a critical report (Morse and Berger, 1992), did the Bank withdraw its financial support of the Sardar Sarovar project in India. (This report demonstrated a remarkable and unprecedented willingness to look publicly and extensively into its record.) In other cases, error correction meant banning some activities outright. In June 1986 it decided to stop lending for projects in fragile ecosystems and in July 1991 declared an end to support for commercial logging in tropical forests. Although blanket interdictions are probably the easiest way to avoid controversies and promote bureaucratic compliance, they are not necessarily the best means of promoting environmentally sustainable development. Countries need foreign exchange. Yet Operations finds it more appealing since such blanket policy rids it of complicated headaches.

Environmental assessments seek to change the norms that govern behavior. The Bank promotes a new model of the world around a classical economics approach to environmental issues. Much has been learned about the sociological, cultural, and political contexts of sustainable development. EAs, especially sectoral ones, are potentially powerful instruments of change and can serve as primary vehicles for reorientation.

More important though, learning is essentially a political process. Consensual knowledge and stable coalitions are important when they foster common expectations about the organization's performance. The Bank has acted chiefly when it could make an economic, social, or political link between environmental degradation and human welfare. EAs aim to facilitate the development of political consensus inside and outside the Bank in order to minimize future political controversies; their content then becomes secondary. Organizations that learn are able to create environments they can control.

The Bank hopes to improve performance by limiting its involvement in controversial projects, by creating the conditions for effective national implementation of agreed-upon procedures, by internalizing environmental concerns through institutional and policy frameworks, by creating local constituencies, and by relying on NGOs for supervision. The emphasis is on gaining local support and commitment as well as increasing local capacities. The Bank tends to believe that design and the involvement of the borrower, more than supervision, improves projects. Yet the Wapenhans and Morse reports also underlined the importance of supervision. Accordingly, the Bank decided in 1993 to pay closer attention to the implementation of its environmental policy in the field.

This strategy has allowed the Bank to improve considerably its access to funds, projects, and political support. In that sense it has "learned." But it also faces a new dilemma because the new policy reduces the control that it has over its own performance. EA procedures, intended to protect the Bank from economic and political project failures, create new vulnerabilities as they throw the organization into the thicket of national politics. Other factors reinforce this trend: the pressure to include local participation, the role of broker among national administrations and social groups that the Bank plays through NEAPs and EAs, the use of environmental and human rights issues by ambitious local politicians, and the use of environmental issues by governments as a means of gaining access to international capital. The assumption that transparency and pluralism will contribute to consensus building behind a set of criteria governing development projects and process (Goodland, Juras, and Pachauri, 1992) runs the risk that the outcome of environmental debates will rest not on sustainable development considerations but on internal political power struggles. Transparency identifies winners and losers, and pluralism ensures that the aggrieved parties will stay involved. Environmental learning, therefore, has reduced the autonomy of the organization by forcing it to assume a larger political role.

NOTES

1. Amendment to the 1992 International Financial Institutions Act, Section 1307(d). *Federal Register* 57, No.112 (10 June 1992):24544-46.

2. Jeremy Warford and David Wheeler in a paper presented in November 1991, quoted in *Environment Bulletin* 4 (2):6.

3. Excerpted in *The Economist*, 8 February 1992:66.

7

The U.S. Congress and the World Bank: Impact of News Media on International Environmental Policy

Priya A. Kurian

In a world marked by intractable ecological problems and an anarchical international system that has no governing authority, international organizations play an increasingly important role in shaping global environmental policy. Scholarly research on international organizations (IOs) and the environment has generally been directed at examining the ways that specific organizations have dealt with particular environmental problems, whether IOs are independent actors or merely pawns of powerful nation-states, and, to a lesser extent, developing theoretical understanding of their functioning and their ability to adapt and change (Caldwell, 1990b; Le Prestre, 1989; P. Haas, 1990; E. Haas, 1990; Boardman, 1981). One area largely unexplored by scholars is the nebulous process of agenda setting and problem definition by IOs.

The literature on sources and processes of influence on international organizations, and especially on environmental policy making by IOs, remains sketchy. The stabs that have been taken in hazarding possible sources of influence are, with a few exceptions, rarely empirically or theoretically grounded. The policy process within IOs is seen as primarily influenced by member-states, who view international organizations as a forum wherein national interests play themselves out in policy formulation (Feld and Jordan, 1988; P. Haas, 1990). The environmentally conscious public, represented by nongovernmental organizations (NGOs); other international organizations that form part of the external environment of an IO (Mikesell and Williams, 1992); and especially, the policy ideas put forward by relevant epistemic communities (P. Haas, 1990) all play critical roles in influencing the agenda of IOs. Yet there is as yet no systematic discussion of the agenda-setting processes at work in IOs. What makes IOs focus on one set of issues and not others? How do they define problems? This chapter seeks to address a small part of this gap in the literature by empirical investigation of one possible source of influence on agenda setting by IOs: the news media.

One set of international organizations that play a significant role in the international environmental policy arena are the multilateral development banks (MDBs)—the World Bank and the regional development banks for Asia, Latin America, and Africa. While these are not primarily environmental organizations, their activities have been instrumental in influencing the nature of environmental problems in the Third World. The MDBs are the biggest sources of external financial assistance to the Third World and have been influential in shaping the developmental processes in these countries. But they have been sharply criticized in the last two decades for the adverse environmental consequences of the projects they have funded. It is in the wake of these critiques as well as their own realization of the economic failure of projects that have harmed the environment that the MDBs have discovered the importance of the environment and resource conservation.

The World Bank is the largest of the MDBs that fund development in the Third World. It has exerted significant influence on the contemporary Third World, and more than any other international agency, it has been "instrumental in creating new values and redistributing old ones" (Le Prestre, 1989:12). The World Bank is important too because it has taken the lead among international funding agencies in integrating environmental considerations into decisions on project funding. Especially in the 1980s, it has helped set standards for other developmental agencies in cooperation with the United Nations Environment Programme (Le Prestre, 1989:134) and has also sponsored national and international workshops to train consulting firms in environmental assessment (Goodland, 1991:812). The significance of the World Bank to international environmental policy notwithstanding, the process of policy change in the Bank has, with a few notable exceptions, received little scholarly attention. Indeed, even where the role of national governments and nongovernmental organizations in shaping Bank policies is acknowledged, there is little by way of substantive analysis of the actual process of influence. Most striking by its absence is any serious attention to the role the news media may play in influencing the Bank's environmental policy by helping set the Bank's agenda on the environment—either directly or through mediating institutions.

Studying the processes of influence can take many paths. In a democratic society with a free press, one such way is to examine agenda setting of the public and of public policy by the news media. Although it is possible that the media have direct effects on the public's and policymakers' opinions and attitudes, establishing this empirically has been difficult (Rogers and Dearing, 1988). Agenda-setting research, thus, appears to "offer an alternative approach to the scholarly search for direct media effects" (1988:560), and has generated evidence of the significance of the media in the policy-making process.

Recent studies have shown that the media have an impact on U.S. federal policy making. Linsky concluded that the press can speed up the decision-making process by positive coverage of an issue, as well as slow down the process through negative coverage by pushing "the decision making up the bureaucracy to a higher level of officials" (1986:87). Rogers and Dearing offer three generalizations on policy agenda-setting research:

> (1) The public agenda, once set by, or reflected by, the media agenda, influences the policy agenda of elite decisionmakers...; (2) the media agenda seems to have direct, sometimes strong, influence upon the policy agenda of elite decision makers...; and (3) for some issues, the policy agenda seems to have a direct, sometimes strong, influence upon the media agenda. (1988:579)

It is the second of these that is especially of interest here. To what extent, in other words, does the media agenda affect the policy agenda of the U.S. Congress with reference to the World Bank's environmental policy?

Research on agenda setting in the U.S. context has shown the impact the media have on aspects of foreign policy (Linsky, 1986, for example). Given that the U.S. Congress is an acknowledged influence on the World Bank's functioning and decision-making process (Sanford, 1982; Le Prestre, 1989; Mikesell and Williams, 1992), it is possible that the media exert an indirect influence on the World Bank through the actions of Congress. Thus, to understand more fully the decision-making process within the Bank, it becomes necessary to study those factors that affect the Bank both directly and indirectly.

The United States controls 16.5 percent of the shares of the World Bank (Mikesell and Williams, 1992)[1] and is the single largest shareholder in the Bank. Because of the policy of weighted voting (whereby the number of votes a country can cast is in direct proportion to the number of shares it holds), the United States is in a position to influence decisions on the projects to be funded by the Bank. Furthermore, two other factors help maintain the dominance of the richer countries, led by the United States, within the Bank. First, the executive directors of the Bank or the governors (appointed by and representing member countries) interpret the constitution of the Bank. This, in addition to the informal lobbying done to take care of U.S. foreign policy interests—of primary concern to Congress—ensures that Congress maintains some influence on the Bank. And second, the World Bank has to negotiate International Development Association (IDA) replenishments periodically and thus has to solicit national governments annually for grants (Le Prestre, 1989:93). If Congress chooses, it can withhold U.S. contributions to the Bank; hence Congressional concerns about the Bank's decisions and actions have to be addressed by Bank officials. This is not to argue, of course, that the United States, by its position as the most powerful member of the bank, can dictate Bank policy. Indeed, as Ernst Haas points out, "Power as direct imposition does not explain anything" (1990:13). Instead, power may be seen in the ability of a coalition "to impose its will simply by virtue of its superior voting strength or as a result of its Gramscian ability to socialize and persuade its opponents into the position the coalition prefers" (1990:13). Given all this, the question remains, what role if any have the media played in shaping congressional attempts to influence the Bank?

This chapter explores the role of the media in influencing the agenda of the World Bank's environmental policy through its impact on Congress. Thus, in this two-step process of the media's potential influence on Congress facilitating in turn Congress's impact on the Bank, I focus on the first part, namely, media's influence on Congress. I examine the relationship between media coverage of and congressional interest in the World Bank over a twenty-one-year period beginning in 1972 to identify a possible correlation between the two. Specifically, I analyze all committee and subcommittee hearings on the World Bank, as well as the coverage of World Bank-related environmental issues in the *New York Times*, the *Washington Post*, and the *Wall Street Journal* to see whether an increase in media attention to the issues of the global environment and the World Bank can be linked to the holding of congressional hearings on the same subject.

MEDIA AND AGENDA SETTING

Agenda setting has been defined as the process by which problems gain salience as political issues "around which policy alternatives can be defined and support or opposition can be crystallized" (Erbring, Goldenberg, and Miller, 1980:17). It forces political institutions and actors to "confront political issues and consider making policies to cope with them" (Studlar and Layton-Henry, 1990:274). The complexities inherent in this process make for a messy reality best captured by the garbage can model of choice—problems, policies, and politics vault along independently until the right combination of them come together to form a "policy window" in which decisions can be made (Kingdon, 1984).[2]

The significance of media to the agenda-setting process has been evident to media and communication scholars for a long time. Bernard Cohen, for example, observed that the press:

> may not be successful much of the time in telling people *what to think*,
> but it is stunningly successful in telling its readers *what to think about*. .
> . . The world will look different to different people, depending . . . on
> the map that is drawn for them by writers, editors, and publishers of the
> papers they read. (1963:13)

The literature on the role of mass media in agenda setting that focuses on the influence of the media on the public is relatively clear that the public's attention to governmental issues follows closely on the media coverage of those issues (McCombs and Shaw, 1972; Erbring, Goldenberg, and Miller, 1980; and MacKuen and Coombs, 1981). McCombs and Shaw's study focused for the first time on agenda setting as a process, thus adding the time element to the study of media effects (Rogers and Dearing, 1988:564). These studies have shown definitively that mass media do affect the public opinion agenda. More controversial, however, is the notion that the media influence the government agenda.

Kingdon (1984) argues that the media have little independent effect on setting the policy agenda, although he acknowledges its significant role in allowing communication between policymakers, in magnifying issues, and in influencing public opinion. According to Kingdon, the short duration for which stories and issues gain salience in the press makes for a limited impact of media on the policy agenda; and newsworthy or dramatic stories come invariably at the end of the policy-making process, thus diminishing the role of the media.

But Kingdon ignores the significant role the media play in deciding which real world occurrences become the "focusing events, crises, and symbols" that he sees necessary to get an issue on the agenda. The ability to exercise influence over international environmental policy is determined in part by the salience of international environmental issues. And it is here that the media have a role to play. As Cook (1989) points out, reporters do more than reflect events; because they are selective in their coverage of issues, they help mold national priorities and also act as powerful gatekeepers to the political arena. Making news can, thus, become a constructive part of the legislative process.

Although there is a fair amount of general literature on media coverage and congressional behavior and the role of the media in election campaigns (Badgikian, 1974; Miller, 1978), virtually no attention has been directed at the possible effects of the media on Congress's decisions to wield influence over international organizations. Nor has much attention been paid to agenda setting within IOs. Cox and Jacobson argue that the mass media rarely have an impact on the decision-making processes in international organizations, primarily because "the organizations seldom deal with matters that arouse wide public interest" (1973:401). Especially since the 1980s, however, the perceived impact of IOs, such as the World Bank, on the global environment has been a matter of intense public interest, bringing with it media scrutiny. There are certainly other sources of influence on IOs' agendas, particularly the member-states, the organizational bureaucracy, NGOs (especially in the United States and Western Europe), and other IOs (Cox and Jacobson, 1973; Mikesell and Williams, 1992).

This chapter examines only the media's agenda-setting role and only its potential indirect impact on the World Bank's environmental policy through Congress, but this is not to discount either the direct effects the media may also have on the Bank or the other possible routes of indirect influence. The Bank has always been sensitive to adverse publicity (see Chapter 6) and tends to shy away from actions that give it bad press. As environmental awareness has spread, and especially as international nongovernmental organizations have begun to focus their attention on MDBs for their role in environmental crises, the Bank has taken steps to ensure its continued credibility in the eyes of the international community. Indeed, bad publicity is one of the mechanisms available to enforce the informal law of regimes (see Chapter 9).

METHODOLOGY

I used the Congressional Information Service index to identify all congressional hearings dealing with the World Bank from 1972 through 1992.[3] I examined each of these hearings to determine which contained references to the World Bank and the environment, locating forty-four hearings in all. Along with noting the number of hearings per year, these hearings were content analyzed to identify the specific environmental themes they contained.[4] The forty-four hearings were held before nineteen committees and subcommittees of the House and Senate (see appendix to this chapter).

All stories relating to the World Bank in the *New York Times*, the *Washington Post*, and the *Wall Street Journal* during the same twenty-one-year period were examined to identify the items dealing with the environment and the Bank. To classify the newspaper articles, I developed a framework, based on those used by other media scholars, to evaluate the prominence given to items relating to the World Bank and the environment.

The prominence score for each year was correlated with the number of congressional hearings in a year to determine if increased media prominence given to the environment and the World Bank was paralleled by an increase in congressional interest in the subject. A detailed description of the methodology and framework of analysis may be found in the appendix at the end of the chapter.

FINDINGS

To what extent does Congress really respond to media attention to issues? Before analyzing the correlation between media coverage and congressional hearings, I offer a brief sketch of the pattern of coverage of the issue in the *New York Times*, the *Washington Post*, and the *Wall Street Journal* (see Figure 7-1).

The coverage of environment-related World Bank issues was sporadic from 1972 to 1978. This was followed by a more consistent coverage from 1979 to 1982. Environmental stories disappeared from newspapers in 1983 but were back in print in 1984. Then the last eight years of the period studied reveal

Figure 7–1
Media Coverage of Environment-related World Bank Issues

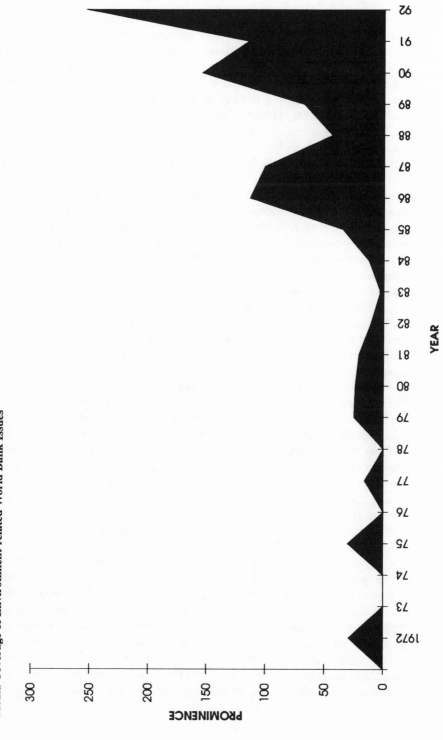

significant media activity, when the World Bank's environmental policy came under increasing scrutiny from all three newspapers.

Reviews of World Bank projects on forestry and forest protection showed up in the press in 1979. The apparent attempt of the Bank to respond to past congressional criticism was also noted by the media. Human rights, energy development projects, and poverty alleviation, all stressed by Congress and reported by the media, suddenly became a new focus of the Bank.

The prominence of such stories increased sharply in 1986 when both the *Times* and the *Post* carried a series of scathing reports on the environmentally damaging consequences of projects funded by the World Bank. In 1987 editorials in both papers called upon the U.S. representative at the World Bank to push the Bank into taking up environmentally linked debt relief programs. Even the *Wall Street Journal*, a predominantly financial newspaper that had, except for a brief story in 1977, ignored the environmental issue as linked to the World Bank until 1986, ran a large double-column, front-page spread entitled, "Saving the Earth: U.S. Asks World Bank to Make Safeguarding the Environment a Priority" in its issue of 3 July 1987. The reduced environmental coverage of 1988 was followed by stories the subsequent years highlighting efforts (or a lack thereof) of the Bank to use its economic clout in protecting the world's environment. The intensity of coverage more than doubled in 1990, remained high in 1991, and peaked in 1992. The coverage in 1992 was, of course, partly a response to the United Nations Conference on Environment and Development held in Rio de Janeiro.

In the twenty-one years from 1972, forty-four congressional hearings were held that focused on or referred to the World Bank and the environmental implications of the projects it was funding. The political and economic implications of reducing U.S. aid to the Bank are issues that figured in 1972, and they surfaced repeatedly in the next ten years, even as the executive branch sought to uphold U.S. international commitments. It was, however, the attempts by Congress since the late 1970s to influence the operations of the Bank more closely that provide the "most salient example of attempts to exercise leverage through IDA replenishments" (Le Prestre, 1989:93).

The issue of the environment figures in the congressional hearings on the World Bank only from 1980, and the annual frequency of these hearings in the thirteen-year period until 1992 ranged between zero and seven (see Figure 7-2). There was a perceptible thematic change in the hearings in the 1980s. Congressional committees decided to try withholding aid to bring about changes in the Bank's environmental policy, and they took up the issue of tropical deforestation. Between March and May 1980, technical subcommittees discussed not only the role of the United States in encouraging proper management of tropical forests, but also the potential role of the World Bank in tropical forest preservation. For the first time also, the environment was added to the agenda of all hearings for fund appropriation for the Bank.

Figure 7–2
Hearing on Environment-related World Bank Issues

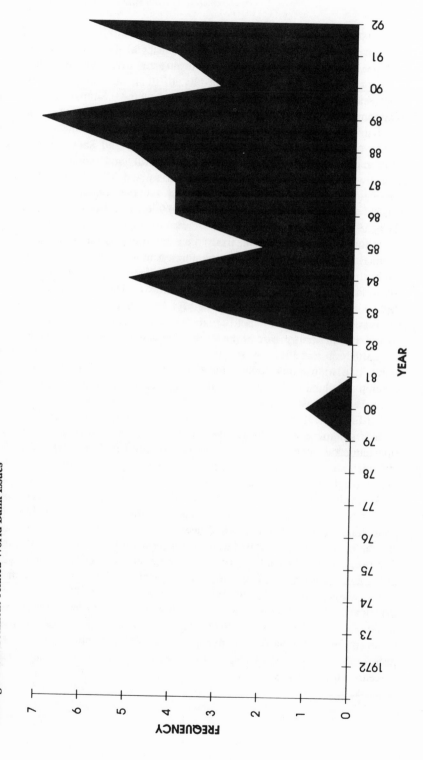

In 1983 Congress held its first hearing devoted entirely to the environmental impact of MDB-funded projects. The inadequacy of the World Bank's policies and procedures for implementing environmental objectives and the adverse effects of many of the projects funded by the Bank were among the topics that were featured (and would be from then on). In 1984 the House adopted nineteen recommendations to improve the environmental performance of multilateral banks. These included provisions to strengthen the environmental review capabilities of the Departments of Treasury and State, ways to foster environmental programs in the developing world, and guidance to the U.S. executive director on how to vote. Congressional hearings that focused on international development organizations and the environment totaled four each in 1986 and 1987, five in 1988, seven in 1989, three in 1990, four in 1991, and six in 1992.

Although many of these hearings were routine appropriations hearings for international organizations and other foreign operations including the World Bank, they recorded, for the first time in Congress, testimony on the Bank's environmental performance in taking funding decisions. Apart from these routine hearings, beginning in late 1983, congressional committees and subcommittees began to hold hearings that focused exclusively on the environmental performance of the Bank. The witnesses that appeared before the committees in the 1980s were often environmentalists who were playing an active role in forming links with environmentalists in other countries and attempting to lobby Congress to hold hearings on the environmental implications of the World Bank's policies.

As Figures 7-1 and 7-2 reveal, media stories first peaked in 1986, followed by a sharp increase in the number of hearings on the World Bank and its environmental policy. The pattern thus appears to indicate that the media do influence the number of Congressional hearings. To what extent is this borne out by a quantitative analysis of the data?

The following table reveals the results of a correlational analysis of the frequency of congressional hearings per year with the corresponding media prominence scores. The individual newspaper prominence scores for the year and the combined media score were correlated with the frequency of hearings. The results show a strong correlation between congressional hearings and the prominence scores which is statistically significant.[5] Although the data strongly co-vary, it is problematic to infer causality from this only. The figures indicate that other factors may be at work here that are likely to have influenced the workings of both Congress and the media. For example, the amount of attention given to the World Bank by congressional committees especially for the first peak (1982-1984) appears disproportionate to the amount of media attention preceding it (1979-1981).

NYT-PR	WP-PR	WSJ-PR	MED-PR
.65	.53	.51	.63
(P=.001)	(P=.014)	(P=.019)	(P=.002)

CONCLUSIONS

Charting the pattern of influence wielding through the muddy waters of international environmental policy is a risky task. For, too often, influence is a matter of subjective perception. Clearly, much more needs to be done to understand the multifarious factors underlying environmental policymaking. The analysis offered in this chapter, however, does indicate the need to appreciate the role the media play in shaping international environmental policy. And, as Rogers and Dearing point out, "[A]n agenda-setting process must occur in an organization, and, in fact, must be fundamental to understanding how change occurs in an organization" (1988:581). Agenda setting is continuously underway in organizations, and it is the way in which problems are defined during this stage that determines the response of the organization to the issue at hand. Both by helping set the congressional agenda on the Bank and by offering particular perspectives on international environmental issues, the media have shown themselves as deserving a place in the complex equations at work here.

As the figures show, the swings in congressional hearings on environment-related World Bank issues from the 1980s show Congress as seeming to respond to a new influence that prompts its interest in the environmental aspects of the World Bank's policies. The significant correlation between media prominence and congressional hearings suggests a strong relationship between media attention and congressional hearings. We may infer impact of the media on Congress's attempts to influence the Bank's policies on the environment from the frequent references by members of Congress to news stories. (Congressional actions on the Bank, on the other hand, are rarely mentioned in the news media coverage.) Media coverage of World Bank-related environmental issues create salience for these issues that conceivably help shape congressional interest in the World Bank. Of course, no claim is being made here that the media act independently in choosing to cover such issues. Thus, it must be kept in mind that the 1980s was the time when environmental organizations in the United States and elsewhere turned their attention to international development agencies. Together these groups lobbied the press and

Congress to take note of environmental issues that were created or affected by the development agencies. Thus, it appears likely that the media and NGOs, among others, acted in tandem to create an environment conducive for Congress to act.

A qualitative analysis of the hearings shows the United States as increasingly attempting to influence the environmental activity of the World Bank. Along with directives to the U.S. executive director to the World Bank to vote against any project that potentially has environmentally damaging consequences, members of Congress have repeatedly sought to increase the Bank's accountability to the United States. Irked by the Bank's apparent unresponsiveness to environmental issues, Senator Robert Kasten (chairman of the Appropriations Subcommittee on Foreign Operations) wrote to Bank president A. W. Clausen in 1985 threatening congressional economic reprisals (Mikesell and Williams, 1992:268). In addition, Congress passed legislation in 1989 making environmentally sustainable development a necessary condition to U.S. support of the World Bank's policies, projects, and programs.

The World Bank's sensitivity to adverse publicity makes sense inasmuch as the cumulative net influence of media on its agenda is much greater than that exerted only through the United States. Besides Congress, there are other routes of influence—governments of other countries that are shareholders in the Bank, U.S. courts, the U.S. president, and so on. The World Bank has responded to the pressures brought on it, albeit in a belated fashion. Its environmental policy has evolved over time and, in 1989, it formalized the requirement for environmental impact assessment (EIA) of all major projects it funds. Of course, EIA in itself is no guarantee of the environmental viability of a project. And as was evident in the case of the Sardar Sarovar project in India, there still exists among Bank officials the tendency to condone noncompliance with EIA requirements (Morse and Berger, 1992). Yet, the Bank has shown a capacity to learn (see Chapter 6). The changes in its environmental policy from the 1980s show an organization reluctantly shedding a perspective that allowed economic and technical rationalities to reign supreme to one that recognizes the significance of ecological, political, and social rationalities. It is, of course, a different question altogether whether the Bank (or any other organization for that matter) will ever fully succeed in reconciling Western notions of "development" with long-term environmental protection. Too often, the inherent contradictions between these two goals have resulted in the achievement of neither. Within the bounds of this developmental paradigm, however, the creation of a milieu that allowed environmental concerns to surface and remain significant to Bank policies is to be attributed in part to the role the media have played in assuring salience to international environmental issues.

APPENDIX

Methodology and Framework of Analysis

The framework of analysis involved classifying an item according to the page on which it appears (editorial, page one of the main section, page one of any other section, or an inside page), the main focus of the item (environment and the World Bank, as opposed to a reference to environment in a story on another aspect of the World Bank's functioning), and the display it was accorded in terms of either boxing the item or carrying a visual with the item. These were rated on a scale of 1 to 14, as shown below. Separately, I recorded the space taken by an article as an indicator of prominence, using a scale ranging from 1 to 5 (see below).

The first framework thus uses the criteria of placement, content, and display (together referred to as "placement" in the equation given below) to evaluate the prominence of an item. It is generally accepted by professional journalists and media experts that page one is more important than any other page in terms of its audience impact (Klein and Maccoby, 1954; Markham and Stempel, 1957; Stewart, 1943; Lewis, 1960). The reason for rating a story with its main focus on environment higher than one making a passing reference to it is obvious. And, the importance of display by either boxing an item or using visuals is also widely acknowledged by journalists and scholars.

Though the size of the headline and issue frequency are valid criteria to measure prominence, it has been found that the performance of the three different measures of space, issue frequency, and headline size are nearly identical (Markham and Stempel, 1957:190). Considering the headline size and issue frequency with space would, therefore, be redundant, and, hence, only space is taken here as an indicator of prominence.
Thus:

Placement + space = prominence

Sum of prominence
for NYT, WP, & WSJ = Score/year

The prominence ratings of newspaper articles from the newspapers for each year were added to give the media prominence score per year. The media prominence and the frequency of congressional hearings have been graphed separately as seen in figures 7.1 and 7.2 respectively.

Placement Scale:

Item	Rating
Editorial on World Bank and environment	14
Front page, front section, main focus on environment, boxed/visuals	13
Front page, front section, main focus on environment, not boxed/no visuals	12
Front page, any other section, main focus on environment, boxed/visuals	11
Front page, any other section, main focus on environment, not boxed/no visuals	10
Inside page, main focus on environment, boxed/visuals	9
Inside page, main focus on environment, not boxed/no visuals	8
Editorial with reference to World Bank and environment	7
Front page, front section, reference to World Bank and environment, boxed/visuals	6
Front page, front section, reference to World Bank and environment, not boxed/no visuals	5
Front page, any other section, reference to W. Bank and environment, boxed/visuals	4
Front page, any other section, reference to W. Bank and environment, not boxed/no visuals	3
Inside page, reference to World Bank and environment, boxed/visuals	2
Inside page, reference to World Bank and environment, not boxed/no visuals	1

Space Scale:

Size	Rating
Single column, small	1
Single column, medium	2
Single column, large or double column, small	3
Double column (or more), medium	4
Double column (or more), large	5

Congressional Committees:

The list of congressional committees and subcommittees that held hearings on the World Bank are as follows:

House Committees and Subcommittees:

1. The Subcommittee on International Organizations of the Committee of Foreign Affairs
2. The Subcommittee on Mining, Forest Management, and Bonneville Power Administration of the Committee on Interior and Insular Affairs
3. The Subcommittee on International Development Institutions and Finance of the Committee on Banking, Finance, and Urban Affairs
4. The Subcommittee on Foreign Operations Appropriations of the Committee on Appropriations
5. The Subcommittee on Natural Resources, Agricultural Research, and Environment of the Committee on Science and Technology
6. The Subcommittee on Human Rights and International Organizations and the Subcommittee on International Economic Policy and Trade of the Committee on Foreign Affairs
7. The Committee on Banking, Finance, and Urban Affairs
8. The Select Committee on Hunger

Senate Committees and Subcommittees:

1. The Subcommittee on Hazardous Wastes and Toxic Substances of the Committee on Environment and Public Works
2. The Committee on Foreign Relations
3. The Subcommittee on International Economic Policy
4. The Subcommittee on European Affairs
5. The Subcommittee on Western Hemisphere Affairs
6. The Subcommittee on East Asian and Pacific Affairs of the Committee on Foreign Relations
7. The Subcommittee on Foreign Operations Appropriations
8. The Subcommittee on Foreign Assistance and Related Programs of the Committee on Appropriations
9. The Subcommittee on Technology and National Security of the Joint Economic Committee (U.S. Congress)
10. The Select Committee on Indian Affairs
11. The Committee on Governmental Affairs

NOTES

I thank Sylvo Lenart, Madhu Malik, and especially Robert V. Bartlett for helpful comments and suggestions on earlier versions of this chapter, and Ines Monte for invaluable research assistance.

1. The number of shares the United States has controlled has fluctuated with time, and the present figure of 16.5 percent is down from 1980 when it controlled approximately 21.5 percent of the votes (Sanford, 1982) and 18.97 percent in 1982 (Hayter and Watson, 1985:69).

2. Agenda setting is, of course, only one of several ways in which media influence public opinion and the policy-making process. Iyengar (1991) points out other effects of the media (although his discussion focuses solely on television): framing effects (i.e., the manner in which an issue is "framed" significantly influences decision outcomes); priming effects (the ability of news programs to affect the criteria by which individuals judge political leaders); and bandwagon effects (where political campaign news stories focus on candidates' electoral prospects rather than on their policy positions or personal characteristics).

3. I chose to begin the study from 1972, as reliable data for all three newspapers were available only from that year. Collecting data on media without the help of published indexes (as would have been the case for the *Washington Post*) would have raised problems of reliability and feasibility. Admittedly, published indexes are not error free, but it is reasonable to assume that their errors are random, not systematic.

4. The content analyses of the media stories to evaluate their prominence and of the congressional hearings to ascertain their frequency and themes were replicated independently during this research project.

5. It is a conceptually defensible argument, however, that it takes time for Congress to respond to media coverage. The mechanics of arranging the holding of a hearing itself takes time, and this is especially true in the case of an issue such as the environment, which, although significant, does not usually carry the urgency or immediacy of, say, a political scandal or upheaval. Hence, it would be worthwhile to lag the media prominence scores by a year and see how this affects the correlation figures.

NYT-L	WP-L	WSJ-L	MED-L
.63	.38	.49	.60
(P=.003)	(P=.10)	(P=.03)	(P=.006)

The results of the correlation between congressional hearings and the lagged prominence scores of the media show that the correlation between the combined media score and the frequency of hearings continues to be high at .60, significant at the .006 level. This is a weaker correlation than the non-lagged correlation, indicating that if there is indeed a lag between media attention and congressional response, it probably is a lag of less than one year.

On aggregating the data into six-month intervals, the correlations went down (overall media prominence and the hearings had a .53 correlation significant at the .00 level). An inspection of the graphed data reveals there is consistently a wide variation between the first six months of a year and the second as most hearings are held in the first part of the year. This background variation obviously masks the relationship between media coverage and the holding of hearings and suppresses the correlations when data are aggregated at six-month intervals.

Although there is no theoretical basis for expecting a two-year lag, we get a slightly stronger correlation of .71 (significant at the .001 level) when allowing for a lag of two years.

NYT-L2	WP-L2	WSJ-L2	MED-L2
.72	.44	.67	.71
(P=.001)	(P=.058)	(P=.002)	(P=.001)

8

The Institutionalization of International Environmental Policy: International Environmental Law and International Organizations

Dimitris Stevis and Clifton Wilson

The role of international organizations (IOs) in international environmental policy (IEP) has been a subject of interest for some time (Kay and Skolnikoff, 1972; Boardman, 1981; Kay and Jacobson, 1983; Council on Environmental Quality, 1985:ch. 11; Council on Environmental Quality, 1989:ch. 7; Stevis, Assetto, and Mumme, 1989; Caldwell, 1990b; Haas, Keohane, and Levy, 1993). Moreover, since the late 1970s the broader debate over international organizations has also cast a shadow on what their role should be in the area of environmental policy (Gallarotti, 1991). The ensuing debate has taken the form of three questions. First, should there be more or less resort to IOs in the area of international environmental policy (Young, 1989b)? Second, if IOs are to be used, should these be new or existing ones (Plant, 1990; Kimball, 1992)? Finally, how can IOs be made more effective (World Commission on Environment and Development, 1987:ch. 12; Sand, 1991b; General Accounting Office, 1992; Kimball, 1992)?

We do not deal here with the role of specific organizations nor do we address the desirability or effectiveness of IOs. Our goal is to examine the broader context within which the above debates are taking place: the degree to which multilateral international environmental law (IEL) prescribes the use of IOs, whether newly formed or existing ones. Undeniably the formal evocation of an IO is no guarantee of an effective policy. Yet the prescription of a role for IOs in international politics is rarely a routine matter (Kennedy, 1987; Plant, 1990; Keohane, 1990:740-48). Stated differently, the "move to institutions" is expressed both in terms of the functions of IOs once established as well as in terms of the decisions to establish them.[1] Although in-depth case studies are necessary in order to understand fully the role of IOs in IEP, they are not sufficient. We cannot infer that IOs play a significant role solely by virtue of their numbers nor by the prominent role of a select few.

In order to examine this quantitative aspect of institutionalization we report data regarding the relationships between IEL and issue area structure, on the one hand, and the prescription and types of IOs, on the other. Drawing on these data we argue that the presence of IOs in IEP is far from being episodic. In fact, the numbers suggest the ubiquity and resilience of IO prescription. This result lends credence to a functionalist understanding of IOs, broadly construed, and it casts doubt on what we call the epiphenomenalist trends in recent academic and political thinking about IOs.

THE EPIPHENOMENALIST VIEW OF INTERNATIONAL ORGANIZATIONS

Post-World War II politics is characterized by movements both toward and away from multilateralism and IOs. Aggravations of global cleavages, the choices of particular governments, or the impacts of crises may be factors inhibiting the formation of multilateral policy (Krasner, 1985; Keohane, 1990; Snidal, 1990:330). Moreover, the policies of the Reagan administration toward the International Seabed Authority and the United Nations Educational, Scientific, and Cultural Organization (UNESCO) suggest that IOs can be the core of international controversy, especially when lead countries challenge multilateralism (Gallarotti, 1991).

In addition to the political challenges, IOs have been subjected to academic disregard (see Chapter 14; also Kratochwil and Ruggie, 1986). Institutional analysis, particularly regime analysis, has sought to rectify this problem (Haggard and Simmons, 1987; Young, 1989b). Regimes are defined as social institutions with common principles, norms, rules, and decision-making procedures regulating single-issue areas, and they may or may not include IOs. Institutional analysis, however, has not accounted for the ubiquity and necessity of formal regime components, such as legal instruments and IOs. Although there are regimes that do not utilize IOs, these are clearly the minority in IEP.

The instrumentality and vulnerability of IOs are manifested in a variety of ways that are not examined in this chapter, including the cutting of budgets and the exercise of formal and informal vetoes. It stands to reason, however, that fluctuations in attitudes toward multilateralism will also be manifested in oscillations to and away from the prescription of IOs by international environmental policy instruments. The absence of such patterns would clearly weaken the epiphenomenalist interpretation. Moreover, if IOs are a consistent element of IEP this should provide a strong incentive for integrating them into institutional analysis.

THE FUNCTIONALIST VIEW OF INTERNATIONAL ORGANIZATIONS

A second perspective can be derived from the functionalist view, broadly construed (Mitrany, 1966; Jacobson, 1984:62-66; Keohane, 1984:chs. 5 and 6). In its prescriptive form, functionalism suggests which types of IOs are more appropriate to deal with particular problems (Claude, 1984:ch. 17). Although we address this dimension here, in-depth case and comparative studies are more appropriate as a starting point (Haas, Keohane and Levy, 1993). Our primary goal, therefore, is to investigate functionalism's explanatory dimension. Functionalism claims that the fragmentation of the modern system and the exigencies of solving and managing common international problems drive the formation and use of IOs. Moreover, IOs are likely to be formed in issue areas that are less politicized and more subject to technocratic management—areas of "low politics."[2]

If the functionalist logic has merit, then the prescription of IOs ought to be driven by the growth of IEL and the structure of the issue areas. Stated differently, if IOs are an integral part of the structure of international politics, this should clearly mitigate the impacts of political hostility on the prescription of IOs.

INTERNATIONAL ENVIRONMENTAL LAW AND ORGANIZATIONS

Prescription of a role by a legal instrument does not cover all of an organization's activities. The role of IOs in catalyzing international law (IL) is clearly an important dimension, even when the ensuing policy does not assign a role to IOs (Young, 1993a). Moreover, IOs are involved in much of policy that is not manifested in formal ("hard") international legal instruments. Third, IOs may exist only on paper or, once created, may not operate as intended. With the above clarifications in mind we nevertheless assume that the formation or prescription of a role for IOs, whether in the environmental or other issue areas, is not normally a routine policy output and requires serious examination.

International Environmental Law

Regime analysis has had the same impact on IEL as it has had on IOs. It has properly challenged both the formalist analysis and the outright disregard of international law. Yet, it has not paid the necessary attention to the central role of law in establishing and reinforcing the principles, norms, rules, and procedures of regimes (see Chapter 9). Although international law does not account for all types and stages of international policy, it is the exceptional policy that will not be anchored in a significant legal foundation. In general, our research has persuaded us that treaty-based IEL provides a valid measure of IEP.

The major sources of international law are customs, general principles, treaties, judicial decisions, and certain decisions of IOs. In the environmental issue area, treaty law provides a fairly comprehensive picture of international law; historically, the other major sources of IL have not been as prominent (Kiss and Shelton, 1991; Birnie and Boyle, 1992). International environmental law, as used in this chapter, consists of a variety of instruments, including treaties, conventions, agreements, understandings, protocols, annexes, and amendments. These instruments are formally binding on the parties, once in force.

Here we deal only with multilateral IEL, involving three or more countries, from the middle of the 19th century to the end of 1992. The United Nations Environment Programme (UNEP) provides a broadly recognized compendium of current multilateral treaties and agreements (UNEP, 1989). Additional instruments and information have been gathered using Ruster, Sima, and Bock (1975-), *International Legal Materials*, *United Nations Treaty Series* (UNTS), and a number of auxiliary sources (Kiss and Shelton, 1991; Brown-Weiss, Szasz, and Magraw, 1992; Bergesen, Nordenhaug, and Parmann, 1992; Birnie and Boyle, 1992; Handl, 1991; Robinson, Hassan, and Burhenne-Guilmin, 1992).

The boundaries of what may be considered environmental law are imprecise. We have used UNEP and the above mentioned sources as our beacons. Even so, the environmental pedigree of some of the instruments counted (locust control as well as some fisheries and water basin management arrangements) could be subject to debate.

Protocols have been counted separately, unless they simply streamline the original treaty. Amendments have *not* been counted separately.[3] On the basis of the above standards, we have identified and examined 253 multilateral instruments. Although our count may not exhaust the universe of multilateral IEL, we believe it is extremely close to doing so.

International Organizations

Each IEL document was reviewed in order to establish whether it forms a new IO or prescribes a new role to an existing one.[4] To be counted, these IOs had to be assigned at least some secretarial responsibilities beyond being depositaries. Programs within existing IOs were not counted separately.[5] Moreover, in each case, we counted only the leading organization.[6] Almost all the organizations referred to are intergovernmental. We have, however, noted the instances where other types of organizations were used. Finally, we have not included the European Union (EU).[7]

THE DIACHRONIC GROWTH OF INTERNATIONAL ORGANIZATIONS

Time Periods

We have tried to capture the impact of international political dynamics by delineating six periods: before 1920, 1920-1945, 1946-1958, 1959-1972, 1973-1980, 1981-1985, and 1986-1992.[8]   Each of these periods is delimited by important turning points and, on the whole, they exhibit distinct characteristics in terms of world and environmental politics (McCormick, 1989b; Caldwell, 1990b). The year 1958 is used because of the first United Nations Conference on the Law of the Sea (UNCLOS) and because it follows the International Geophysical Year, both heralding extensive multilateral collaboration. Moreover, the late 1950s initiated the rapid increase in the numbers of new countries as a result of decolonization. The period from 1959 to 1972 witnessed the maturation of detente, the enlargement of the world community, and the delineation of the north-south debate. The period from 1973 to 1980 was characterized by the playing out of multilateralism at its highest, for example, the results of the Stockholm Conference, the Law of the Sea Conference, and the New International Economic Order debates. This period came to a formal end in 1981 with the start of the Reagan administration, aided as it was by the Thatcher government. Beginning in 1986 there is an evident move away from the new Cold War. In environmental affairs this was presaged by the signing of the Ozone Treaty in 1985 and the commitment, in late 1986, to negotiate what became the Montreal Protocol (Benedick, 1991b).

In order to focus further on the impacts of the changing moods toward multilateralism and IOs, we pay closer attention to three five-year periods: 1976-1980, 1981-1985 and 1986-1990. The middle period exemplifies a vigorous rejection of multilateralism and is both preceded and followed by periods with varying commitment to multilateralism.

IEL and the Prescription of IOs

The first question that we examined is the relationship between IEL and the prescription of IOs. The second column of Table 8-1 indicates that IEL has grown steadily throughout the last century. Using periods with approximately the same number of years, we note that the number of IEL has risen from thirty-five during 1946-1958 to fifty-five during 1959-1972 to eighty-seven during 1973-1985.

Similarly, the third column of Table 8-1 indicates that the numbers of IEL which form or prescribe a role to IOs have also grown. Most important, as the

Table 8-1. IEL and IO Prescription, 1868-1992

Period	IEL	IEL with IOs	IEL with IOs (%)
1868-1919	16	3	18.75
1920-1945	17	9	53
1946-1958	35	27	77
1959-1972	55	43	78
1973-1980	53	42	80
1981-1985	34	30	88
1986-1992	43	40	93
Total	253	194	77

fourth column shows, the relationship between IEL and IOs has continued to grow, reaching 93 percent during the 1986-1992 period, compared to 77 percent during the 1946-1958 period.

We have also examined the period from 1976 to 1990 more closely to see whether and to what degree the hostility of the Reagan administration toward multilateralism in general, and IOs in particular, affected the prescription of IOs

Table 8-2. IEL and IO Prescription, 1976-1990

Period	IEL	IEL with IOs	IEL with IOs (%)
1976-1980	35	31	88
1981-1985	34	30	88
1986-1990	27	24	89

by IEL. The second column of Table 8-2 shows that the number of IEL instruments did not drop appreciably during the early 1980s. Quite possibly there was a time lag effect; the numbers of IEL instruments did decline during the second part of the 1980s. As columns three and four report, however, this temporal decline had no effect on the proportion of IEL prescribing IOs. If anything, then, these findings suggest a persistent relationship between multilateral IEL and IOs, even when the number of multilateral agreements drops.

The Growth of Environmental IOs

A second temporal dimension that we have investigated is that of the growth of primarily environmental IOs. In doing this, we were motivated by the fact that earlier IEL was mostly managed by primarily nonenvironmental organizations, some of which had expressed their opposition to the formation of primarily environmental IOs (Boardman, 1981; McCormick, 1989b).

With respect to responsibilities we have distinguished between those IOs that are *primarily environmental* and those that are *primarily nonenvironmental*. Our findings are reported in Table 8-3. The absolute number of different IOs pressed into service by IEL has reached a total of 107, but the rate of increase has slowed in recent times (Table 8-3, column 2). In absolute numbers, the largest category is that of primarily nonenvironmental IOs. Examples include the Food and Agriculture Organization (FAO), the United Nations Economic Commission for Europe (UNECE), and the Council of Europe. The numbers of nonenvironmental IOs whose use was prescribed for the first time remained relatively stable during the 1959-1985 period (24 from 1959 to 1972 compared to 23 from 1973 to 1985; see Table 8-3, column 4). If the numbers for the 1981-1992 period are an indication of an emerging pattern, however, the balance may be shifting away from primarily nonenvironmental organizations (Table 8-3, columns 3 and 5).

The shift away from the utilization of primarily nonenvironmental IOs and toward primarily environmental ones is evident in Table 8-4, which reports the frequency of IO prescription, by primary responsibility. While primarily nonenvironmental IOs are still the instrument of choice, the use of primarily environmental IOs has grown. During the period from 1959 to 1972, for instance, the ratio was more than one to seven in favor of nonenvironmental IOs; during the period from 1981 to 1992, environmental IOs were used almost as frequently as nonenvironmental IOs (Table 8-4, column 5).

The strict diachronic analysis of the data does not exhibit any strong divergence between IEL and the prescription of IOs. It is quite possible that opposition to multilateralism does affect the growth of IEL; it has not affected, however, the numerical relationship between IEL and IOs.[9]

IEL and the Organizational Type of IOs

A second question that we have investigated is the possibility that political opposition may affect the organizational types of IOs prescribed from period to period.[10]

We have used *membership* (universal or limited) and *policy focus* (general

Table 8-3. The Growth of Environmental and Nonenvironmental IOs

Period	IOs[1]	Env IOs[2]	Nonenv IOs[3]	Env / Nonenv[4]
1868-1919	3	1	2	.5
1920-1945	6	1	5	.2
1946-1958	26	8	18	.45
1959-1972	29	5	24	.2
1973-1980	21	5	16	.3
1981-1985	10	3	7	.4
1986-1992	12	8	4	2.0
Total	107	31	76	.4

1. Absolute number of different IOs prescribed from the mid-19th century to 1992, by period.

2. Absolute numbers of different, primarily environmental, IOs prescribed from the mid-19th century to 1992, by period.

3. Absolute numbers of different, primarily nonenvironmental, IOs prescribed from the mid-19th century to 1992, by period.

4. Ratio between primarily environmental and primarily nonenvironmental IOs; derived from columns three and four.

or specific) to construct four categories of IOs. To these four types we have
added the category of programs and services—organizational entities created by
IOs that possess some financial and administrative autonomy. Finally, we have
also traced the use of nongovernmental organizations (NGOs).[11]

We have included the UN proper (but not UNEP) in the *universal-general*
focus category. The secretary-general of the UN has had, in the past, some
secretarial responsibilities in the area of IEP. The second category, *universal-
specific*, is that of conventional IOs, such as specialized agencies and their

Table 8-4. Prescription of Environmental and Nonenvironmental IOs

Period	# of IEL with IOs[1]	Env IOs[2]	Non-env IOs[3]	Env / Non-env[4]
1868-1919	3	1	2	.5
1920-1945	9	1	8	.12
1946-1958	27	7	20	.35
1959-1972	43	5	38	.13
1973-1980	42	13	29	.45
1981-1985	30	14	16	.88
1986-1992	40	21	19	.90
Total	194	62	132	.47

1. Numbers of IEL agreements that prescribe an IO, by period.

2. Numbers of IEL agreements that prescribe a primarily environmental IO, by
period.

3. Numbers of IEL agreements that prescribe a primarily nonenvironmental IO, by
period.

4. Ratio between the prescription of primarily environmental and primarily
nonenvironmental IOs; derived from columns three and four.

specific programs. We have also included UNEP in this category.

The third category is that of *limited membership-general focus* IGOs, such as the Association of Southeast Asian Nations (ASEAN), the Organization of African Unity (OAU), and the Council of Europe (we have not included the EU). The fourth category is that of *limited membership-specific focus*, such as various fisheries and water commissions.

The information reported in Table 8-5, columns 3 and 5, indicates that specific policy focus organizations, whether limited or universal in membership,

Table 8-5. Prescription of IOs by Organizational Type

Period	Uni Gen[1]	Uni Spe[2]	Lim Gen[3]	Lim Spe[4]	Pro& Ser[5]	NGO
1868-1919	0	2	0	1	0	0
1920-1945	0	5	2	2	0	0
1946-1958	2	7	0	16	1	1
1959-1972	2	13	5	16	5	2
1973-1980	3	13	6	17	3	0
1981-1985	1	13	8	4	4	0
1986-1992	0	11	4	22	3	0
Total	8	64	25	78	16	3

1. IOs that are universal in membership and have general policy focus.

2. IOs that are universal in membership and have specific policy focus.

3. IOs with limited membership and general policy focus.

4. IOs with limited membership and specific policy focus.

5. Programs and services with some administrative autonomy, set up by one or more IOs from the previous categories.

are more likely to be prescribed by IEL. This pattern is even stronger if we consider that the increases in the limited-general category are mostly due to the role of the Council of Europe. These findings suggest that any impact that temporal fluctuations may have is tempered by additional factors having to do with the type of IOs or the structure of the issue area.

Worth noting in this context is the role of UNEP. Since its formation, UNEP has become the secretariat for at least eighteen international agreements, twelve of which are in force.[12] In addition to the numerical patterns, we have identified an important qualitative pattern. UNEP has become the foremost IO in terms of the breadth of the agreements for which it serves as a secretariat, a pattern resembled only by the UN Secretariat and the Council of Europe. According to our issue area categories, UNEP serves as secretariat to legal instruments in at least five issue areas.

On first sight, this proliferation in UNEP's utilization may strengthen the functionalist argument. There are, however, alternative hypotheses. One explanation for this pattern may be the antiorganizational mood of the early 1980s. That resistance may have, by default, broadened the responsibilities of an otherwise weak entity. Another explanation may have to do with the relative openness of UNEP to various environmental actors, whether government agencies or international nongovernmental environmental organizations. Accordingly, UNEP's use may be driven by factors other than its designated function.

ISSUE AREA STRUCTURE AND THE PRESCRIPTION OF IOs

The characteristics of a particular issue area are arguably instrumental in determining the appropriate policy strategy (Vasquez and Mansbach, 1983; Krasner, 1985; Young, 1989b; Keohane, 1990; Snidal, 1990). If IOs are a manifestation of shifting political strategies, we would expect that issue area structure should have a marginal impact on the prescription of IOs by international environmental policy instruments. To the degree, however, that the structure of the issue area does affect the prescription of IOs, then they must be considered an integral part of international environmental politics. We have used *participation* in IEL agreements and the *functional scope* of these agreements to capture the impact of issue area structure on the prescription of IOs.

IEL Participation and IO Prescription

We have used the criteria of *geographic area* (global or regional) and *entrance eligibility* (open or closed) to create four participation categories:

global open, *global closed*, *regional open*, and *regional closed*.[13] For the sake of simplicity, these categories have been used as broadly as possible to accommodate the variety of IEL. Accordingly, an IEL is considered global both when the activity it regulates is naturally global, such as ozone depletion, and when it is potentially global, such as export of hazardous wastes. As Table

Table 8-6. IEL Participation and IO Prescription

Period	Global Open[1] IEL IOs	Global Closed[2] IEL IOs	Regional Open[3] IEL IOs	Regional Closed[4] IEL IOs
1868-1919	2 2			14 1
1920-1945	9 5		2 2	5 2
1946-1958	11 8		9 9	15 10
1959-1972	21 17	1	16 14	17 12
1973-1980	12 12	2 2	18 17	22 11
1981-1985	6 6		23 22	5 2
1986-1992	11 10		22 22	10 8
Total	72 60	3 2	90 86	88 46

1. IEL agreements that are global in geographic area and are open to all parties.

2. IEL agreements that are global in geographic area and allow limited entrance.

3. IEL agreements that are regional in geographic area and are open to all potentially affected parties (including, on occasion, nonregional parties).

4. IEL agreements that are regional in geographic area and allow limited entrance (including, on occasion, nonregional parties).

8-6, column 2, indicates, there are seventy-two IEL agreements in this category. On the other hand, there are so few instruments in the global-closed category that no conclusions can be drawn. The regional-open category accommodates IEL that is regional in geographic scope and is open to all countries in the region and, occasionally, to outsiders. Examples of this category would be the environmental agreements on the Black Sea. Finally, the regional-closed category refers to regional geographic scope and delimited participation, complemented by a few cases of intercontinental memberships. Such would be the case with the nuclear treaty system in the Pacific as well as the Antarctic system.

Regional instruments with open participation have become more prominent (Table 8-6, columns 6 and 7). This trend, however, has had no impact on the relationship between IEL and IO prescription within any of the four categories. Until recently, the likelihood that an IO would be prescribed has been much higher when participation has been open, regardless of whether the instrument is global or regional (Table 8-6, columns 2,3,6,7).[14] It would seem, therefore, that larger (global) or smaller (regional) participation eligibility is not the reason behind the use of IOs (Kahler, 1992).

This finding says nothing about the quality of IEL or the practical significance of the prescribed IOs. Quite possibly, the IOs prescribed by closed IEL are much more active. Yet, the guarded inferences that we can draw may add credence to the contractual approach to the formation or utilization of IOs (Keohane, 1990:744-45). Accordingly, IOs are more likely to be used in order to improve transparency and lessen the transaction costs in situations where participants do not have access to other means of communication. Additionally, IOs may serve as a shield against the unintended modification of existing understandings resulting from open entrance. In general, then, IOs may offer a measure of stability and predictability.

Functional Scope and IO Prescription

The second dimension of issue area structure is that of the functional scope of IEL. We have chosen to present the information in a disaggregated fashion both because of its substantive use and because it allows us to focus on the relationship between IEL and IOs in specific issue areas.

As Table 8-7 reports, IEL has come to cover a wider number of issue areas over the years, and IOs have kept pace. Some of these issue areas, such as nuclear energy or space, are new, whereas others, such as health or culture, have been around for some time but have not been salient.

Transboundary pollution and natural resources continue to dominate, with marine pollution becoming the most prominent. These are also the issue areas that account for the larger numbers of IOs. It is evident, moreover, that as we move closer to the present the numbers of IEL and IOs are converging, with the exceptions of general IEL, fauna and flora on land and, to a lesser degree, marine resources.

A further observation raises some intriguing suggestions. Generally speaking, traditional functionalism puts a premium on low politics. If, however, we include nuclear energy and military activities under high politics, we observe that the ratio between IEL and IO prescription is no different from the ratio in

Table 8-7. Issue Areas and the Prescription of IOs

Issue Area[1]	1868-1945 IEL	1868-1945 IOs	1946-1972 IEL	1946-1972 IOs	1973-1992 IEL	1973-1992 IOs	Total IEL	Total IOs
General[2]			2		11	8	13	8
Marine Poll			9	6	43	41	52	47
Marine Res	7	1	23	17	15	10	45	28
Fauna&Flora	7	4	15	12	16	11	38	27
Pests	3	2	6	6	9	8		
Inl Water Poll	3	1	4	4	3	3	10	8
Inl Water Man	9		6	5	4	3	19	8
Air&Noise Poll					5	5	5	5
Climate			1	1	4	4	5	5
Space			2	1	3	2	5	3
Wastes					2	2	2	2
Ind&Infra			1	1	3	3	4	4
Haz Products			2	2	1	1	3	3
Nuclear Enrg			5	4	6	5	11	9
Military			3	1	3	3	6	4
Work Envi	1	1	2	2	6	6	9	9
Health					1	1	1	1
Culture[3]	1	1	5	4	3	3	9	8

1. An additional category consisting of the instruments setting up multipurpose environmental organizations, such as the IUCN or UNEP, has not been included.

2. This category refers to framework agreements that span a variety of issue areas.

3. Culture refers to the preservation and management of artistic and architectural heritage.

low politics issue areas with similar numbers of IEL, such as inland water management or culture.

This suggests that when there is an international agreement in high-politics areas, IOs are considered necessary. Another explanation, however, may be related to the nature of the specific IOs prescribed. In the area of nuclear energy, for instance, the primary role has been played by the Nuclear Energy Agency of the Organization of Economic Cooperation and Development and the International Atomic Energy Agency. In military activities it is the UN secretary-general who plays that role. The fact that all of these entities are tightly controlled by the major participants may explain the reason why they are used. Stated otherwise, the prescription of IOs may not be limited to low-politics areas. Under certain conditions—when appropriate IOs already exist and they are controlled by the dominant members—international environmental instruments in areas of high politics do prescribe a role for IOs.

FINDINGS AND CONCLUSIONS

We close this chapter by recapitulating our findings, by pointing out some of the implications for international organizations and international environmental policy, and by suggesting some possible extensions of this research agenda.

What has been the diachronic relationship between IEL and the prescription of IOs? There is a clear and positive relationship between the growth of IEL and the prescription of IOs. Even though there has been a small decline in the rate of growth of newly used or newly formed IOs since the early 1970s, that decline is not matched by a decline in the frequency of IO prescription. One reason for this pattern may be that, by the early 1970s, the range of IOs was adequate for the new IEL. A second explanation may be the resistance of some industrial countries to the formation of new IOs, thus leading to the use of existing ones.

Has the primary policy focus of the prescribed or formed organizations changed through time? The absolute number of primarily environmental IOs has grown, as has the frequency of their prescription. Although primarily nonenvironmental IOs continue to be extensively utilized, they are not as predominant as they used to be.

Are there any patterns with respect to organizational types? Generally speaking, organizations with a specific policy focus continue to be most prominent, whether these are regional or global. Regional, multipurpose organizations have also been prominent, particularly because of the environmental activism of the Council of Europe. Among global, specific focus organizations, the growing role of UNEP is worth noting.

Looking at the structure of the issue areas has also generated some intriguing results. IEL with open participation has had a consistently stronger relationship with the prescription of IOs than IEL with closed participation. This leads us to believe that IOs are intended as mechanisms for reducing uncertainty and transaction costs. Stated somewhat differently, IOs are indicative of efforts to manage common problems in a segmented world of states.

The rate of IO prescription has been largely uniform across issue areas with the notable exceptions of marine resources and fauna and flora on land. The most intriguing finding, however, suggests that traditional high-politics issue areas may not necessarily be less likely to make use of IOs, provided that some agreement has been reached. The use of IOs may, in fact, depend on the nature of existing IOs as much as it may depend on the structure of the issue area. If, for instance, an IO is controlled by the leading states then they may be willing to utilize it.

What do the above findings suggest regarding IOs in international environmental policy? As noted earlier, there are clear limitations to the inferences we can proffer given the absence of in-depth case studies. There is strong evidence, however, that IOs are an integral part of the broad discourse of international environmental policy. At least in that sense IOs are not epiphenomenal—they do not appear and disappear in response to shifting moods toward multilateralism and international organization. Moreover, the rates and patterns of IO prescription suggest that institutional analysis must pay closer attention to the existence and role of IOs.

This is not to suggest that the formation or prescription of IOs is impervious to the oscillations of international politics. One interesting, if unintended, result of these oscillations may have been the organizational concentration of international environmental policy. A primary example of this is the expansion of the role of UNEP, as well as that of the Council of Europe. Nor are we suggesting that IOs cover the spectrum of international regulation in the specific issue areas where they appear. But their ubiquity and resilience cannot be dismissed or downplayed.

Clearly, IOs can be manipulated by governments, and their particular (ab)uses vary over time. In this sense we have no argument with instrumentalists. Yet, it may be illusory to expect that they are bound to disappear or be replaced by spontaneous international governance. This is not to say that IOs are always necessary or appropriate (Young, 1989b). Quite frequently, IOs legitimate inaction or improper action. In light of the evidence presented, however, one of the key tasks confronting government policymakers in the area of environmental policy will remain that of crafting appropriate organizations and properly managing existing ones, provided that there is commitment to deal with international environmental problems. Stated somewhat differently, IOs may not be merely an option when multilateral problems face governments with no alternative forms of communication and coordination; they may be the primary means of discourse and, on occasion, problem solution.[15]

The study of the relationship between IEP and IOs, even in this aggregate form, can be pursued in a number of additional directions. One issue that requires further exploration is the relationship between IEL participation and IO prescription. Are there some identifiable combinations of countries or issue areas wherein IOs are more or less likely to be used? If so, what are the characteristics of these countries or issue areas?

A related issue is that of the apparent move toward specific policy focus organizations. Are primarily environmental or primarily nonenvironmental organizations preponderant? Does the issue area, region, or availability of IOs play a role?

Finally, the relationship between high- and low-politics issue areas and the prescription of IOs requires closer attention. The traditional functionalist hypothesis that low politics areas may be more likely to be subject to international organizational arrangements may require modification. IOs, once in place and under certain conditions, may strengthen the probability of their own use, even in high-politics issue areas.

NOTES

We thank Georgia Carvalho and Mary Van Buren for their assistance.

1. A number of authors distinguish between institutions and organizations (Young, 1989b). We have no objections to the validity of such a distinction. We consider, however, that the combination of international law and organizations is strong evidence of institutionalization.

2. "Low politics" refers to issue areas that are not very salient and controversial; on the other hand, "high politics" denotes issues that are salient and controversial. Traditionally, international welfare issues have been considered low politics whereas security issues have been considered high politics. Economic issues have been considered somewhere in the middle (Snidal, 1990:330).

3. Protocols usually specify the operational requirements of framework treaties and may require the utilization of IOs not clarified in the treaty itself. Amendments, on the other hand, are intended to bring up to date existing arrangements. In that sense, protocols may be thought of as auxiliary treaties.

4. The instruments of formation of primarily nonenvironmental organizations who were later assigned environmental responsibilities, such as the United Nations or UNESCO, were not counted. Those of primarily environmental organizations, such as the International Union for the Conservation of Nature or the Rhine Commission, were counted.

5. On occasion, existing IOs set up a program or service that they also administer (i.e., the program or service reflects an extension of their functions). In other instances, one or more IOs will set up a program with some operative independence. UNEP is a

program of the United Nations. It has some administrative autonomy, however, and throughout the years it has developed its own policy niche and politics (for background, see Caldwell, 1990b).

6. Since our goal is to establish the degree to which IEL utilizes IOs, counting only the lead IOs does not create serious problems. Moreover, by avoiding double counting, we ensure that the numbers and the role of IOs are not exaggerated.

7. There has been a debate as to whether EU policy constitutes international law. We believe that it is neither international nor domestic law. In any event, EU law, by definition, utilizes the institutions of the EU, thus presenting no counting problems.

8. The variable length of these periods does not present a problem since our intent is not to capture historical patterns that are dependent on the number of years. What we are interested in is not the rate of growth of IEL, which may be dependent on the number of years, but the relationship between IEL and IOs, which is dependent on the historical characteristics of the different periods.

9. This does not mean that opposition to multilateralism may not affect the internal organization and the effectiveness of existing or new IOs.

10. A persistent temporal shift in the type of IOs prescribed would be consistent with our previous findings. On the other hand, oscillations could strengthen an instrumentalist, but not necessarily epiphenomenalist, interpretation.

11. With respect to organizational type we have adopted a modified version of the typology used in the *Yearbook of International Organizations*, published by the Union of International Associations (also see Jacobson, 1984:app. A; Caldwell, 1990b).

12. In fact, the number rises to twenty-four if we relax our standards for counting protocols, amendments, and subsidiary agreements (on the role of UNEP, see Young, 1993a).

13. Most IEL agreements, as well as IOs, have more or less specified conditions of entrance (see Keohane, 1990:750-51). Unless these conditions are clearly intended to limit entrance to specified parties, we have counted them as open.

14. During the 1986-1992 period, the relationship between IEL and IOs in the regional-closed category has also become stronger (see Table 8-6, columns 7 and 8).

15. Our conclusions here are limited to governments and do not imply that other social forces cannot have their own priorities as well as construct their own networks and coordination mechanisms.

9

International Regimes and Environmental Policy: An Evaluation of the Role of International Law

Lynne M. Jurgielewicz

The successful implementation of international environmental policy has been the subject of much recent research within various disciplines. One promising approach for cross-disciplinary explorations of environmental policy invokes the concept of international regimes.

Although international regimes were addressed much earlier by international law (IL) as a means of describing the prospect of legal regulation in unregulated areas (Goldie, 1962),[1] the theory has gained prominence primarily within the discipline of international relations (IR), where it was developed to explain stability in the international system despite the absence or decline of a hegemon (Krasner, 1983a; Keohane, 1984; Young, 1989b). It is only recently that regime theory has again become the focus of legal scholars searching for methods to induce international cooperation (Abbott, 1989; Williamson, 1990; Gehring, 1990).[2] This requires the integration of the disciplines of IR and IL, the relations between them having been one of mutual neglect, as noted by Hurrell and Kingsbury:

> Regime theorists have tended to neglect the particular status of legal rules, to downplay the links between specific sets of rules and the broader structure of the international legal system, and to underrate the complexity and variety of legal rules, processes, and procedures. On the other hand, theoretical accounts of international . . . law have often paid rather little explicit attention to the political bargaining processes that underpin the emergence of new norms of international . . . law, to the role of power and interest in inter-state negotiations, and to the range of political factors that explain whether states will or will not comply with rules. (1992a:12)

This chapter will incorporate the work of both IR and IL scholars to evaluate regimes as instruments of environmental policy, using ozone layer depletion and climate change resulting from global warming as specific examples.

STRUCTURE OF AN INTERNATIONAL REGIME

Definition

There is no complete agreement on what exactly constitutes an international regime.[3] Goldie, in his earliest work in this area, identified regimes as:

> (1) the acceptance, amongst a group of States, of a community of laws and of legal ideas; (2) the mutual respect and recognition accorded by certain States to the unilateral policies of others acting in substantial conformity with their own, enmeshing all the States concerned in a regime with respect to those policies; (3) a common loyalty, among a group of States, to the principle of abstention regarding a common resource. (1962:698)

He added:

> when this is mutually and equitably administered in the light of scientific knowledge, the participation of these States within a regime of this kind most clearly illustrates the possibility of restraining pre-emptive acts which might be otherwise permitted under international law. (698)

Within IR, the most frequently cited definition of regimes is attributed to Stephen Krasner, who states that international regimes are "principles, norms, rules and decision-making procedures around which actor expectations converge in a given issue-area" (Krasner, 1983b:1). Within this framework, principles are defined as "beliefs of fact, causation, and rectitude"; norms are "standards of behavior defined in terms of rights and obligations"; rules are "specific prescriptions or proscriptions for action"; and decision-making procedures are "prevailing practices for making and implementing collective choice" (Krasner, 1983b:2).[4] Although he makes no mention of any discipline, Krasner might well be describing IL.

Thomas Gehring (1970) offers a more integrated work in this area, particularly as it better addresses the role of IL in international regime theory. He explains regimes as the regulations, developed within the context of a conference of parties (which addresses both political and technical issues) to the regime, governing a specific area of IR.

Within this framework, lawmaking is the search for consensus and agreement on the priorities and strategies for international action. Once these are established, norms will evolve as to how to carry out these priorities and strategies, resulting in accepted norms or "shared expectations" regarding the behavior of states (Gehring, 1990:37).[5] Of course, this process from priority setting to norm evolution takes time, but it is the regime framework that allows for the process to take place at all. Thus, regimes provide the building blocks for evolving norms and rules.

Norms may be only partially articulated in formal legal instruments. Thus, differing degrees of formal law are utilized in regimes (Gehring, 1990:47-50).[6] Indeed, there may be reasons why the parties to a regime might desire an informal agreement instead of a treaty, such as when states are uncertain about future benefits and wish to remain easily open to adjustment, or for reasons of wanting to act quickly (Lipson, 1991).[7]

Dispute settlement functions are also internalized within regimes. Since states rarely use third-party dispute settlement procedures to resolve critical issues of policy, internalizing judicial functions is a practicality and reflection of the present state of international affairs. Yet there is an additional benefit in that such internal dispute procedures can utilize IL to guide decisions and can also incorporate the normative expectations developed within the regime. This method of dispute settlement ensures greater cooperation (settlement is no longer based on a traditional win-lose outcome) and is of great importance since the "legal relations would be based on more highly articulated rules and standards . . . than those generally obtaining [within international law]" (Goldie, 1962:699).

International Organizations and Regimes

It is important to distinguish between the two concepts of regimes and organizations, particularly within IL.[8] Regimes are a conceptual part of the legal order, whereas organizations are a tangible component.

Most legal scholars advocate an international supervisory mechanism to ensure compliance within a regime.[9] Although it is possible that international organizations can advance the prospect of international agreements "by fostering new norms, values, and expectations" (*Harvard Law Review*, 1991:1579), the concern of states with their individual sovereignty cannot be ignored. The extent of the role that international organizations can play in a regime, therefore, is limited by state sovereignty.

Nevertheless, the influence of international organizations within environmental affairs cannot be ignored as the environment in general has increasingly become a matter of international concern.

Of the many international organizations and specialized agencies dealing with environmental issues, the one predominantly associated with such work is the United Nations (UN). Among its bodies and specialized agencies, the UN Environment Programme (UNEP) is most closely involved in environmental affairs.

UNEP's role as guardian of the global environment is often described as "catalytic"—its primary function is that of a coordinating body vis-à-vis other

UN agencies, as well as non-UN organizations concerned with the environment. Although UNEP admittedly has not received a formal mandate to develop international law, the driving force of the legal activity of UNEP is drawn from the decisions of its Governing Council and documents such as the Report of the Ad Hoc Meeting of Experts held in Montevideo in 1981.

The 1992 environmental conference in Rio de Janeiro called for the establishment of a UN Commission on Sustainable Development to supervise the implementation of the environmental goals set out at the conference, and the UN General Assembly adopted a resolution outlining its duties (UNGA Res. 47/191 1992). It remains to be seen how effective it will be.

Regimes, IR, and IL

Notwithstanding the fact that IL and IR have been working in relative isolation concerning regimes, the two disciplines may be drawing closer together in their analysis of cooperation in general and the concept of regimes in particular (Schechter, 1993; List and Rittberger, 1992:89-90; Porter and Brown, 1991:20). The IR viewpoint appears to be moving toward a greater rule-oriented view of order, while the IL view is moving away from the traditional positivist view of rule-making (Hurrell, 1993:54). Keohane, a leading IR scholar of regime theory, currently defines regimes as "institutions with explicit rules, agreed upon by governments, that pertain to particular sets of issues in international relations" (Keohane, 1989:4). Compare that with Patricia Birnie, a legal environmental specialist, who describes the purpose of international agreements as providing a framework for the facilitation of ongoing negotiations for the development of rules of law (Birnie, 1992:57). Although these are just two viewpoints, they reflect a gradual movement of the two disciplines toward each other in this area.[10]

THE LEGAL STATUS OF REGIMES

Even if there was unanimity as to the exact definition of regime, there is dispute amongst the theorists as to how valuable the concept of regimes is within the international order (Strange, 1983:337). Within IL, a critical question must be to what extent a regime can be classified as "legal." It has been argued that because of the internalization of the making and application of law, and by virtue of "dispute settlement procedures consistent with the consensus-building process of communication," regimes develop into "comparatively autonomous sectoral legal systems" (Gehring, 1990:37). Oscar Schachter agrees that a regime may eventually achieve a significant degree of autonomy (1991:80-81). Indeed, he believes that IL is shifting away from its focus on state sovereignty and that regimes will form the "new centers of authority" because of the inability of states to deal unilaterally with complex problems.[11] Birnie supports this view of states' shift toward "responsible" sovereignty, at least within the area of environmental regulation, as a necessity for self-preservation (1992:84).

Others, however, see regimes as something short of formal law or a legal order, but somewhat more structured than an arrangement based on power politics (Williamson, 1990:740). A great deal depends, of course, on the definition of what exactly constitutes the international legal order or, indeed, whether IL exists at all. The use of regimes to cope with environmental change should help prove that IL does exist, so long as regimes are able to apply and prescribe normative behavior—in effect, to provide a source of obligation.

The source of obligation of IL has been the center of debate within the discipline, and it is not the purpose of this chapter to provide a detailed summary of this debate.[12] But it is useful to point out some of the leading work in this area in order that the legal legitimacy of regimes can be established.

Schachter, pursuing the path of the policy-oriented approach to international law,[13] states that five processes are necessary for the establishment of obligatory norms:

> (1) the formulation and designation of a requirement as to behavior in contingent circumstances;
> (2) an indication that designation has been made by persons recognized as having the competence (authority or legitimate role) to perform that function and in accordance with procedures accepted as proper for that purpose;
> (3) an indication of the capacity and willingness of those concerned to make the designated requirement effective in fact;
> (4) the transmittal of the requirement to those to whom it is addressed (the target audience);
> (5) the creation in the target audience of responses—both psychological and operational—which indicate that the designated requirement is regarded as authoritative (in the sense specified in (3) above) and as likely to be complied within the future in some substantial degree. (1968:308)

For Schachter, as well as the policy-oriented school, the critical test is the response of the target audience to the express or implied assertion of authority, a test of legitimacy and effectiveness that is a psychological as well as a political event (1968:311). The psychological factor is not new to IL; it has been addressed with respect to customary law and *opinio juris et necessitatis* (Brownlie, 1990:7-9). But Schachter differs from the usual approaches to characterizing the psychological factor (consent of states, state conduct, will of the international community) and instead focuses on the shared expectations of the target audience. For him, "[t]he question with regard to any given possible norm or practice is whether the target audience *will* regard it as authoritative and effective, not simply whether it has done so in the past" (Schachter, 1968:314).[14]

Critics counter by arguing that law cannot depend on shared expectations and cannot be measured in degrees. Support for the relevance of expectation in IL, however, comes from strange places. IR specialists argue that cooperation is facilitated by environmental law and environmental regimes due to the benefits they provide "in the form of an order based not on coercion, but on the coordination of interests and of patterned expectations" (Hurrell and Kingsbury, 1992a:25). Schachter, in turn, argues that legal obligation may indeed involve degrees and that when deciding whether an obligation exists, the decision will need to be made on the basis of the relevant variables (expectations, perceptions, and compliance). To "impose hard-and-fast categories on a world filled with indeterminacies and circularities can only result in a pseudo-realism which does justice neither to our experience nor to our higher purposes" (1968:322).

The legal status of the normative expectations created (as opposed to their source of obligation) will depend on their ability to fall within one of the traditional sources of IL: customary law, treaties, or general principles of law.[15] Under a positivist analysis of international law, it may be difficult to place some regimes within the legal order, as that school of thought limits its analysis to a reliance on rules alone.[16] A policy-oriented analysis, however, takes the perspective of the decisionmaker. While the positivist is concerned with the identification of sources of law, the policy-oriented school is concerned with social choices encountered in decisionmaking: "the prescription and application of policy in ways that maintain community order and, simultaneously, achieve the best possible approximation of the community's social goals" (Reisman, 1992:120).

The essence or necessity of the policy-oriented approach can be summed up with regard to its role in three critical areas of lawmaking: determining legal obligation when there are competing legal principles at play, when legal rules have fallen into disuse, and when new legal rules have come into existence.[17] In each of these three areas, policy must be taken into account to determine the existence and context of legal obligation. This does *not* mean that the traditional sources of international law are discarded. Rather, policy is taken into account during the decision-making process in order to determine the presence (or not) of a legal norm "by the use of analogy, by reference to context, and by analysis of the alternative consequences" (Higgins, 1993:34).[18]

Thus, whereas a positivist view of international law might find that some regimes are composed of "soft law" only and so are not legally binding, nonformalized regime norms and rules may share the same "legally significant expectations" as formalized rules.

In a similar manner to the policy-oriented approach, the difference between legal and nonlegal norms has been attributed to the interpretation or construction of norms and rules, "a skill transmitted through a socialization process which people undergo when they become 'rule handlers,' i.e., either judges or advocates" (Kratochwil, 1989:205). The similarity to the "shared expectations" ascertained in the prescriptive process of the policy-oriented school is evident.[19]

EFFECTIVENESS OF REGIMES: PROSPECTS FOR COMPLIANCE

The degree to which regimes can ensure compliance with their regulations is arguably the most important factor, in terms of usefulness, to consider in the evaluation of regimes.[20] A regime, although not a traditional form of legal entity, can provide an effective level of compliance.   Indeed, not being formalized may prove to be its best asset for achieving compliance.   For example, one U.S. State Department legal adviser questions the effect on compliance of traditional dispute settlement procedures involving the International Court of Justice or an arbitral tribunal, stating that "from the standpoint of environmental effectiveness, it may not matter whether state A or state B has the better legal argument; what is needed is a process that identifies the impediments to full implementation and seeks to overcome them" (Donoghue, 1992:9-11).

To illustrate the role of regimes in the international legal order, the example of climate change and ozone layer depletion will be considered.

Evolution of Norms into Legal Rules

As stated earlier, the evolution of normative or shared expectations within regimes is an important process, as it creates legal rules within the regime, which in turn create an obligation to comply with those rules. Thus, as Goldie has suggested, regimes provide for the

> development of a legal consciousness and moral awareness and sensitivity
> concerning the self-seeking and exclusionary qualities of pre-emptive
> activities and following from that consciousness and that sensitivity, the
> making of legal rules limiting and channelling its drives, in brief, the
> "detailed shaping of legal consciousness into manageable rules of law."
> (1962:698)

Within the regime, this common effort to solve a problem results in the underlying goal or purpose of the regime being "more universally accepted, gradually transforming pragmatic arrangements into normative constraints on behavior" (Williamson, 1990:743).

Regarding the evolution of norms, as knowledge is gained by member-states of the regime, normative or shared expectations will develop. The ozone-depletion regime is evidence of this, as documented by historical accounts of the issue (Dotto and Schiff, 1978; Roan, 1989). The 1992 Copenhagen Revisions to the 1987 Montreal Protocol on Substances That Deplete the Ozone Layer have taken into account new knowledge concerning the extent of ozone layer depletion, with the result that the relatively weak norms outlined in the Vienna Convention for the Protection of the Ozone Layer (1985) have evolved into greater legal restrictions on behavior. Thus, the schedule for phasing out ozone-depleting substances has been steadily tightened.

But normative prescriptions or rules within the regime may evolve even without new technical knowledge as a result of discussion and negotiation among regime members (Gehring, 1990:55). For example, the negotiations on the Framework Convention on Climate Change (FCCC) resulted in an agreement in 1992 to attempt to limit fossil fuel emissions, almost two years after potential harm from climate change was forecast by the publication of the Intergovernmental Panel on Climate Change report in 1990. The important point to remember is that legal rules evolve over time. Thus, Richard Benedick, chief U.S. negotiator for the earlier ozone treaty, stated that the Earth Summit "should not be judged by immediate results, but by the process it sets in motion," namely the evolution of norms (Stevens, 1992:2).

Notwithstanding discussion and knowledge creation, then, norm evolution within regimes depends on consensus or shared expectations. Consensus building was achieved in the ozone negotiations. For example, specific attempts to accommodate the differing needs of developing states were made in the Montreal Protocol and in the 1990 London Revisions to the Protocol. These include providing for access to alternative technology as well as the financial means for such access (London Revisions, 1991:art. 10 and 10A). They also allow developing states to delay compliance for ten years, so long as chlorofluorocarbon (CFC) use remains below a certain limit (art. 5).[21] In addition, new requirements under the 1992 Copenhagen Revisions to the Protocol will not apply to developing states before a 1996 review of the Protocol, and then only if the review determines a need for doing so (Copenhagen Revisions, 1992:decision IV/4:29).

Climate change presents a more difficult road to achieving consensus than ozone depletion; scientific, economic, and development issues are much more complex. Thus, there is currently not enough consensus or shared expectations to allow for strict emission targets in the FCCC. So, although the stated objective of the FCCC is to stabilize greenhouse gas emissions, the "aim" of returning to 1990 emission levels is to date required only of developed states (art. 4[2]b).

Dispute Settlement

Within a regime, disputes are normally resolved among the parties themselves. The ozone regime is a good example. An Implementation

Committee was established at the Second Meeting of the Parties to the Montreal Protocol to receive complaints from any malcontented party (London Revisions, 1990:annex III). Pursuant to Article 8 of the Montreal Protocol, a revised noncompliance procedure was formulated at the Fourth Meeting of the Parties to the Protocol, held in Copenhagen.

The Implementation Committee is to consider and report on submissions made to the Secretariat regarding possible noncompliance, "with a view to securing an amicable solution of the matter on the basis of respect for the provisions of the Protocol" (Copenhagen Revisions, 1992:annex IV). The Implementation Committee is then to report to the Meeting of the Parties with its recommendations. An indicative list of measures that might be taken for noncompliance by the parties was also adopted. Included in the list was "appropriate assistance" (such as assistance for data collection and reporting, technology transfer, and financial assistance), the issuing of cautions, and suspension of specific rights and privileges under the Protocol. Possible examples of noncompliance were, however, not adopted. While it did not establish an Implementation Committee, the FCCC calls on the Conference of the Parties to consider at its first session the establishment of a "multilateral consultative process . . . for the resolution of questions regarding the implementation of the Convention" (art. 13).

This internal judicial system, which allows for settlement without the constrictions of formal IL, can either "confirm or modify authoritatively . . . the normative structure of the regime," thereby "shaping consensus on the interpretation of norms in light of the factual circumstances," "reinforcing the stability of the sectoral legal system as a whole" (Gehring, 1990:54). The composition of the Committee has been criticized, however, as "a political body," since it is composed of parties, rather than so-called independent experts, suggesting bias (Barrett, 1991:200). Nevertheless, Schachter affirms the probability of achieving high compliance within a regime, attributable in part to a representative decision-making body, which "tends to limit the sphere of autointerpretation by the states of their obligations" (1991:75).[22]

Accountability and Transparency

The absence of a global government means that regime members will need to find a "substitute for coercion" that a domestic legal system can usually provide. In most regimes, this is accomplished through "the exploitation of *accountability* of states by rendering their performance *transparent* to scrutiny by the international community" (Chayes and Chayes, 1991:290). In other words, despite state sovereignty, states are accountable for their actions: to their own populations, to other states, and to the international public. States are held accountable, then, through the information available about their actions, generated by the regime itself.

Various means have been noted for achieving accountability and transparency within a regime. They include reporting and monitoring, target setting and surveillance, and negotiation and conciliation. These methods distinguish accountability from mere reciprocity. Within the ozone regime, these mechanisms are used in requirements for reporting and target setting, as well as through the Implementation Committee outlined above ("Montreal Protocol," 1987:art. 7, 6). The FCCC allows for the monitoring of compliance with the treaty provisions by the Conference of the Parties (1992:art. 12). The agreement commits parties to provide periodically to the Conference of the Parties a national inventory of anthropogenic emissions by sources, as well as their removal through sinks, of all greenhouse gases that are not covered under the Montreal Protocol; to prepare national programs to mitigate climate change; and to report on steps taken to implement the Convention. For developed states, there are more stringent reporting requirements, to be carried out "with the aim of returning individually or jointly to their 1990 levels" (art. 4, 12).

While linked to the techniques of reciprocity between states, accountability within a regime has the added support of the regime itself. Stated another way, if the regime has evolved legitimate expectations regarding obligations, it is easier for delinquent states to be held accountable, particularly when the regime has strengthened to a degree that sanctions for nonperformance can be established.

CONCLUSION

The study of regimes may not fit in well with the traditional view of IL, where the emphasis is on formal sources of law. But the traditional view of IL is no longer sufficient for examining the legal order, since it fails to take account of how states come to regulate an area. Thus, a policy-oriented view of IL is warranted by the success of regimes in implementing regulations in such contentious and global areas as the environment. In so doing, international legal scholars will have to become more seriously involved in interdisciplinary research, to a greater extent than mere collaboration on joint projects. There is between the disciplines of IL and social science: "a deeper division concerning not only what we know but also what there is to know and how we come to know what we know" (Young, 1992:39).

Although IL is not politics or economics, it is surely shaped by these areas, and understanding not only that but also the manner in which those disciplines go about their scholarly pursuits is essential. While legal practitioners may realize this linkage in their everyday work, legal academics do not always take account of it. This may explain the internal schism within the discipline of IL itself, but that could be the subject of another piece of research. The use of regime theory within IL provides—indeed requires—that this interdisciplinary linkage be observed and studied as part of the international legal order.

The brief examination in this chapter of the climate change and ozone-depletion regimes reveals that there is prospect for progress in the international legal order. But these successes have also shown that merely studying the resulting obligations is not the best method for examining the legal order. A better method is to observe the regime process whereby consensus is formed, critical issues are agreed upon, and obligations ensue. Not to do so is to ignore the fact that IL does not exist in a vacuum. Although the idea that the legal order is a process is not a new idea, the exploration of that process in the context of institutional arrangements or governance systems has not previously been undertaken in great detail within IL.

Regimes provide a structure whereby behavior can evolve into rules reached through shared expectations or consensus, which can be modified when necessary, as shared expectations change. More important, they are able to do this when there remains uncertainty that prevents general principles of IL from regulating the issue at hand:

> a deterring effect [on potential polluters] does not exist presently, not in international law anyway, because of the uncertainties of the enforcement of responsibility rules. Thus, the only remaining solution is to adopt regulations and, in some cases, to set standards. (Kiss, 1991:12)

As a decision taken at the Fourth Meeting of the Parties to the Montreal Protocol stated, "the responsibility for legal interpretation of the Protocol rests ultimately with the Parties themselves" (Copenhagen Revisions, 1992:decision IV/5). This is true of all IL, since the international legal order is self-enforcing. Although legal interpretation is always open to charges of self-interest, it is more likely that states involved in the shaping of the rule will interpret that rule in the spirit in which it had been negotiated. (Hard-core realists can take comfort in the fact that disputes about interpretations within regimes are settled by the parties with the aim of upholding the principles of the regime.) Knowledge of the formation and further development of the regime conceiving those negotiations will make the interpretation less open to inconsistency and surprise.

Because laws heighten public expectations, it is important that policymakers ask whether prospective laws are consistent with a government's ability to achieve the goals established by those laws (Bryner, 1993:34). Since regimes take account of the underlying critical issues, they are adept at realizing regulations that the regime states can implement and, in the process, strengthen the overall legal order, of which they are an integral part. If IL changes or evolves, it will be the result of pressure on states to make that change. Knowledge of how that occurs is of great importance in bringing about change.

Regimes, then, are worthy of study in IL, not least because they are already part of the legal order.

NOTES

1. Goldie (1962) thus introduced the concept of regimes into international law more than a decade before it was introduced into the international relations literature.

2. These legal scholars are not just examining regimes to describe legal institutional arrangements and practices, as Goldie (1962) did, but they have begun to take a preliminary look at the conceptual and theoretical issues underlying regime theory.

3. Regimes as defined in this chapter are distinct from the legal concept of "objective regimes," defined as treaties that create rights and duties for third states, such as treaty regimes for international waterways or demilitarization. Although regimes as advocated in this chapter may eventually create third party duties or lead to formal treaties, they do not necessarily do so (Brownlie, 1990:633).

4. Predictably, there is disagreement among regime analysts as to these meanings (Haggard and Simmons, 1987:494).

5. Gehring argues that technical and normative aspects of regimes are mutually reinforcing: "changing knowledge demands an adaptation of normative prescriptions, whereas agreed-upon norms induce the generation of technical knowledge" (1990:55).

6. See Lang, who maintains that "treaties are . . . a major component of . . . regimes" (1993:118).

7. Lipson (1991) states that the choice between treaties and informal agreements is not based on whether either are "legally binding," which, for Lipson, is a misleading term since states must act for themselves to enforce their bargains. Rather, states choose treaties over informal arrangements when they wish to raise "the credibility of promises by staking national reputation on adherence" (1991:511). Although I agree with Lipson that states must decide for themselves whether to comply with their agreements, I disagree that only formal treaties can raise the credibility of promises, since regimes can also infer a source of legal obligation.

8. Haas, Keohane, and Levy distinguish between regimes and bureaucratic organizations, with regimes being "rule-structures that do not necessarily have organizations attached" (1993:5).

9. See, for instance, Palmer, 1992; Plant, 1991; Barratt-Brown, 1991:569, and, more generally, Fisher, 1981, esp. ch. 10.

10. An examination of the recent texts dealing with the environment and cooperation may leave one feeling somewhat pessimistic, however. This is reflected in the scope of four of the most recently published IR books on the environment and cooperation: Rowlands and Greene, 1991; Porter and Brown, 1991; Thomas, 1992; and Hurrell and Kingsbury, 1992b. Only Hurrell and Kingsbury give adequate space to the important linkage between IR and IL in environmental cooperation, although Porter and Brown make a point of defining regimes in terms of legal instruments. Rowlands and Greene allot space only to a traditional analysis of the formal legal institutions involved in environmental cooperation, and Thomas does not allude to the role of law at all, except to formal legal instruments already in place. International law, of course, with its well-

known disregard for the behavioral aspects underlying legal instruments, is in no position to cast the first stone.

11. It should be noted that Schachter is referring here to regimes that include a treaty.

12. See, for example, Oscar Schachter's well-known "baker's dozen" list of the proposed sources of obligation within IL: (1) consent of states, (2) customary practice, (3) a sense of "rightness"—the juridical conscience, (4) natural law or natural reason, (5) social necessity, (6) the will of the international community (the "consensus" of the international community), (7) direct (or "stigmatic") intuition, (8) common purposes of the participants, (9) effectiveness, (10) sanctions, (11) "systematic" goals, (12) shared expectations as to authority, and (13) rules of recognition (1968:308).

13. Myres McDougal is the best-known advocate of this approach. For his earliest work in this area, see, McDougal and Lasswell (1959).

14. Thomas Franck (1990) has also focused on legitimacy, but with regard to compliance with international law.

15. See Statute of the International Court of Justice, Art. 38, reprinted in Brownlie (1983:397).

16. For a "pure" view of positivism, see Kelsen (1952). While "neopositivists" have begun to take account of nonstate actors, they still fail to take account of decision or choice in the legal process and give insufficient attention to the policies for which rules are devised (Chen, 1989:11-12).

17. I am grateful to Professor Rosalyn Higgins of the London School of Economics, a former student of McDougal, for pointing this out to me.

18. In order to understand fully the policy-oriented model of lawmaking or prescription, it is necessary to speak of it as an ongoing process wherein the observer can identify the participants, the perceptions of the participants, the situations or arenas in which these perceptions are mediated, the resources or knowledge and skill used by the participants, the modes of communication used, and the outcome of the process, measured in terms of expectations shared by politically relevant groups that certain policies are authoritative (legitimate) and controlling (effective and likely to be carried out) (Chen, 1989).

19. Schechter (1993) notes the similarity between the policy-oriented school and regime theorists in general.

20. The argument could be made that the formation of a regime is an equally important aspect with regard to identifying the presence of international law; space does not allow for that evaluation here.

21. During the negotiations for strengthening the Protocol, "most observers were . . . unprepared for the intensity of concerns subsequently expressed by many developing countries" (Benedick, 1991b:148). The industrialized countries' push for a total phase out of CFCs convinced the developing states that they would have to acquire new technology as soon as possible; they sought also to ensure that the developed world would help them accomplish this. Thus, the London Amendment to the Montreal Protocol ensures that parties will "take every practicable step" to transfer technology to developing states "under fair and most favorable conditions" (1990:art. 10A). Actions such as these are needed to counter developing states' fears that environmental factors will become a new component of conditionality affecting financial aid and international trade.

22. For a recent article evaluating the Implementation Committee, see Koskenniemi (1993).

10

International Organizations, Environmental Cooperation, and Regime Theory

Paul D'Anieri

The imposing scope of environmental problems facing the world has provoked wide debate on what, if any, remedies are possible. One policy that seems obvious to many is that international cooperation to protect the environment must increase. While some environmental issues are localized, some of the most pressing are international "tragedies of the commons," requiring international cooperation for their resolution.

There is significant disagreement, however, on what the scope of such cooperation should, and will, be. Some argue that the conventional piecemeal approach taken to cooperation in arms control and trade simply will not work on the environment. On environmental issues, they contend, the complexity of the problems and solutions requires that states cede some sovereignty to international regulatory bodies, rather than negotiate new treaties for every new issue (Chayes and Chayes, 1991; Prins, 1990).

Thus it seems that the nature of environmental problems will make international organizations more necessary for their solution than for other problems. If so, we can expect that states pursuing their self-interest will have a greater demand for international organizations (IOs) than in the past, and that IOs will play a larger role in the solution of environmental problems than they have in arms control and trade, the areas most focused on in the past.

Such expectations are debatable. In particular, one can argue that because environmental issues are less conflictual than trade and especially arms negotiations, less formal arrangements will be needed to create and maintain cooperation in this area. Indeed, some would argue that many environmental issues are problems of coordination rather than cooperation,[1] and are therefore more easily solved without formal institutions (Young, 1989b:ch. 2).

This difference in views raises the question: what roles are international organizations likely to play in the future of international environmental cooperation? I investigate this question first from the perspective of mainstream regime theory and then ask what we can learn about the question by going beyond regime theory and rethinking the potential role of IOs in international environmental cooperation.[2]

Regime theory, which is dominant in political science approaches to international cooperation, regards international institutions, including IOs, as a means by which states solve collective action problems. The utility of IOs as solutions for collective action problems is difficult to assess in general terms because theoretical debates on the question diverge. Not surprisingly, it will depend largely on the particular issue involved.

By looking beyond regime theory, however, we see a different potential role for IOs. Regime theory, as well as most current studies of cooperation in international politics, treats institutions only as means to an end—as intervening variables between states' interests and international cooperation. It is possible, however, to treat international organizations not only as tools, but as independent actors. If IOs are not only the results of states' interests, but can also play an independent role in changing states' interests—and especially in promoting cooperation—they can be important even on issues where they are not needed as tools for solving collective action problems.

I evaluate the plausibility of this argument by reviewing the role of the United Nations Environment Programme (UNEP) as an independent actor in promoting cooperation on Mediterranean pollution and ozone depletion. The point is to assess the value of reconsidering the way in which international relations theorists think about IOs in international cooperation.

INTERNATIONAL ORGANIZATIONS AS INTERVENING VARIABLES

The study of international organizations has long tended to view organizations from a utilitarian or functionalist perspective (Krasner, 1988; Ness and Brechin, 1988). In the 1960s, functionalist integration theory explained the creation of IOs in terms of the functions those IOs were supposed to serve.[3] In the 1980s, regime theory was driven by the attempt to use rational choice analysis to meld neorealist assumptions with liberal views of cooperation.[4] The goal was to show that, even with realist assumptions about the primacy of state actors and the anarchical nature of international politics, cooperation could still occur. Regime theorists therefore deliberately assumed that state interests were fixed and that actors other than states could not be independent variables (Krasner, 1983b).

International politics, as presented in standard versions of regime theory, could be represented as a prisoner's dilemma or a collective action problem, the basic paradox being that individually rational acts lead to Pareto-inferior outcomes (Axelrod, 1984; Oye, 1986a, 1986b; Keohane, 1984). States therefore need mechanisms to coordinate their behavior and to reassure each other that they are not cheating. Regimes, in essence, provide such mechanisms.[5] In this view, regimes do not themselves cause cooperation, but they are created and used by states as state interests dictate. And they are not an end in themselves, but a means to the end of cooperation. Regime theorists therefore attribute little causal significance to regimes.

For regime theorists, IOs are unimportant in and of themselves. The regime literature focuses on regimes defined as social institutions, but not necessarily as formal organizations (Young, 1989). Some regimes have organizations as part of them—for example, the International Atomic Energy Agency (IAEA) in the nonproliferation regime—but organizations are just a subset of regimes, providing the link between interests and cooperation. International organizations that are not part of a "regime" are therefore of little interest to regime theorists (Stein, 1990:27).

In considering the potential role of IOs in environmental cooperation, the question from the functionalist perspective of regime theory is whether something about the nature of the issues themselves will require regimes supported by organizations, as opposed to regimes not requiring a formal organization. Regime theory is based largely on "the demand for regimes" (Keohane, 1983), so the question is whether IOs will be viewed as necessary to solve environmental problems.

Two basic arguments can be made here, and they unfortunately have opposite implications. First, environmental issues, being inherently less conflictual than economic issues, may require a lower degree of formal organization. Second, the extreme complexity of environmental issues may make IOs necessary for cooperation because less formal regimes simply will not suffice. I address these two issues, the degree of conflict involved and the complexity of the issues, in turn, and then try to show how the two points may be complementary.

Collaboration vs. Coordination in Environmental Problems

It is important to distinguish between problems of collaboration and those of coordination (Hardin, 1982:chs. 10, 11; Stein, 1990:27-44). Problems of collaboration are represented by the standard prisoner's dilemma game, wherein each state follows a dominant strategy that leads to suboptimal payoffs for both (in formal terms, the single Nash equilibrium is Pareto suboptimal). The problem in moving to the optimal outcome is that each fears the other will cheat (each has the incentive to do so), leaving the cooperating state with the worst possible outcome. The problem of cooperation has been represented by the prisoner's dilemma and the tragedy of the commons metaphors so widely used to represent international politics. The shepherd who agrees to graze a limited number of animals knows that others have an incentive to cheat and to leave the cooperator with a deteriorating feed supply and a limited number of animals, the worst of both worlds.

Some issues are less conflictual games of "coordination." The players may agree on the worst outcome, but disagree on the optimal solution. This situation, which Stein calls the "dilemma of common aversions with divergent interests" (1990:37), may be more easily solved. In such a situation, unlike in a prisoner's dilemma, once an equilibrium solution is agreed upon, neither side can improve its payoffs by cheating (there are two Nash equilibria, and both are Pareto optimal). So while there is still conflict over which solution should be chosen (Krasner, 1991), neither side would benefit from cheating the other or from abandoning the coordination (Hardin, 1982:157-58; Stein, 1990:42). In the game of common aversions, uncoordinated activity, not unreciprocated cooperation, is the worst outcome, and converging on a solution, not promoting compliance with the solution, is the function of regimes.

Solving coordination games may require less use of international organizations (Young, 1989b), because the necessity of formalizing cooperation increases with the conflict in the issue. Whereas regimes formed to solve collaboration problems will need to prevent cheating, regimes dealing with coordination problems will not, because states have no incentive to cheat (Stein, 1990:42). Coordination regimes merely need to assist in helping states converge on one of the possible equilibria, and therefore may not need permanent formal organizations. So organizations will be less needed on environmental issues where states are unified in their desire for joint action, but it remains unclear exactly which issues are problems of coordination rather than of collaboration.

If the United States and Canada disagree over the best policies to abate acid precipitation, but agree that coordinated action is preferable to uncoordinated action, there may be little need for international organizations. The provisions of a coordination agreement may be difficult to negotiate, but there will be no incentive to defect from such provisions, so much of the justification for regimes is absent. If, however, each hopes to continue to pollute while the other stops (and fears that the other will do the same), the solution of collaboration is obvious, but states may hesitate to cooperate for fear of being cheated. Some type of formal monitoring organization may be required.

The extent to which environmental issues are problems of coordination rather than of collaboration is difficult to assess. In addition, the degree of conflict and the incentive to cheat on a given issue are likely to vary by issue. If one general statement could be made, it is that the tightness of the link between a given environmental issue and international trade issues is likely to have a large effect on the degree of conflict on that issue.[6] No one opposes environmental protection itself in principle, but where there is large financial incentive to cheat on agreements, environmental issues will correspond better with the prisoner's dilemma view typically used in analyses of international cooperation.

The point here is not to identify the proper game model for different issues.

Rather it is that there is reason to believe that environmental issues are better described as coordination games than collaboration games. If this is true, the "demand" for international regimes may be low.

The Complexity of Environmental Problems

Whereas some derive the demand for formal organizations from the degree of conflict on the issue, others derive this demand from the nature of the issue itself, arguing that the nature of the issues—not the degree of conflict on them—determines what type of regime is necessary. This is the view of those who both advocate and predict a proliferation of international organizations to deal with environmental problems.

Two characteristics of environmental problems, complexity and dynamism, may make international organizations more necessary for them than for other issues. The first argument is that these issues are so complex—and so intertwined with each other and with economic issues—that coordination of policies will be extremely difficult, manageable only by an ongoing international regulatory agency. The second argument is that environmental issues change so quickly that the typical process of international cooperation—conferences, treaty, ratification—simply cannot keep up with the pace of change, and that formal organizations, which can react more quickly, will be demanded.

There are a number of ways in which problems—and proposed solutions—are more complex than the issues typically dealt with in international cooperation. First, the scientific issues involved are extremely complex technically. This is particularly problematic on issues where there is no inherent opposition to such coordination, but detailed regulations are extremely difficult to coordinate between countries. One solution is to give greater scientific authority to international organizations to conduct research and establish technical standards, as the World Health Organization does on public health questions (Sand, 1991a:254; Wijkman, 1982).

Organizations are also necessary to implement certain types of solutions. In the case of fisheries regulation, dividing up a fishery and giving states property rights over portions of it may require no organization. If the goal, however, is to ascertain on an annual basis what the maximum sustainable yield of the fishery is, and then to apportion the rights to the catch, some type of organization will probably be the most efficient way to achieve the goal (Young, 1989b:46). Even a market-based scheme of trading emissions credits internationally is likely to require a regulatory body (Tietenberg, 1991:210).

A third function in environmental cooperation that may require organizations is dispute resolution. Interpreting agreements, modifying them, and resolving disputes over them may be an ongoing process, rather than an occasional task, and permanent adjudicative organs may be the most efficient way to address this task (Chayes and Chayes, 1991:286). In addition, although bilateral arms control agreements and trade agreements have been largely self-monitored, such a possibility seems infinitely more complex for those issues involving many industries in many countries. Monitoring organizations to play a role analogous to that of the IAEA in the nonproliferation regime will be more likely.

Finally, the high transaction costs of noninstitutionalized cooperation among a large number of states create a demand for institutions (Keohane, 1984). While some issues can be resolved on a bilateral or regional level, many of the most important issues will involve a large number of states. Where a ban is enacted, as in the ozone case, adoption and implementation of an agreement may still be feasible on an ad-hoc basis. But more formal mechanisms will likely be necessary to implement more complex agreements involving ongoing processes of adjustment among many states.

The second major reason why international organizations may be more necessary in environmental cooperation than in other areas is the rapidity of change in the environment and in our understanding of it. Change in the issues may take place too quickly for noninstitutionalized processes to keep up.

Abram Chayes and Antonia H. Chayes (1991) contend that a key facet of any arrangement to deal with environmental problems will be its adaptability. Because political, cultural, economic, and technical factors concerning the environment are all changing rapidly, that which appears necessary or sufficient today may appear unnecessary or insufficient tomorrow. This problem was exemplified by the need to revise the Montreal Protocol on ozone depletion almost as soon as it was drafted, and even before it had been ratified. The traditional method of setting international standards, "the ad-hoc diplomatic conference," with its delays for negotiation and ratification, simply cannot keep up (Sand, 1991a:240). Chayes and Chayes therefore argue that environmental cooperation requires not a series of contracts, but "a constitutive document," establishing an ongoing and binding process for setting environmental standards and resolving the attendant disputes (1991:281).

In sum, they contend, international regimes on the environment simply will not be effective without formal organizations to provide adaptability and to deal with the complexities of compliance. They chastise other proponents of international cooperation on the environment for demonstrating "an impoverished institutional imagination" (1991:308).

Summary: International Organizations as Intervening Variables

In examining the potential demand for international organizations as a solution to international environmental problems, we see arguments pointing in opposite directions. Some look at the degree of conflict on the issues and say formal organizations will not be necessary to preserve coordination on many environmental issues. Others look at the complexity and speed of change on the issues and conclude that organizations will be essential.[7] These two perspectives are based on different assumptions about what the function of international organizations is and should be, but because they share an underlying functionalist view of international institutions, there is no reason to expect the two views are mutually exclusive.

Those who view the function of international organizations primarily as one of reassuring states about each others' intentions and activities may be correct that such a function is less necessary on environmental issues.[8] It may still be true, however, that IOs are more required in environmental cooperation than on other issues because of the second major function they can fulfill: doing the actual nuts-and-bolts organizational work involved in coordinating complex policies across a large number of states. Even those issues that are coordination rather than cooperation problems might be extremely complex or divisive, requiring formal organizations to deal with these characteristics.

INTERNATIONAL ORGANIZATIONS AS INDEPENDENT ORGANIZATIONS

The discussion so far has been from the view of international institutions held by mainstream regime theorists who build from the neorealist view of international politics. In this "functional" view of regimes, institutions have little autonomous role but are driven by state interests and the distribution of power in the world.

Beyond Regime Theory: Autonomous Organizations

While the view of institutions as nonindependent factors in international politics has dominated the study of cooperation in recent years, there has always been dissent on the question.[9] Stephen Krasner (1983a) explicitly defines regimes as intervening variables in the first chapter of his edited collection on the subject, but in the conclusion he raises the question of whether regimes might have independent causal capabilities. More recently, various authors writing on the subject of "epistemic communities" have emphasized the importance to outcomes of how issues are defined by institutions (P. Haas, 1990, 1992b, 1992c; Adler, 1989). In addition, the independent role of organizations has been a major focus of work in sociology on organizations (Ness and Brechin, 1988).

These lines of research, as well as empirical evidence of the roles of some IOs in recent cooperative efforts, indicate that formal organizations may be important to the study of international cooperation as independent variables. The key argument is that, once formed, IOs can play an important role in shaping states' interests on future issues, as well as in negotiating processes, thus affecting outcomes on those issues (Krasner, 1983b:361). It is therefore worth considering what independent role IOs might play in international cooperation on the environment.

International organizations are not able to coerce states, particularly the developed industrialized states, nor is it likely that states will increasingly surrender authority to them. But IOs can generate their own sources of influence, involving the promotion of consensus on solutions of collective action problems. Functionalist arguments that IOs should be more used as tools to solve environmental problems and that IOs should be given more authority focus on only one of the possible roles which IOs can play in environmental cooperation. International organizations can independently affect outcomes in international cooperation in two fundamental ways: by shaping how states' interests are defined and by committing resources to promote certain outcomes.[10]

It is possible to conceive of IOs as actors that in some cases will have a degree of autonomy from state actors, resources (in terms of money, information, and prestige), and a specific goal or set of goals that the organization itself chooses to pursue. If an organization has all three of these things, it can use its resources to try to bring about its desired policies, just as other actors do, although it may not succeed.

Each of these attributes (autonomy, resources, and organizational goals) will vary from issue to issue and from organization to organization. On security issues, states take a high interest and are more likely to monitor and control an organization. Organizations concerned with less politicized issues, such as the environment, may have greater autonomy simply because states do not exert the resources to monitor them closely. Many organizations are formed specifically to reduce the "transaction costs" of closely monitoring complex interactions, but in doing so they gain power to alter those transactions. On the other hand, even an autonomous organization may be divided in its goals and strategies. While organizations presumably seek survival, at a minimum, it is unclear how organizational goals develop beyond that point (Ness and Brechin, 1988).

For example, in dealing with ozone depletion, UNEP was not closely monitored or directed by the states that make up the United Nations. In addition, under strong leadership and with internal agreement about the nature of the problem, it was able to press for a certain solution and to put resources behind it (see Chapter 11). On the other hand, the International Whaling Commission (IWC) is much more closely watched by governments and participating industries, and it does not have a unified solution or even a unified goal (Peterson, 1992). The IWC therefore has had much less independent influence on cooperation than UNEP.

In sum, IOs can affect international cooperation not only when given a specific mission and resources by states, but also when they choose to pursue specific goals and are left enough latitude to maneuver. The resources and autonomy of IOs will always be limited, as will their influence, but such influence may be crucial in some cases. Thus I do not contend that IOs will rule the world, but rather that they cannot be ignored in understanding international cooperation, particularly on the environment.

International organizations can shape states' definition of their interests through their role as providers of information and through the large role they play in setting the agenda for international discussion and negotiation. Organizations that conduct research, or are responsible for its dissemination, can affect the solutions that states choose for problems and even the issues that are defined as problems. To the extent that states rely on IOs for technical and scientific data, and for coordination of international research, IOs can have an effect on what the states' representatives end up believing (see Chapter 5).

The importance of setting the agenda is a truism in negotiation (Craig and George, 1990:ch. 12). Deciding what the issues are, defining them, and setting the range of possible outcomes can determine the outcome of a negotiation as much as the bargaining itself. Organizations affect agendas at two stages. First, if states decide to conduct a set of negotiations under the auspices of some IO, that organization may have significant input in how the negotiations are conducted and hence on their outcome.

More subtly, however, IOs can put items on the international agenda themselves by drawing attention to them and committing resources to their research. Ness and Brechin point out that organizations can often collect and disseminate data on air and water quality without getting specific permission from the states involved (1988:262), and Benedick attributes considerable importance to the public relations effort waged by UNEP in favor of the Montreal Protocol (1991:5).

International organizations can also help resolve coordination games by creating and promoting focal points or principles on which actors' expectations can converge.[11] In many cases, states seek to cooperate but cannot agree on the form in which to do so. A precedent, principle, or focal point may help resolve such problems. International organizations often try to create principles through declarations. That such principles are not binding may be less important than the fact that they provide those who seek to coordinate actions with a ready-made solution.

Even if it is theoretically plausible that international organizations can act as independent variables, the question remains what significance this has for environmental cooperation. I return now to the question of whether we can expect international organizations to play a larger role in future environmental cooperation than they have in other areas in the past. There are three reasons to believe they can play a larger role as independent actors in environmental issues than in other areas.

First, IOs in the environmental sphere are likely to have more autonomy than those in other areas because they are only tenuously linked to security (defined traditionally) on which states most closely guard their sovereignty. They are more closely linked to trade and economic development issues, but are still distinct. As the economic repercussions of environmental programs become more important, however, states are likely to pay more attention and limit the autonomy of IOs.

Second, the nature of environmental issues plays to the strengths of international organizations. International organizations' primary independent role is in shaping agendas and debates. To the extent that environmental issues are new items on the international agenda, organizations have more room to influence how those issues and agendas are defined. In addition, the lack of scientific certainty on many questions means that neither state interests nor the international agenda are firmly set. Organizations that sponsor research and engage in public education will have a relatively open field in which to work.

And third, at least in some areas, international organizations are likely to be more unified and goal oriented than those in other areas. Because environmental protection is perceived as a universal goal, there is a greater chance of staffers in environmental organizations coming to agreement on a common plan and putting that ahead of the narrower interest proposed by each of their countries. In addition, because many of the issues are seen as technical issues, there is a presumption that there is a best solution that can be found. There is less room for a perception of inherent conflict of interest on environmental issues. This will be particularly true when staffers and delegates to the IOs come from states' environmental ministries rather than their foreign ministries (P. Haas, 1990).

None of these factors, however, will operate universally; each aspect of environmental cooperation will have its own characteristics. These overall trends, however, seem plausible and merit further examination.

UNEP, the Montreal Protocol, and the Mediterranean Action Plan

To demonstrate that IOs can play an independent role in environmental cooperation, I consider the role that one, UNEP, has played in the past. I focus on two issues which have recently been given much attention as examples of successful environmental cooperation: the Mediterranean Action Plan (MAP) on pollution in the Mediterranean and the Montreal Protocol on ozone depletion. UNEP's role as an independent forger of consensus on these issues was at least as important as its role as a tool to be used by states. In both cases UNEP had a consistent goal, as well as autonomy from states and resources, to pursue the goal.

While Peter Haas's (1990) study of cooperation to control pollution in the Mediterranean focuses on the role an "epistemic community" played in promoting cooperation, it also points to the important role played by UNEP in that process.[12] UNEP had the autonomy and unity to devise a goal and pursue it, and it had the resources (not necessarily financial) to make a difference in the process of cooperation.

UNEP became deeply involved in negotiations on Mediterranean pollution when it essentially took oversight of the issue from the Food and Agriculture Organization (FAO) in 1974. The fact that UNEP chose to pursue this issue so vigorously demonstrates a large degree of autonomy, as it was not a major priority in the 1972 Stockholm Action Plan from which UNEP ostensibly took its mandate (Agesta Group, 1982). UNEP immediately sought to broaden the scope of the contemplated program and undertook a series of programs to do so (P. Haas, 1990:91-96). Although UNEP's initial involvement in Mediterranean pollution fits the functionalist view of IOs as tools, UNEP soon took an independent role.

UNEP had a strong "ecological orientation," which Peter Haas describes as an "ideology."[13] Maurice Strong's view was that the role of UNEP was "to speak for the environment" (Thacher, 1993:134). It is particularly noteworthy that this "ideology" was initially "not shared by national foreign affairs officials, nor by most of the scientific community" (P. Haas, 1990:79). For example, the Land Based Sources Protocol of 1980 was initially opposed by both northern and southern states, but was pursued by UNEP nonetheless (Boxer, 1983:292).[14] UNEP independently defined a set of goals and sought to attain them with such determination that many complained that UNEP was "heavy-handed" (Boxer, 1983:288; McCormick, 1989b:110).

From the beginning, UNEP-sponsored research was aimed at convincing national governments of the need for certain policies, such as the need to limit a wide variety of pollutants (P. Haas, 1990:95; Thacher, 1993:127). Among its goals for the Barcelona conference in 1975, which initiated the Mediterranean Action Plan, UNEP sought "to initiate a change in the way of thinking of riparian countries" (quoted in Thacher, 1993:127). The goal of persuasion affected the way in which UNEP presented its information. When many officials erroneously believed that movement of pollution from one country's shore to the next made Mediterranean pollution a true "commons" problem, UNEP officials "hoped to complete an agreement, so they just smiled and nodded" (P. Haas, 1990:70-71).

UNEP's research support also indicates the autonomy of the organization and the resources available to it in pursuing its goals. Although the financial resources available were quite limited, UNEP used them strategically to maximize their effect (McCormick, 1989b:107-10; Young, 1993b:248). For example, UNEP promoted research in less developed states, rather than use the more efficient facilities in France, because the goal was not so much to produce the highest quality research, but to gain advocates in the less developed countries' governments. Only two of the seven main laboratories sponsored by UNEP performed satisfactorily (P. Haas, 1990:79), but that was not the main point. In this way, UNEP was able to use the limited resources at its disposal to alter the debate in several states (P. Haas, 1990:78-82). UNEP essentially played old-fashioned patronage politics to further its goals.

In addition, UNEP made a considerable effort to avoid giving state representatives direct input in decisionmaking on MAP. Rather than negotiating research agreements with state governments, UNEP worked directly with the individual research institutions. Moreover, UNEP distinguished between "government" and "independent" scientists and used independent scientists as much as possible to bypass government interference and to prevent interstate rivalries from hampering the process (Boxer, 1983:289-92).

Peter Haas attributes at least one specific result to UNEP's varied efforts: the list of pollutants covered by the Land Based Sources Protocol (1990:110). He credits UNEP with broadening the scope of cooperation on Mediterranean pollution: "UNEP's leadership envisioned and masterminded an entire interlinked program for broadly defined environmental protection" (P. Haas, 1990:76). Others attribute much broader significance to UNEP's role in the Mediterranean Action Plan (Boxer, 1983:293; McCormick, 1989b:115).

UNEP has been able not only to catalyze the creation and implementation of the Mediterranean Action Plan, but also to make the program largely independent of UNEP's finances. In this way, UNEP has been not simply a regime, but the creator of a regime (Young, 1993b:245-46), a role reserved for states in most regime theory. In addition, by presenting the process of MAP as a successful method of cooperation, UNEP has been able to exert its influence on a wide range of issues.[15]

One issue to which the techniques used on the Mediterranean Action Plan were successfully transferred by UNEP is the treaties on ozone depletion, particularly the Montreal Protocol of 1987.[16] In the ozone case, it can first be established that UNEP had sufficient autonomy to decide internally what policies it would pursue and what solutions it would seek to solve the problem of ozone depletion. Also, under the leadership of Mostafa Tolba, the organization was unified enough to formulate a preferred policy and strategy.

Even though UNEP's financial resources were limited, its ability to promote certain points of view and take steps to achieve them was not tightly constrained. Thus while UNEP was at times severely hampered by its lack of financial resources (McCormick, 1989b:124; Thacher, 1991:438-39), it derived significant influence from its other primary resource: expertise (Stoel, 1983:66; Szell, 1993:47; Young, 1993b:248). Stoel asserts that UNEP was able to play the key role in early research on ozone because it was recognized as best qualified for the job (1983:66).

In this case, as in MAP, UNEP made a unilateral decision early in the process to get involved and to pursue a particular goal (see Chapter 11). Among other things, the executive director of UNEP was given the power, by its governing council, to call international meetings as he saw fit. In the following years, UNEP used this power to bring specialists together and to disseminate findings aimed at raising concern about ozone depletion and making it a priority item on the international diplomatic agenda (Benedick, 1991b:40-43).

UNEP took a partisan role in the diplomatic arena once negotiations started, pursuing its preferences rather than objectivity. Mostafa Tolba, speaking of "UNEP's interests" in the issue, made it clear that he viewed the role of UNEP as that of interested advocate, not merely as a coordinator of others' interests (Tolba, 1979). Rather than trying to play an impartial coordinating role, Tolba "unequivocally placed UNEP behind tough international regulations" (Benedick, 1991b:27; see also Chapter 11).

The actions of UNEP and its leader Tolba affected the negotiations at many different points. Because the negotiations "were conducted entirely within the framework of UNEP" (Szell, 1993:40), UNEP and Tolba were able to exert considerable influence on setting the agenda, in building consensus on technical issues, and in steering negotiations in directions it saw as useful. Tolba varied the nature of the meetings to achieve the goals he favored. For example, he created a group of delegation heads that met in closed session to negotiate the crucial parts of what became the Montreal Protocol (Benedick, 1991b:72-73) and insisted on many "informal" meetings in order to allow differences in positions to be narrowed. More fundamentally, Tolba successfully advocated pursuing a deliberately vague framework initially, one that committed no one to anything. This tactic obtained an early commitment to a treaty that developed a momentum of its own (Rubin, 1993:283, 286). Later, when new data made the Montreal Protocol appear inadequate, UNEP and Tolba worked to delay reconsideration of the Protocol and instead sought ratification of the first steps before moving on (Benedick, 1991b:112-13).

Whether UNEP was in some way decisive in causing the agreement is a matter of speculation, but the question is moot.[17] One can debate the relative importance of different key actors—the U.S. government, the European Community, the German government, DuPont, and UNEP—in promoting or allowing cooperation to reduce ozone depletion. It is difficult to deny, however, that UNEP was one of these key actors and was not merely a tool of others.

This cursory examination of UNEP's role in two issues, pollution in the Mediterranean and ozone depletion, indicates that international organizations have in the past played significant autonomous or independent roles in promoting environmental cooperation. This raises the question of what impact UNEP or other IOs might have on significant future issues such as global warming. Indeed, many authors argue that MAP and the Montreal Protocol—and UNEP's role in their negotiation—should provide a model for successful future cooperation.[18] While a detailed analysis of this question is beyond the scope of this chapter, it is worth noting the relationship of UNEP to other actors.

The main argument of this chapter has been that international organizations are not merely the epiphenomenal products of state actions, but are actors in their own right. This leaves open the question of how powerful they are. Can UNEP be expected to be as influential on other issues as it was on the two discussed here? Why has UNEP been so much more successful on these two issues than on others?

As Kay and Jacobson (1983) and Young (1993b) point out, UNEP is only one of many actors involved and, as with any other actor, will not always prevail. Young, in a useful formulation, distinguishes between the internal and external sources of UNEP's success (1993b:248). Although the internal sources of success such as technical expertise, strong leadership, and skillful maneuvering may be applied to other issues, the external situations on those issues may be much more difficult to cope with. Several factors, including public opinion, scientific consensus, willing states, and reduced industry opposition, made UNEP's task on ozone easier (Young, 1993:252). Thus Sebenius (1991) argues that the methods used to achieve the Montreal Protocol may not work for global warming, which is a much more difficult issue for many reasons.

Not only is abatement of global warming more complex and costly than reduction of ozone-depleting chemicals, but other actors are much less supportive. The most notable example is the United States, which was a leader from the beginning on efforts to prevent ozone depletion but has dragged its feet on global warming. As the abundant literature on hegemonic stability in international political economy indicates, cooperation is much easier when the most powerful state in the world supports it.

A much more mundane factor also contributes to an inherent limit in UNEP's effectiveness: its meager budget. This chapter has emphasized the necessity of resources of one type or another for institutional effectiveness, and whereas many analysts comment on UNEP's skill at maximizing the impact of a small budget, the amount of success remains limited by budgetary constraints (Young, 1993b:248; Thacher, 1991:438; McCormick, 1989b:109-10, 121). Although UNEP has strong resources in terms of international respect and expertise, "its principal handicap remains: it is rarely in a position to back up its warnings and advice with either money or technical assistance" (McCormick, 1989b:124).

The Mediterranean Action Plan and the Montreal Protocol were successes in part because UNEP decided to make these issues priorities. The corollary to making one issue a high priority, however, is making another a low priority. As long as UNEP's budget and staff are minuscule, it will be able to put its skill and expertise behind only a few issues. And even on those, other actors or difficult structural factors may prevent success.

CONCLUSION: INTERNATIONAL ORGANIZATIONS AND ENVIRONMENTAL COOPERATION

Regime theory, as well as functionalist integration theory before it, conceived of international institutions primarily as tools. In this conception, international organizations that were not part of a "regime" were irrelevant. UNEP, which was not in itself a regime or part of one, was therefore unimportant. In broadening the conception of institutions to entertain the possibility that institutions can be independent variables, we see the important differences between formal organizations and less formal institutions.

Krasner has argued that international regimes can "feed back" on the structural factors that created them, thus having an autonomous effect. Formal organizations, however, can go a step further: they can deliberately seek to change the system, design strategies to do so, and attempt to implement the strategies. They can attain the status of "actors." And even if they remain weak in traditional power factors, they can make a difference in negotiations and in outcomes.

The broad theoretical conclusion of this chapter is that, in assessing the roles of IOs in general, and especially with respect to environmental issues, the lens of regime theory focuses on only one of two broad roles that IOs can play. This narrow focus may lead to misunderstanding not only the actual and potential role of IOs, but also the reasons cooperation occurs (or does not) and who the relevant actors are. Regime theory is better at explaining the reasons for creating IOs than the effects they might have once created.

To assess the potential importance of IOs in environmental cooperation, then, two potential roles of IOs must be examined: the IO as tool and the IO as independent advocate. There is dissent concerning the necessity of IOs as tools to implement state interests. On issues defined as problems of coordination, IOs may be needed only to help states overcome the complexity of issues to arrive at coordination equilibria. On issues that remain traditional prisoner's dilemmas or commons problems, states will remain concerned that others will exploit them, and IOs will be needed to increase confidence in compliance.

As independent actors, international organizations may be expected to play a significant role in the debate on environmental cooperation. Increased autonomy of IOs on some environmental issues and the increased needs of states to rely on them for information and coordination will allow those organizations with unified leadership and significant resources to have independent effects.

The power of IOs will vary greatly by organization and by issue, and IOs will not be able to overcome the wishes of determined states on highly politicized issues. But these constraints may leave more room for IO action on the environment than on trade and security issues. This potential role for IOs merits further study by advocates and students of international environmental cooperation.

NOTES

An earlier draft of this chapter was presented at the Summer Workshop on International Organization Studies, Dartmouth College, July 1992, sponsored by the Academic Council on the United Nations System and the American Society of International Law. I am grateful to the conference participants and to several anonymous referees for their suggestions.

1. The difference between coordination and cooperation is discussed below and in Hardin (1982) and Stein (1990).

2. I do not attempt to predict the extent of environmental cooperation that will occur, which is a separate question. I am investigating the potential role of international organizations in whatever cooperation does occur. The two may be linked if states that are protective of their sovereignty refuse to cooperate on issues where they perceive such cooperation would require surrender of authority to international organizations.

3. See the discussion of the link between regime theory and functionalism and utilitarianism in Krasner (1988).

4. For examples of this approach, see Keohane (1984); Krasner (1983a); Oye (1986a); and Stein (1983, 1990). The most explicit formulation is found in Keohane (1984, chs. 5-6).

5. The standard definition of "international regime" is that used by Krasner: "International regimes are defined as principles, norms, rules, and decision-making procedures around which actor expectations converge in a given issue-area" (1983b:1).

6. For a more thorough discussion of the impact of distributive issues on international environmental cooperation, see D'Anieri (1993).

7. A third point of view is that of Oran Young, who contends that the nature of the issues does not tell us much about the role of organizations. Young (1989b:46) contends: "A more compelling argument centers on the proposition that incentives to create organizations in conjunction with international regimes flow from the character of the regime under consideration," rather than on the objective structure of the issue. This view throws even more uncertainty into the question of the potential role of IOs as tools in international cooperation.

8. Many, including Chayes and Chayes (1991), would contend that compliance issues on international environmental cooperation are extremely problematic and that formation of organizations is necessary to overcome the problem.

9. Jacobson (1984), Kay and Jacobson (1983), and Le Prestre (1986) have discussed IOs as independent actors in international cooperation. I am grateful to an anonymous referee for bringing these sources to my attention.

10. Krasner posits four ways in which institutions can "feed back" on "basic causal variables": altering "actors' calculation of how to maximize their interests," altering "the interests themselves," providing "a source of power to which actors can appeal," and by altering "the power capabilities of different actors, including states" (1983c:361-67). My categorization is not meant to contradict or supersede his; it is simply a different categorization. These categories are neither distinct nor all encompassing, but rather provide a general scheme of examining a set of interrelated phenomena.

11. On the role of focal points and principles in resolving coordination problems, see Schelling (1960).

12. I will not analyze the interaction between the "epistemic community" and UNEP here, but the interaction between the epistemic community and the organization clearly merits further study. The (apparently) mutually reinforcing relationship between the two poses a dilemma if one seeks to unravel the two and sort out the relationships among ideas, individuals, and institutions. For additional discussions of UNEP, the Regional Seas Program, and the Mediterranean Action Plan, see Boxer (1983); Hulm (1983); Kuwabara (1984); McCormick (1989b); and Thacher (1993).

13. See P. Haas (1990:74-79) for a detailed description of the epistemic community's ideology. Demonstrating the unified outlook and prescriptive beliefs of the epistemic community and UNEP is a major thrust of Haas's book. UNEP's role as an advocate is discussed also by Boxer (1983).

14. For a discussion of the negotiation and content of the Land Based Sources Protocol, see Kuwabara (1984).

15. Peter Hulm (1983:2-3) shows how the success of MAP has led to its emulation in the other areas of the Regional Seas Program. Moreover, in contrasting the success of the piecemeal approach of MAP with the failure of the comprehensive approach of the UN Conference on the Law of the Sea, he argues that the piecemeal approach should be used in other areas of environmental cooperation.

16. The similarity between UNEP's approach to the ozone negotiations and that of MAP is emphasized by Szell (1993:45-46). For general discussions of the negotiations on preventing ozone depletion, see Benedick (1991b, 1993); Szell (1993); and Stoel (1983).

17. For evaluations of the role of UNEP compared to other actors and factors, see Young (1993b:248); Szell (1993:36); and Benedick (1993:224-25).

18. This argument is examined most thoroughly by Sebenius (1991).

11

UNEP and the Montreal Protocol

David Leonard Downie

In 1974 researchers at the University of California discovered that an important family of chemicals commonly known as chlorofluorocarbons (CFCs) posed a serious threat to the earth's protective ozone layer (Molina and Rowland, 1974).[1] Created in 1928 to replace inflammable and noxious refrigerants, CFCs are inert, noninflammable, nontoxic, colorless, odorless, and profitably adaptable to a variety of uses. By the mid-1970s, CFCs had become the chemical of choice for propellants in aerosol sprays, coolants in refrigerators and air conditioners, solvents in the cleaning of electronic components, and blowing agents for the manufacture of flexible and rigid foam.

Because of this economic importance, establishing controls on CFCs proved extremely difficult. The absence of firm scientific consensus on the nature and seriousness of the problem, a strenuous antiregulatory campaign by corporations producing or using CFCs, concerns for the cost of unilateral regulation, and opposition by the European Community prevented effective action for many years.[2]

Nevertheless, states have created a series of very important ozone-protection agreements, including the 1985 Vienna Convention for the Protection of the Ozone Layer, the 1987 Montreal Protocol on Substances That Deplete the Ozone Layer, and the Amendments and Adjustments to the Protocol agreed to in London in 1990 (UNEP/OzL.Pro.2/3) and Copenhagen in 1992 (UNEP/OzL.Pro.4/15). These agreements form the core of the "Ozone Regime"—widely hailed as a historic development in global environmental policy and a worthy blueprint for other international environmental agreements (Benedick, 1991b:1, 7-8).

The United Nations Environment Programme (UNEP) played a critical role in the development of the ozone regime. Although other factors were important, UNEP significantly assisted the creation and influenced the content of the ozone regime.[3] Remarkably, there has been little detailed analysis of UNEP's contribution. This chapter focuses on three issues: What role did UNEP play in the international response to stratospheric ozone depletion? Why was UNEP able to play this role? And do existing theories of regime creation and change explain UNEP's contribution?

INTERNATIONAL REGIMES

International regimes are evolving sets of agreed upon principles, norms, rules, and procedures that regulate and coordinate action in particular issue areas of international relations.[4] Created primarily through a series of international agreements and often administered by international organizations, regimes are best seen as ynamic sectoral legal systems (Gehring, 1990) composed of "interlocking sets of rights and rules" (Young, 1990:339). When effective, regimes manage interactions, augment policy coordination and collaboration, cause international behavior to conform, reduce conflict, and facilitate the making of further agreements (Keohane, 1984:65-134).

An international regime is not patterned interaction, an ad hoc agreement, or a single organization. Each, however, may be part of a regime. Rather, an international regime consists of the principles, norms, rules, and procedures contained in a *set* of interrelated agreements, organizations, and norms of behavior that together regulate international action in a particular issue area. For example, the nonproliferation regime includes the Partial Test Ban Treaty, the Non-Proliferation Treaty, and the relevant activities of the International Atomic Energy Agency. The ozone regime includes the Vienna Convention, the Montreal Protocol, the London and Copenhagen amendments, the Ozone Secretariat, and the Secretariat for the Multilateral Fund.

Regimes exist in most areas of international relations, including trade, money, security, and the global commons.[5] The ozone regime is an example of the increasing diplomatic attention being given to environmental issues. It is the success of the ozone regime that makes it particularly worthy of scholarly study.[6]

UNEP'S ROLE IN THE DEVELOPMENT OF INTERNATIONAL OZONE POLICY

UNEP has played five roles critical to the evolution of the ozone regime. In the late 1970s, UNEP *initiated* international action by organizing the first scientific and political meetings focusing on ozone depletion. UNEP then *sustained* international attention on the issue when interest in ozone depletion waned significantly during the early 1980s.

Once substantive negotiations began, UNEP *facilitated* regime creation by establishing a procedural foundation and reducing transaction costs. UNEP also acted as a *negotiation manager*, actively pushing the parties toward strong agreements. Finally, UNEP has served as a *regime administrator*, performing key organizational tasks, implementing regime rules, and managing the review process.

Regime Origins: UNEP as Regime Initiator and Sustainer

In the first phase of the regime's development, 1974 to 1983, the CFC-ozone problem was discovered, its impact was explored, and international regulatory negotiations were begun. During this period, UNEP *initiated* and *sustained* an international response to ozone depletion by coordinating the first international meetings on the issue. In doing so, UNEP built the scientific, political and procedural foundation necessary to create an ozone regime.

UNEP was the first international organization to respond to the Molina-Rowland hypothesis. Its initial plan, released in January 1976, called for reviewing existing scientific research, outlining areas requiring further study, creating an international program to monitor ozone, and examining the need for controls on potential ozone depleting substances (ODS). Putting this plan into action in April 1976, UNEP called for an international conference "to review all aspects of the ozone layer" (UNEP, 1989:6).

In March 1977, scientific experts and representatives from thirty-two countries met in Washington, D.C. Following several days of discussion, the conference adopted the World Plan of Action on the Ozone Layer—the first international agreement on the issue (UNEP/WG.7/25/Rev.1, Annex III). Strongly influenced by UNEP's January 1976 plan, this twenty-one-point research program included monitoring stratospheric ozone and solar radiation, assessing the impact of ozone depletion, and studying the consequences of possible control measures. The plan also formalized UNEP's coordinating role by instructing the organization to establish a Coordinating Committee on the Ozone Layer (CCOL).

UNEP organized regular CCOL meetings at which scientists from national governments, specialized UN agencies, environmental organizations, research institutions, and the chemical industry met to exchange scientific and technical information. CCOL issued eight authoritative reports between 1977 and 1986 that assessed current research concerning possible causes and impacts of stratospheric ozone depletion.

UNEP used the scientific discussions as the basis for initiating a similar series of regulatory meetings (Usher, 1993; Mansfield, 1993). Because there was little initial support for even discussing international controls, UNEP's effort to initiate and sustain this process is especially important.

The first official discussion took place in April 1977. Convened by UNEP and hosted by the United States, this intergovernmental meeting was a follow-up to the March scientific conference. Participants discussed plans for possible national programs and agreed on the importance of exchanging scientific, economic and other information. They reached no consensus, however, on the necessity for international regulation. At a similar meeting held in Munich in 1978, delegates could not even agree on coordinating voluntary CFC reductions (Benedick, 1991a:118).

In 1980 the CCOL believed it had sufficiently reliable scientific assessments to conclude there was a definite and serious threat to the ozone layer. Using the expanding scientific consensus to push the political process forward (Mansfield, 1993; Usher, 1993), in 1981 UNEP established the Ad Hoc Working Group of Legal and Technical Experts for the Elaboration of a Global Framework Convention for the Protection of the Ozone Layer (UNEP/GC/9 1981:118, Decision 9/13). The Working Group, open to representatives from all nations and most international governmental, industry, and environmental organizations, met seven times under UNEP's direction between 1982 and 1985 (UNEP/WG.69/10; UNEP/WG.78/8; UNEP/WG.78/13; UNEP/WG.94/5; UNEP/WG.94/10; UNEP/WG.110/4; UNEP/IG.53/4).

Discussions began with the expectation that the convention would cover only "cooperative research . . . not international regulation" (Benedick, 1991a:119). UNEP's goals were to have nations formally acknowledge the threat, commit to its study, and resolve to address it (Usher, 1993). Experience with other issues and the unwillingness of several governments even to discuss binding controls caused UNEP to pursue only a framework treaty in the expectation that this would lead to the greatest level of ozone protection in the long run (UNEP, 1989:7; Mansfield, 1993).

In April 1983, Finland, Norway, and Sweden led nations known as the "Toronto Group" in expanding these discussions by formally proposing a ban on nonessential uses of CFCs in aerosols (UNEP/WG.78/11; UNEP/WG.78/13; UNEP/WG.94/5; Benedick, 1991b:42-44). The beginning of substantive negotiations on mandatory CFC controls closed the first stage of the regime's development.

UNEP's efforts to initiate and sustain regular scientific and political meetings to discuss possible ozone depletion had an important impact. The scientific meetings helped ensure that (1) the CFC-ozone issue received broad scientific attention; (2) there would be a forum for those working on the problem to meet, exchange information and refine predictions; (3) policymakers would have timely information on which to base regulatory decisions; and (4) the public could be educated on the issue through press reports on the scientific reviews. As a result, the meetings established two important regime procedures: there would be regular, international scientific reviews of the issue and scientists and scientific reviews would be part of the policy-making process. Equally significant, UNEP's efforts also helped establish a key regime principle—that scientific concerns would be of equal or greater significance than economic considerations in determining ODS regulation.

More broadly, UNEP's scientific and political conferences began a policy process that created significantly more opportunities for ozone protection than would have otherwise existed. UNEP's meetings placed ozone depletion on the international agenda and attracted representatives of states indifferent or hostile to the issue. Such "agenda setting" is an important and potentially powerful role in highly complex and interdependent environments (Keohane and Nye, 1977:32-35). It was essential to initiate regime building before there was scientific certainty regarding the scope of the problem (Benedick, 1991a:122-23, 144-15). If UNEP had waited, the complex negotiations needed to restrict ODS production would have taken even longer in response to the reports of an Antarctic ozone hole in 1985 (Farman et al., 1985) and of ozone depletion above the Northern Hemisphere in 1988 (NASA, 1988). However, UNEP was operating under the belief that it was important to act preemptively to prevent a more serious problem. This became a central principle of the ozone regime.

Similarly, UNEP's meetings were important to the development of an "epistemic community" dedicated to CFC-ozone science and, eventually, CFC regulation. Epistemic communities are transnational, "knowledge-based networks of specialists who share beliefs in cause-and-effect relations, validity tests, and underlying principled values and pursue common policy goals" (P. Haas, 1992a:187). Members command specialized knowledge and occupy positions within scientific communities, national bureaucracies, lobbying groups, and international organizations. In technically complex issue areas where state preferences have not been established, epistemic communities can significantly affect regime development by producing and controlling information, framing regime options, influencing state preferences, and pushing for international consensus (P. Haas, 1989, 1990, 1992c).

An environmental epistemic community was important to the ozone regime's development (P. Haas, 1992). The community helped build scientific understanding, inform public opinion, refute industry claims, establish contacts between scientists and policymakers, and foster consensus at international conferences. UNEP-organized meetings institutionalized regular gatherings of the epistemic community. The meetings provided a forum and recruiting ground, placed the community at the center of international activity on the issue, and expanded its base of specialized knowledge (an important source of influence in debates on complex domestic and international policy issues).

UNEP was also essential in sustaining these meetings and, consequently, the slow process of regime creation. For more than a decade there was scientific uncertainty concerning elements of the CFC-ozone theory. The absence of empirical confirmation in nature and fluctuating estimates of eventual ozone depletion allowed control opponents to downplay the issue. Following a handful of bans in the late 1970s on most uses of CFCs as aerosol propellants (including restrictions in the United States, Canada, Sweden, Norway, Finland, and Switzerland), states enacted no further significant national or international ODS regulation until 1987.

This was most apparent, and most important, in the United States, the leader in scientific and regulatory activity in the 1970s. A highly publicized CFC-aerosol ban and lack of existing ozone depletion gave many the impression that the issue was under control. These factors combined with effective antiregulatory efforts by the CFC industry and the election of Ronald Reagan—whose environmental skepticism and laissez-faire philosophy heavily influenced Environmental Protection Agency (EPA) appointments and activity—to dampen interest in further regulation.

UNEP, however, maintained its focus and continued the CCOL and working group meetings despite indifference by the United States and active opposition by other states.[7] If it had not, argues a chief American negotiator, "the ozone issue might have died" (Benedick, 1991a:119).

Regime Creation and Expansion: UNEP as Agreement Facilitator, Negotiation Manager, and Regime Administrator

The second phase of the regime's development, regime creation, began in 1983 with the first serious proposal for international regulation, then continued through the negotiation of the 1985 Vienna Convention (a framework treaty), and concluded with the signing of the 1987 Montreal Protocol—the first global agreement restricting ODS production. During the third and current stage, regime expansion, agreements finalized in London in 1990, Copenhagen in 1992, and Bangkok in 1993 have significantly strengthened the regime.

Creating "cooperation under anarchy" is one of the central dilemmas in the study and conduct of international relations (Oye, 1986a). The exigencies of a self-help system, conflicting state interests, and the defections and free-riding associated with collective action often thwart effective cooperation. UNEP *facilitated*, or made it easier for the parties to negotiate and create, the ozone treaties by establishing a procedural foundation that emphasized iteration and disaggregation and by providing organizational assistance that reduced transaction costs (see Chapter 12).

UNEP's ability to initiate and sustain international scientific and diplomatic conferences established the procedure used to create the regime—a pattern of regular meetings (iteration) at which delegates addressed relatively narrow topics (disaggregation). The value of iteration and disaggregation to creating successful agreements is well known (Oye, 1986a:12-18). Each meeting provided the opportunity to build consensus on different aspects of the problem. As a result, by September 1987, there was a formal protocol that few parties would have agreed to initially. This regime procedure has continued during the protocol's expansion.

Disaggregation also helped depoliticize the negotiations. An effective ozone regime required global cooperation. East-west and north-south political divisions, as well as economic competition among industrialized countries, presented serious obstacles. Disaggregation encouraged delegates to focus on the problem at hand and often meant that technical specialists rather than political officers were national representatives. UNEP worked diligently to create an "objective international forum, free of time-consuming debates on extraneous political issues that have too often marred the work of other UN bodies" (Benedick, 1991a:145).

UNEP also facilitated agreement by coordinating negotiations and ensuring the availability of accurate information. The ability of international institutions to assist cooperation in these ways are well known (Keohane, 1984:89-96; Keohane and Axelrod, 1986; Haas, Keohane, and Levy, 1993).

UNEP established the CCOL and working group meetings that led to the Vienna Convention and helped to organize the more complex series that produced the Montreal Protocol—a succession of informal workshops, scientific review conferences, and official working group meetings designed to build consensus on the cause and impact of ozone depletion and to remove various political, legal, and economic obstacles blocking ODS regulation (Usher, 1993; Mansfield, 1993; Sarma, 1993). UNEP helped set dates and locations, sent invitations, handled credentials, issued press releases, secured translators, and provided staff. By allowing delegates to avoid negotiating about negotiations and by handling organization chores, UNEP freed regime advocates to concentrate their efforts on reaching agreement.

UNEP's Ozone Secretariat acted as an information clearing house providing documents from past negotiations; information on scientific, economic, and political developments; and details of upcoming meetings. This lowered information costs, reduced opportunities for market failure, and increased the availability of accurate information to all parties (Keohane, 1984:82-83, 97). Because some developing nations feared they would be unfairly and unnecessarily disadvantaged by the proposed regulations, UNEP's efforts increased the likelihood that suspicious nations would take the problem seriously. As with UNEP's financing of many Third World delegations, this helped ensure broad knowledge of the problem and broad participation in addressing it.

In its fourth role, *negotiation manager*, UNEP actively spurred the parties toward a strong protocol by offering robust control proposals, undercutting the arguments of regime opponents, building consensus, applying political pressure, and providing timely mediation. This was a far more vigorous role than simply facilitating agreement through organizational assistance. Here, UNEP was actively attempting to influence regime norms and rules.

In public pronouncements, formal negotiations and important private consultations with key delegations, UNEP's former Executive Director Mostafa Tolba urged consensus and pressed for a strong treaty (Tolba, 1987, 1989, 1990, 1992; Mansfield, 1993; Sarma, 1993; Benedick, 1991b:6, 40, 71-74, 125, 208). During important negotiations held in December 1986 and April 1987, UNEP advocated a 1990 freeze in CFC production and biannual 20 percent reductions leading to a total ban in 2000 (P. Haas, 1992a:206; Benedick, 1991b:85). This proposal was tougher than the initial positions of other control advocates and served to move the bargaining range toward a more robust regime. Later in the negotiations, Tolba applied political pressure by insisting that UNEP would oppose any protocol mandating only from 30 to 40 percent reductions, even if this threatened reaching an agreement (P. Haas, 1992a:191).

UNEP also organized small negotiating sessions with the heads of selected delegations that proved crucial in formulating key details of the treaties. Meeting informally, away from the glare of press, industry, and environmental observers, delegates were free to explore possible compromises without making formal commitments. Tolba chaired many of these meetings and, if agreement was not forthcoming, UNEP often used the discussions as the basis for new proposals. By combining elements of opposing national positions into a new framework or specific control proposal, UNEP provided a platform for future discussion, driving the process forward.[8]

The most important small group negotiations took place during the Montreal, London, and Copenhagen negotiations. At these meetings, agreement was not certain until the final hours, and Tolba is cited as a forceful mediator who was instrumental in hammering out the final compromises (Sarma, 1993; Campbell, 1993; P. Haas, 1992a:194; Benedick, 1991b:75, 161-88).

Another important example of UNEP's negotiation management occurred in April 1987. Prior to the third round of protocol negotiations in Geneva, UNEP quickly organized a special meeting of leading atmospheric scientists to compare computer models of ozone depletion. Negotiations had stalled during the previous working group meeting as control opponents argued there were still large uncertainties concerning the existence of a serious problem and that these negated the need for strong regulations (UNEP/WG.167/2; Usher, 1993). UNEP hoped that if scientists (in the absence of extraneous political and economic considerations) could reach clear consensus on the extent of the problem, their conclusions would break the political deadlock (Haas, 1992a:211; Usher, 1993).

Meeting for two days in Warzburg, West Germany, the scientists were able to agree on estimates of the total ozone depletion that would occur with no CFC regulation, with a freeze on production, and with a 50 percent cut. Agreeing that even "a 50 percent reduction in CFC emissions would still lead to a 5 to 20 percent depletion of ozone . . . [the] scientists unambiguously concluded that seven substances—CFCs 11, 12, 113, 114 and 115 and halons 1211 and

1301—should be covered in the Protocol" (P. Haas, 1992:211; see also UNEP/WG.167/Inf.1 and Add.1).

These findings altered the political debate, and UNEP officials used them to push the Geneva negotiations forward (UNEP/WG.172/2; Usher, 1993; P. Haas, 1992a:211-12; Benedick, 1991b:71-72). Stating that, because of the meeting, "consensus among the scientific community is confirmed" and that "no longer can those who are against action to regulate CFC release hide behind the charade of scientific dissent," Tolba argued it was necessary to first freeze and then significantly reduce CFC and halon emissions (Tolba, 1987:1-2, 6-7). With the European Community (EC) position undercut and UNEP "unequivocally . . . behind tough international regulations" (Benedick, 1991b:72), the United States and other control advocates were in a better position to press "their arguments for broader scope, deeper cuts, and more rapid entry of the protocol into force" (P. Haas, 1992a:211-12).

Finally, UNEP has served as a *regime administrator* implementing existing regime rules and procedures and helping to establish new ones. After UNEP had campaigned for the duty, the 1985 Vienna Convention mandated that UNEP establish an Ozone Secretariat to organize future meetings, prepare and transmit reports, and perform functions assigned to it by any future protocols. Although UNEP's management of this group was to be temporary and their formal legal relationship is obscure, the Ozone Secretariat has been permanently housed within UNEP's Nairobi headquarters, relies upon UNEP for conference services and administrative assistance, and is, in practice, a part of the larger organization.

The Montreal Protocol contains several basic requirements—control measures on CFCs and halons, trade provisions, noncompliance provisions, and reporting requirements. Subsequent amendments expanded existing regime rules and added new ones. To assist parties in implementing these requirements, the Ozone Secretariat and other UNEP entities organize review meetings, provide legal interpretations, coordinate scientific studies, establish procedures for reporting production data, monitor regulatory compliance, gather and disseminate information on CFC alternatives, and manage the multilateral fund that financially assists developing nations meet regime rules. Through these activities and by offering studies, at the request of the parties, on possible changes to the regime, UNEP continues to be involved in the creation and maintenance of regime rules and procedures.

WHY WAS UNEP ABLE TO PLAY THESE ROLES?

Determining the reasons UNEP succeeded in this case will help us judge UNEP's ability to perform similar roles concerning other environmental issues. Part of UNEP's success is that it adhered to its "catalytic-coordinative mandate"

(Buckley, 1982:6). UNEP emerged from the 1972 United Nations Conference on the Human Environment held in Stockholm. It was intended not to create policy on its own but to act as a catalyst for environmental protection through education, information collection and dispersal, institution building, augmenting government initiatives, and fostering cooperative efforts (UNEP GC/10, 1982:II and III).

By remaining focused on promoting awareness and cooperation, UNEP was able to act effectively during the early stages of the ozone issue. UNEP quickly recognized that broad cooperation was necessary to protect stratospheric ozone, and it charted a gradual education and policy process to build a strong regime (Mansfield, 1993; Benedick, 1991b:40). Fostering scientific consensus in order to push the political process forward was a large part of UNEP's original strategy (Mansfield, 1993; Usher, 1993). By coupling major policy moves (establishing the working group in 1981; proposing a 2000 CFC phase out in 1987) with new scientific developments (CCOL's conclusion that ozone faced a serious threat; the Warzburg modeler's meeting), UNEP avoided the image of crusader and maintained its official standing as international catalyst and coordinator.

Although some have attempted to make UNEP a "development assistance agency," these efforts have been defeated (Buckley, 1982:6). The organization has expanded significantly and possesses a wide range of interests and responsibilities, but it still functions largely as an educating, catalyzing, coordinating, monitoring, and information-providing institution (United Nations Environment Programme, 1990). This focus served it well in protecting the stratospheric ozone.

UNEP also is a largely independent institution within the UN system and the only international governmental organization dedicated solely to environmental protection. The Governing Council, which is composed of national representatives, must approve major policy initiatives, but this body currently meets only once every two years and, in general, gives UNEP broad latitude to carry out its mandate.

These characteristics and Tolba's strong personal interest allowed UNEP to stay focused on ozone depletion during the early 1980s. It continued to coordinate the CCOL and working group meetings and remained at the center of international activity on the issue. UNEP's unique situation also helped divorce ozone negotiations from the political and economic disputes that often impede the effectiveness of other UN organizations.

In addition, UNEP's status as a permanent UN organization enhanced its efforts to place and keep ozone depletion on the international agenda. Even states opposed to international controls found it difficult to ignore UNEP calls to discuss the issue. UNEP's clear commitment to ozone protection also helped build an expectation that the policy process would continue, enhancing prospects for a strong regime by providing "stable expectations" (Keohane, 1984) and a "shadow of the future" (Oye, 1986a:12-18). Negotiators believed that the Vienna and Montreal agreements were not endpoints and that negotiations on production controls, import and export restrictions, and compliance procedures would continue. This pushed the search for both CFC substitutes and political compromise.

UNEP's ability to function as an effective mediator, despite being a control advocate, resulted from its UN status and its assiduous maintenance of good working relations with most delegations. This was of particular importance in attracting the participation and eventually the support of developing countries, many of whom have traditionally mistrusted international attempts at environmental protection. Tolba was especially attuned to interests of developing countries and the need to bring them into the process (Sarma, 1993; Mansfield, 1993). Based in Kenya, sensitive to the concerns of the Third World, and committed to environmental protection, UNEP is uniquely positioned to play this role.

Finally, UNEP's success is also a function of the issue itself. Ozone depletion was a new issue. UNEP was able to become involved at the beginning of international activity and shape the policy process. Ozone depletion was also an extremely complex issue, requiring years of scientific analysis. This enhanced UNEP's influence through its ability to coordinate and disseminate new knowledge about the problem. Finally, although the issue was complex, it was relatively encapsulated (especially in comparison with global warming). This increased the opportunity for eventual consensus on the causes, consequences, and resolution of the problem.

UNEP'S INDEPENDENT ROLE: CHALLENGING REGIME EXPLANATIONS

The four most prominent categories of explanations for regime creation and change—hegemonic stability theory, historical materialism, neoliberal institutionalism, and epistemic communities—provide insights into the ozone regime's development but are unable to explain the important contribution made by UNEP.[9] This argues for incorporating the impact of existing international organizations into such explanations.

Positioned strongly within the neorealist tradition, hegemonic stability theory argues that the active participation of a dominant power is required to create and maintain effective international regimes (Krasner, 1976; Keohane, 1980; Grunberg, 1990). Only hegemons are believed to have the resources to accept the risks inherent in cooperation—nonreciprocity and interdependence—and to take the actions necessary to create a regime—manage bargaining, provide side payments, enforce sanctions against violators, and tolerate defections. Regime terms will reflect the hegemon's beliefs and interests and regime effectiveness will vary with its willingness and ability to absorb disproportionate costs, reward compliance, and punish violators.   No role is seen for an independent international organization.

Hegemonic stability theory suffers from serious theoretical and empirical problems in explaining UNEP's contribution to regime development. The theory ignores UNEP's crucial independent role in initiating early efforts to confront the problem, maintain a procedural foundation, and push negotiations toward a strong regime. More broadly, although the United States was critical to the creation of the regime (Benedick 1992b), it was not a uniquely powerful hegemon in the system or this issue area. The Soviet Union's participation, by definition, invokes bipolarity, not hegemony. The European Community, which was negotiating as a bloc, and Japan had become economic contemporaries of the United States by the mid-1980s. Moreover, by the late 1970s the EC had passed the United States as the world's largest producer and consumer of CFCs (Jachtenfuchs, 1990:263). Indeed, it was EC opposition to CFC controls that kept the 1985 Convention a framework treaty and excluded phase out regulations from the 1987 Protocol (see Chapter 4).

Historical materialism argues that regimes arise through efforts by dominant, First World states to maintain, strengthen, and institutionalize control over the Third World.[10]   Developed states use economic and political coercion, dominance of international organizations, and control of relevant information to structure regimes that support their interests. "Historical materialists are not sanguine that the less developed countries will benefit from environmental cooperation.   Cooperation will be imposed by the North, and its scope will cover issues of concern to the North, not the South" (P. Haas 1990:51).

First World corporations and states did act in ways predicted by this approach. Most important, they pursued phase out targets in a time frame that allowed them to develop and control CFC substitutes (putting the periphery once again at the bottom of the product cycle); they pushed for global and uniform controls that would eliminate costs associated with unilateral regulation; and they used threats of trade sanctions to attract Third World participation.

Historical materialism cannot, however, explain UNEP's efforts to create a strong protocol as these often conflicted with the interests of many developed states and large corporations. Particularly contradictory was UNEP's extensive support for successful LDC efforts to obtain regulatory extensions, historic agreements on financial compensation and technology transfer, and guaranteed access to ODS during the phase out periods.

Neoliberal institutionalism, sometimes called functional explanations, relaxes some neorealist assumptions but maintains the image of states as unitary, rational actors attempting to mitigate the effects of international anarchy (Keohane, 1984; Keohane and Axelrod, 1986; Krasner, 1983a:1-12; Haggard and Simmons, 1987:506-09; Young, 1989c:356-59). Here, however, rather than balancing, avoiding dependence, and maximizing payoff differentials as neorealists predict

(Waltz, 1979; Grieco, 1988), states attempt to create institutions. They do so because such institutions provide goods that are often absent in international anarchy: coordinated policy; stable expectations; official avenues for reciprocity; and established procedures to facilitate decentralized rulemaking and to reduce asymmetries of information, transaction costs, and opportunities for market failure.

As predicted by this approach, the ozone regime assists states to create common ODS regulations. It serves important organizational and information functions, facilitates the making of new agreements, and provides side payments for regime participants and punishments for nonparticipants. Yet, predicting goals does not equal explaining the process. Contrary to this approach, goals were very controversial, control of information was suspect, states often focused on obtaining positional advantages, and UNEP, in addition to state actors, played several very important roles. Indeed, during the regime's creation, UNEP performed and, in some cases still performs, many of the functions that the approach argues the ozone regime would be created to provide. Many of the insights this approach provides concerning the creation and impact of international regimes are equally important for understanding the roles that existing international organizations can play in creating new cooperative arrangements (Haas, Keohane, and Levy, 1993).

Theories focusing on epistemic communities argue that regimes form in issue areas where transnational alliances of like-minded experts and policymakers can influence interstate negotiations. As noted above, an environmental epistemic community was important to the development of the ozone regime (P. Haas, 1992a). Moreover, studying epistemic communities is important because it supplements neorealist analysis by examining knowledge, learning, transnational groups, and domestic politics.

Yet, epistemic communities alone are not a sufficient explanation. What, for example, was the impact of an opposing transnational, industry interest group? What were the conditions that allowed different groups to prevail at different times? And how should we explain UNEP's independent contribution to international ozone protection? It was UNEP taking full advantage of its constitutional mandate and organizational capacity, rather than a new epistemic community, that initiated and sustained scientific and political discussions, facilitated agreement, managed negotiations toward establishing strong rules, and helped administer the regime toward expansion.

CONCLUSION

Contradicting existing regime explanations, the history of the ozone regime argues that an independent international organization can have a significant impact on the development of international environmental regimes. This does not, however, argue for abandoning regimes as an analytical tool. Regimes exist independently of our ability to explain their development. Moreover, the explanations outlined above have proven useful in explaining other types of international regimes.

It does, however, argue for improving our analysis of environmental regimes by considering multiple causal factors to explain their development. Understanding the creation, content, and change of the ozone regime requires examining several factors—UNEP, expanding scientific knowledge, political leadership by key states, epistemic communities, the structure of the negotiations, and international economic competition. Basing regime explanations on one factor can obscure the importance of others.

UNEP's ability to perform similar functions in the future rests upon its ability to stay focused on its original mandate and operational strengths. Although many political, economic, and social issues are connected to environmental problems, and UNEP cannot ignore them, the ozone case demonstrates the merits of a narrow focus and the significant contribution that UNEP can make as a catalyst, facilitator, and manager.

NOTES

I thank the editors and three anonymous referees for their comments on earlier drafts. I also thank Columbia University, the Institute for the Study of World Politics, the University of North Carolina at Chapel Hill, and the Yale Program on Non-Profit Organizations for research support. The responsibility for any remaining errors or omissions is mine alone.

1. Long atmospheric lifetimes allow CFCs to drift into the stratosphere where ultraviolet radiation breaks their chemical bonds. This releases chlorine atoms that act as powerful catalysts in the destruction of stratospheric ozone (Molina and Rowland, 1974). Other ozone-depleting substances include methyl chloroform, carbon tetrachloride, HCFCs (CFC replacements that deplete ozone at .1 to 10 percent the rate of most CFCs), halons, and methyl bromide (the last two destroy ozone by releasing bromine). Stratospheric ozone prevents harmful wavelengths of ultraviolet radiation from reaching the earth's surface. Significant increases in such radiation would depress human immune systems, increase skin cancer and cataracts, reduce crop yields, and threaten several species at the base of the marine food chain (World Meteorological Organization et al., 1991; UNEP Environmental Effects Panel, 1991).

2. For analyses of international ODS regulation, see Benedick, 1991b and Downie, 1995; for the United States, see Dotto and Schiff, 1978; for the United Kingdom, see Maxwell and Weiner, 1993; for the European Community, see Jachtenfuchs, 1990.

3. Additional factors include the structure of the negotiations (Downie, 1995); international economic competition concerning the production and use of CFCs and their substitutes (Downie, 1995); an environmental epistemic community (P. Haas, 1992a);

and pragmatic diplomacy, led by the United States, in response to evolving scientific knowledge (Benedick, 1991b).

4. Following Krasner, "Principles are beliefs of fact, causation, and rectitude. Norms are standards of behavior defined in terms of rights and obligations. Rules are specific prescriptions or proscriptions for action . . . procedures are prevailing practices for making and implementing collective choice" (1983a:2). Compare definitions and discussion in Keohane and Nye, 1977:19-22; Young, 1980:332-33; Krasner, 1983a:2-10; Donnelly, 1986:599-605; Haggard and Simmons, 1987:493-96; and Downie, 1995:ch. 2.

5. Representative analyses of regimes in different issue areas include Aggarwal, 1983; Krasner, 1983a; Keohane, 1984; Donnelly, 1986; Triggs, 1987; Young, 1989c; Gehring, 1990; P. Haas, 1990; and Nadelmann, 1990.

6. Evidence of success includes broad membership (114 parties to the Montreal Protocol as of 30 April 1993, UNEP/OzL.Rat.24) and reductions in ODS releases (Stevens, 1993; Sarma, 1993).

7. The European Community, Japan, and the Soviet Union opposed meaningful ODS controls until the late 1980s. Brazil, China, and India delayed joining the regime until the early 1990s.

8. Mansfield, 1993; Sarma, 1993; Campbell, 1993; Benedick, 1991b:72-74, 82-86, 163-67; and personal observations made during the 1990 London and 1992 Copenhagen negotiations testify to the importance of these meetings.

9. Compare categories and discussion in Aggarwal, 1983:618-19; Krasner, 1983a:1-22; Haggard and Simmons, 1987:498-513; Young 1989c:350-66; and P. Haas, 1990:33-65.

10. As noted by Peter Haas, "The term historical materialism is Cox's (1981). It incorporates Marxists, some non-Marxists, and dependency theorists" (1990:254n, 47-52, 190-213).

12

Iterative Functionalism and Climate Management Organizations: From Intergovernmental Panel on Climate Change to Intergovernmental Negotiating Committee

David Lewis Feldman

Since the 1970s, nation-states, intergovernmental organizations (IGOs) and non-governmental organizations (NGOs) have formulated agreements to explore the causes and consequences of global warming, to monitor climate data, and to stabilize emissions of carbon dioxide and other greenhouse gases. These agreements are designed to be revisited as climate change becomes better understood.

A trial and error process—iterative functionalism—has evolved to identify and resolve stakeholder issues in climate change. This has been accomplished through the development of international organizations able to impose binding rules on nation-states. Decisionmakers view international negotiations on complex, high-risk problems (e.g., global warming, ozone depletion) as learning processes that are successful only if "insurance institutions" can be established to manage them. Iterative functionalism requires unrestricted exchange of scientific information, a focused forum for discussion of reliable feedback mechanisms to correct previous organizational mistakes, and participation by NGOs and IGOs in negotiations (Linstone, 1984; Steinbruner, 1974; E. Haas, 1990; Benedick, 1991b). Four criteria are necessary for its achievement: comparability of voice, equitable financial commitment, prudent activity selection, and signatory trust and confidence. In the context of the evolution of climate change management institutions, the major lesson of the 1972-1992 period is that achieving national compliance with negotiated milestones requires the establishment of durable international organizations with the resources and infrastructure to protect the atmosphere while sustaining economic growth. Until now, climate change negotiators have barely begun to deal with greenhouse gas stabilization and technology transfer issues. Tackling these functions will be long and protracted. If the institutions established by the Framework Convention on Climate Change (FCCC) provide an equitable framework for resolving controversies, an adequate budget, and the means to verify signatory compliance, then iterative functionalism will have succeeded.

FUNCTIONAL COOPERATION IN MANAGING CLIMATE CHANGE

The Concept of Iterative Functionalism

Iterative functionalism is the replication and gradual refinement of procedures, rules, and obligations negotiated by nation-states in previous agreements in larger, more complex contexts. It is iterative because the process may be repeated several times over a lengthy period. It is functional because these agreements, and the organizations they form, bring countries together based upon special skills or resources applicable to a problem rather than on regional proximity (e.g., the European Union or the North Atlantic Treaty Organization), or level of development (e.g., the Group of 77). Iterative functionalism employs national cooperation to carry out vital technical activities for which no single nation is adequately equipped. The tasks (functions) are performed by permanent organizations staffed by legal and scientific specialists. These organizations constitute an independent, international civil service whose decisions are standardized through a code of practice adhered to by member-states. States pool only as much authority as is required for implementing these tasks (Birnie, 1988:95-121).

An example of iterative functionalism is the evolution of agreements to control production of chlorofluorocarbons (CFCs). This process conforms with theoretical approaches to decisionmaking under conditions of uncertainty which presume consideration of well-defined alternatives and institutional learning through reflection on previous mistakes and successes (Linstone, 1984; Steinbruner, 1974).

Iterative functionalism may be contrasted with traditional realist approaches to international organizations, which argue that participants bring preformed positions to negotiations based on concerns with power, sovereignty, and short-term interest (Ashley, 1986:255-300). Iterative functionalism is closer to neo-realist approaches which assume that, although developing countries desire many of the same economic and political goals as developed states, they are likely to pin their hopes for achievement of these goals on authoritative international instruments that equalize access to common property, increase equal representation, redistribute resources, and permit national sovereignty over environmental behavior (Krasner, 1985:4-7). If a problem is seen as unresolvable by countries acting alone, unlikely to produce clear "winners," and posing high risks, nations are likely to form special institutions to manage them (P. Haas, 1990; E. Haas, 1990; Keohane, 1986).

In environmental policy, three examples of such problems are (1) verifying compliance with agreements to reduce air or water pollution or protect resources (e.g., the 1974 Mediterranean Action Plan, the 1979 Long-Range Transport of Air Pollutants Agreement); (2) transferring technical assistance (e.g., CFC substitutes and alternative refrigeration technologies—as occurred under the Montreal Protocol on Substances That Deplete the Ozone Layer); and (3) promoting environmentally benign development (Protocol to the 1979 Convention on Long-Range Transboundary Air Pollution; P. Haas, 1990).

Functional organizations ensure compliance through confidence-building measures that resolve discrepancies (inconsistencies between national records and international audits) and anomalies (unusual conditions that frustrate or restrict an organization's ability to ensure that a country is meeting its obligations). These measures make national behavior transparent to other countries and deter cheating. Unlike punishment, which regulates national behavior through *intrusive* measures (e.g., trade embargoes or diplomatic sanction) likely to be used by developed, industrialized nations against poorer, weaker countries, confidence building acknowledges the sovereignty of all states and avoids selective, discriminatory measures that threaten national independence (Young 1989a).

CREATING AN EFFECTIVE INTERNATIONAL ORGANIZATION

Forging cooperation and joint action through iterative functionalism requires the involvement of an international organization, or several, to provide a comparable voice among countries, an equitable commitment of resources, a careful selection of activities based upon the degree of an organization's internal consensus and expertise, and confidence in administrative structures and their personnel. Thus, examining the process of forging cooperation within those organizations that negotiate binding targets and timetables requires a focus more narrow than that of comprehensive bundles of organizational relationships and rules for resolving conflicts—namely, regimes. The rudimentary organizations that initially draw up and enforce these rules—such as the Intergovernmental Panel on Climate Change (IPCC) and Intergovernmental Negotiating Committee (INC)—are critical.

Comparable Voice

All nations with a stake in the outcome of an organization's activities want, at the least, a comparable voice in its operations. This issue has frequently arisen in international fora established to manage climate change. It arose in IPCC, formed by the World Meteorological Organization (WMO) and the United Nations Environment Programme (UNEP) in 1988. Some contend that

IPCC's assessment favored the economic interests of developed countries because of its emphasis upon gradual emission reductions rather than on immediate, deep reductions to prevent a sea-level rise from adversely affecting low-lying and island nations (Petesch, 1992:20).

Ensuring a comparable voice between developed and developing countries is difficult because it requires reconciling equity issues (i.e., allowing multiple participants with diverse perspectives to be actively involved) with the practical need to focus upon a manageable issue. Involving too many participants can encumber negotiations with extraneous issues that inhibit resolution. It can also render subsequent enforcement of agreements impossible since there will be no consensus on what was agreed to during negotiations (Hampson, 1989-90; Underdal, 1990).

The INC's Framework Convention on Climate Change exemplifies this dilemma. The accord's modest objective, *stabilizing* anthropogenic greenhouse gases, was the best that could be achieved because the 100 nations and ninety-five IGOs and NGOs who attended the negotiations disagreed on the urgency of climate change as a problem (United Nations General Assembly, 1992:3).

Equitable Share Issues

Members of international organizations should contribute a fair share of resources to ensure that an organization performs its tasks effectively. This equitable share issue has been a contentious one in international negotiations aimed at the management of climate change for two reasons. First, developing countries feel particularly vulnerable to the impacts of climate change. They tend to share freshwater resources with neighboring, sometimes hostile, countries. They lack adequate water supplies and coastal barriers. Furthermore, a large percentage of their populations reside along coasts (Glantz, 1990). Sea-level rise will severely affect exposed coastal populations in India, Bangladesh, Egypt, and the Pacific basin.

Second, although most greenhouse gases are currently produced by developed countries, developing countries are likely to increase their emissions through industrialization, power generation, and deforestation. The United States, Russia, and China collectively account for one-half of the world's carbon dioxide emissions (Grubb, 1990). Thus, it is likely that they will be asked to bear the burden for major reductions.

Examples of equity issues advanced by developing nations include proposals for (1) assistance to broaden participation at environmental meetings held by the World Bank, the European Bank for Reconstruction and Development, and the United Nations; (2) not making aid programs to improve national economic development conditional on environmental performance (an idea suggested at various less developed country summits, e.g., the Belgrade Conference of Non-

Aligned Countries of 1989); (3) assistance to reduce risks from sea-level rise and coastal zone erosion (e.g., the Noordwijk Declaration of 1989 ratified by Japan, Canada, and Western Europe under pressure from developing countries); and (4) transferring CFC substitute technologies through the Global Environment Facility (GEF), formed in 1990 by UNEP, the UN Development Programme (UNDP), and the World Bank (Goldemberg, 1990:25-31; Petesch, 1992:76).

Developed nations control the assets of the World Bank, regional development banks, and aid agencies. Thus, developing countries are disadvantaged in negotiations involving allocation of resources for addressing development issues (Krasner, 1985:4, 174-75). Developing country pressures for greater equity as a condition for participation in a global warming agreement have forced a restructuring of the GEF.

Selection of Activities

Activities of an international climate change organization must be precisely defined and carefully selected according to the capabilities of the states willing to participate. Selection of activities tends to evolve through trial and error. Typically, functional integration occurs most effectively when organizations choose narrow, instrumental tasks such as data gathering and information dissemination upon which all participants can agree (Birnie, 1988:95-121; see also Chapter 5). Over time, as an organization proves its ability to manage effectively these tasks in a politically impartial manner, signatory states may broaden its responsibilities.

For instance, the International Atomic Energy Agency's (IAEA) early activities were strongly influenced by U.S. dominance in nuclear technology. In the early 1960s, partly as a result of the reduction in U.S.-Soviet tensions following the Cuban missile crisis (1962) and the signing of the Atmospheric Test Ban Treaty (1963), a new period of Soviet-American cooperation resulted. This cooperation led to negotiation of a Nuclear Non-proliferation Treaty with the concurrence of both nations. Finally, beginning in the early 1970s, less developed countries made their presence felt in IAEA by demanding greater technical assistance and superpower arms reduction (Scheinman, 1987).

As illustrated in Figure 12-1, a similar evolution appears to be taking place in climate change regime building. Two types of efforts—preliminary calls for action and establishment of deliberative processes—have occurred. Preliminary calls for action are rhetorical declarations of a problem, usually issued in the form of a communiqué by an international meeting called to bring attention to an issue. These declarations call for a concerted effort to define the problem better and to obtain data on its scope. Appropriate responses also may be recommended.

The Stockholm Conference (1972) and the First World Climate Conference

Figure 12–1
Sequence of Events Leading to Framework Convention on Climate Change

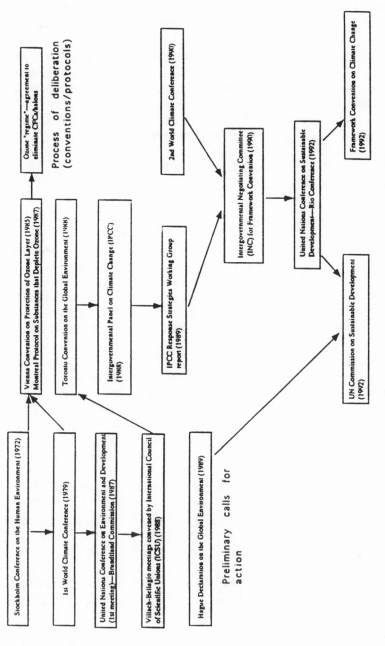

(1979) called attention to the impacts of human activities on the ozone layer, recommended a global atmospheric observation and monitoring system, and identified basic means of preventing climate change (Thacher, 1988; "Final Statement of the Second World Climate Conference," 1991). These actions brought together the efforts of nation-states, IGOs, and NGOs. The World Climate Conference, which led to the Vienna Convention, was sponsored by UNEP, WMO, the UN Educational, Scientific, and Cultural Organization (UNESCO), the Food and Agriculture Organization (FAO), and the International Council of Scientific Unions (ICSU).

Developed and developing countries debated the need for basic science versus policy response in these fora. While conferees at the World Climate Conference agreed on the need "to foresee and prevent potential man-made changes in climate that might be adverse to the well-being of humanity" ("Final Statement," 1991), developing nations criticized conference organizers for concentrating more on data gathering than on adaptation issues.

The 1987 UN Declaration on Environmental Protection and Sustainable Development (issued by the United Nations Conference on Environment and Development) and the 1988 Villach and Bellagio Conferences, convened by the Scientific Committee on Problems of the Environment (SCOPE) of ICSU, recommended increasing reforestation efforts, strengthening energy end-use efficiency, identifying areas vulnerable to sea-level rise, enhancing coordination of global environmental monitoring, strengthening procedures to resolve environmental disputes, and reducing greenhouse gases through negotiation of a global convention and other legal instruments (World Commission on Environment and Development, 1987; Jaeger, 1988). SCOPE's credibility was enhanced by reliance upon ad hoc scientific groups convened for specific problems, such as defining critical scientific issues and reviewing the state of current knowledge—rather than forming permanent subcommittees organized along conventional disciplinary lines (White, 1987:7-13).

As depicted in Figure 12-1, these preliminary calls compel no formal action under international law. They may, however, lead parties to form institutions and adopt standards through a convention, possibly followed by implementation agreements (protocols). At maturity, a global authority with power to regulate national behavior may emerge.

Trust and Confidence

The international civil service that carries out an organization's functions (i.e., secretariat, subsidiary bodies) must earn the confidence and trust of signatory states by revisiting issues in the face of new evidence. Confidence in climate change organizations has proven especially difficult to achieve because the functions these organizations perform are viewed by some as impinging on vital national interests.   To overcome this problem, functional integration specialists point to the need for the organization's secretariat to develop a common set of beliefs about its role and a sense of loyalty to the organization and its purpose that transcend national differences (E. Haas, 1990).

The IAEA has partially achieved a sense of institutional loyalty by its scientific staff (Scheinman, 1987).   A similar sense of competence has developed among scientific advisers involved in the Montreal Protocol.   Structural impediments make achievement of competence and loyalty to a climate change agreement difficult.   Although signatories to the 1992 framework convention have agreed on a secretariat composed of INC states (Algeria, Argentina, France, India, and Romania), its authority is limited to convening meetings of signatories, contracting with other international organizations for research, and communicating draft protocols to signatories (United Nations General Assembly, 1992:add.2).

Iterative Stages of Agreement: Evolution of Climate Issues

Several functional efforts for managing climate change issues have been initiated.   A number of NGOs and IGOs have supported these efforts, including the World Wildlife Fund (WWF), the World Resources Institute (WRI), the World Bank, the International Geosphere-Biosphere Program, the International Association of Meteorology and Atmospheric Physics, WMO, and UNEP.   The principal institutions through which these groups participate in climate activities are the Montreal Protocol on Substances That Deplete the Ozone Layer, IPCC, INC, and the FCCC.

The Ozone Regime-Convention Followed by Protocol

The convention-protocol negotiating process involves formulation of conventions, ratified by nation states, that establish emissions reduction targets. These conventions are followed by *protocols* (amendments or annexes) that require signatories to take specific actions to meet goals, ensure compliance, and show why they are eligible to receive new resources provided under the agreement.

The Montreal Protocol (1987) was a valuable precedent for a greenhouse gas stabilization agreement because it permitted variable compliance standards for developed and developing nations; pragmatically defined consumption, production, and export limits; and relied on close consultation between scientists, diplomats, and industry representatives (Benedick, 1991; Morrisette, 1991; Feldman, 1991).   The FCCC, prepared by INC, acknowledges a debt to the Montreal Protocol by committing signatories to preparing national inventories of greenhouse gases "not controlled by the Montreal Protocol (through) using comparable methodologies" and to "tracing all sources and potential sinks of greenhouse gases" (United Nations General Assembly, 1992:add.2).

The Protocol encouraged cross-validation of national research findings by permitting cooperation among scientists and NGOs and by focusing on narrow functional tasks. Scientists representing national scientific advisory bodies and UNEP offered input into the environmental impacts of CFCs, resource vulnerability, and effectiveness of proposals for concerted action. Open cooperation, in turn, permitted governments to take concerted, prudent action to reduce CFCs. If leaders had waited until adverse impacts were certain, agreement on control measures might have been impossible and impacts might have been irreversible (Benedick, 1991b).

Efforts to accelerate the phase out of CFCs have occurred since the signing of the Protocol. The GEF, established as an "Interim Multilateral Fund" (1990), provides $240 million over three years for technology development; it induced India and China to endorse the protocol (Petesch, 1992:76). Moreover, IGOs have hastened acceleration of the Montreal timetable and the refinement of its science. WMO has formed an Ozone Network to monitor total ozone distribution in the atmosphere through a series of ground-based stations—a process begun under UNEP in 1988 (United Nations General Assembly, 1990; United Nations Environment Programme, 1988).

Deliberative Process: Toronto and IPCC

The 1988 Toronto Convention on the Global Environment urged the establishment of a comprehensive global energy policy and a world atmosphere fund paid for by a fossil fuel consumption tax. Its goal was to stabilize carbon dioxide concentrations through a 20 percent reduction of emissions by 2005. This was to be achieved by greater end-use efficiencies, the use of lower carbon dioxide emitting fuels, and greater reliance on nuclear energy and renewables (Statement of the Meeting, 1989). Although the Toronto Convention was never ratified (due to its insistence on specific targets and timetables), its recommendations led to the formation of IPCC and its Response Strategies Working Group.

IPCC, formed in 1988, is composed of three working groups: group 1, scientific assessment; group 2, impact analysis; and group 3, risk reduction. These groups are chaired by the United Kingdom, the former Soviet Union (Commonwealth of Independent States), and the United States, respectively.

As shown in Table 12-1, IPCC is an "intergovernmental" organization—emphasizing government-to-government discussions and a functional framework for research and education. Reflecting the dominance of developed countries, NGO influence in IPCC is diffuse—NGOs communicate concerns to IPCC by way of WMO or UNEP. Moreover, the functions of science and policymaking are explicitly separated in IPCC.[1]

Group 1's assessments underwent peer review by over 300 scholars nominated by national academies of science. Underscoring IPCC's narrowness of functions, however, these assessments contained no policy recommendations. Even though group 2 assessed the impacts of global warming on human settlements, industry, energy, and transportation, it did not consider impacts upon *institutions*. Despite criticism from many quarters, groups 1 and 2 garnered much scientific consensus over the causes and consequences of climate change. Group 1 also produced a critically well-received report (Houghton, Jenkins, and Ephraums, 1990).

Developed country dominance in IPCC is also exemplified by its integrated assessment, whose conclusions urged gradual responses to global warming through the formulation of a "global warming potential" or "carbon intensity" index. This index will rank countries according to their contributions to global warming. Inclusion of both "sources" and "sinks" of greenhouse gases in attributing national responsibility for climate change led developing countries to oppose this index for three reasons.

First, it was feared that highly industrialized countries could be rewarded (i.e., given emission "credits") for changes now taking place in their economies that might ultimately reduce greenhouse gases—such as reforestation, substitution of noncarbon or low carbon fuels, or increased reliance on nuclear energy. Second, within the next twenty to thirty years, greenhouse gas emissions from developing countries may double or triple without massive introduction of energy efficient technologies (Environmental Protection Agency, 1990). Third, many developing nations contend that the current flux of greenhouse gases, particularly carbon dioxide, is caused by past activities of industrialized countries.

IPCC's purpose was to gather information and coordinate research, to evaluate preliminary proposals for greenhouse gas reduction, and to assess the viability of compliance mechanisms for a greenhouse gas treaty. It has neither the resources nor the infrastructure to address redistributive issues—it lacks a full-time staff, permanent committees to study issues and advise signatories, formal means to incorporate new information on the science of global warming, or an executive council to manage a budget, collect dues, or oversee policy (Nitze, 1990).

The newly formed secretariat of the Conference of the Parties to the FCCC will have access to its own sources of scientific information through special subsidiary bodies, but the conference will continue to consult IPCC for advice (United Nations General Assembly, 1992:L.15).

Table 12-1
Current Climate Change Negotiations Regime: Institutions, Issues, and Expectations

INTERGOVERNMENTAL PANEL ON CLIMATE CHANGE (IPCC): 1988-1991

SPONSORS	GOALS	STRUCTURE	RESULTS	PROBLEMS
U. S., WMO, UNEP.	Concerted effort to identify problems and implications.	Three working groups: Science, Impacts, Response Strategies; chaired by U. K., USSR, USA.	Avoid technological "quick fixes" for emissions.	Dominance of developed countries in work groups.
	Establish common understanding of science and of trade-offs among impacts.		Develop comprehensive emissions strategy.	Criticism by less developed nations in UN GA resolution (1/1991).
	Establish international framework for further research/education.			Lacked NGO input.
				Lacked permanent working group, budget, director-general, policy oversight authority.

INTERGOVERNMENTAL NEGOTIATING COMMITTEE FOR A FRAMEWORK CONVENTION ON CLIMATE CHANGE (INC): 1991-PRESENT

SPONSORS	GOALS	STRUCTURE	RESULTS	PROBLEMS
UN General Assembly; at urging of "G-77." meeting.	Draft framework Convention on reducing greenhouse gas emissions for ratification at 1992 UNCED organizations (NGOs) participate.	102 nations, 95 United Nations, Intergovernmental organizations, (IGOs), non-governmental (9/1991, 12/91), New York	Conferences in Chantilly, Virginia (2/1991), Kenya (8/1991), Switzerland (4-5/1992).	Limited success in gaining consensus at modest convention at UNCED.
	Establish permanent treaty implementation organization.	Two working groups: Commitments, Aid, and Technology Transfer (Brazil, Japan, Senegal); and Institutional Mechanisms, Scientific Exchange, Monitoring, Verification and Compliance, and Adaptation (Bulgaria, Canada, Vanuatu).	Agreement that all nations should pursue "appropriate commitments" to reducing greenhouse gases.	Disagreement between US and EC countries on need for specific reduction targets, milestones, and forms of assistance to LDCs.
		Permanent Secretariat—(France, Algeria, Argentina, India, Rumania)	Agreement (in principle) on special assistance to Less Developed Countries.	Difficulty in building a durable consensus among over 100 nation-states.
		Establishing own research headquarters and Budget; designated as acting secretariat for Framework Convention on Climate Change.		

Toward Global Authority

Following passage of General Assembly resolution 4353 in 1988, IPCC's Working Group 3 (response strategies) met in Geneva, Switzerland, and in October 1989 recommended a climate convention modeled after the Vienna Convention on Protection of the Ozone Layer. UNEP, a cosponsor of IPCC, urged that a separate INC be formed for this task, reporting directly to the General Assembly.

Theoretically and practically, the significance of the transition from IPCC to INC is twofold. INC was created at the behest of G-77 countries which argued that only a negotiating body reporting directly to the General Assembly would address climate impact and adaptation issues affecting poorer nations. Also, INC strategically empowered less developed countries by establishing two working groups that addressed redistributive issues (technology transfer and exchange of scientific information). These issues were largely ignored during the developed country-dominated IPCC process. INC's working groups have sought to achieve centralized allocation of resources for climate change mitigation and adaptation.

After endorsement by UNEP's director Mostafa Tolba, INC established a commitments group (group 1) to examine aid, technical assistance, and technology transfer issues and an institutional mechanisms group (group 2) to consider scientific cooperation, monitoring, information exchange, and compliance. Group 1 is composed of representatives from Brazil, Japan, and Senegal. Japan is viewed as a major donor with the capacity to play a significant role in leading technical assistance efforts, but Brazil and Senegal are major actors in prevention (because of their large rainforests) and potential beneficiaries of energy efficiency research and development transfer.

Group 2, consisting of Canada, Bulgaria, and Vanuatu, follows the same philosophy. Canada is a strong proponent of independent verification of treaty compliance, whereas Bulgaria, like other Eastern European countries, seeks technical exchange to stabilize its emissions. Vanuatu, a Pacific island nation threatened by sea-level rise, has demanded consideration of refugee relocation measures. It is the acknowledged leader of the Alliance of Small Island and Low-lying States (AOSIS), and its prime minister, Walter Lini, has frequently criticized developed countries for their alleged lack of interest in the impacts of global warming on Pacific nations (Petesch, 1992:20).

A permanent headquarters for INC's research and negotiating activities will be established. Voluntary donations for a permanent operating budget have been solicited, and a governing secretariat, with representatives from France, Algeria, Argentina, India, and Romania, has been formed (National Climate Program Office, 1991). In 1992, INC completed a draft of the FCCC for signing at the United Nations Conference on Environment and Development (UNCED) in Rio. INC's secretariat was subsequently designated as secretariat for the framework convention—responsible for convening the Conference of the Parties (COP), cooperating with international organizations, and mobilizing finances (see Figure 12-2).

This evolution of climate change organizations illustrates the concept of iterative functionalism in four ways. First, comparability of voice, essential to acceptance of agreements by developing countries, is addressed by the lower standards for their compliance under the Montreal Protocol (delayed CFC phase out) and the Climate Change Convention (exemption from greenhouse gas reduction targets). It is also exemplified by the creation of the INC at the behest of developing nations to ensure a developing country voice in formulating mitigation strategies. Second, equitable share has been addressed by the inclusion of technology transfer programs under the ozone and climate change treaties. The Interim Multilateral Fund and its offspring, the GEF, discussed in the next section, are responsible for promoting this elusive goal. Third, selection of activities by global change organizations has been gradual. Only after basic agreement on CFC reduction was reached was a phase-out timetable accelerated—and then, only because scientific confidence warranted such action. Likewise, climate change convention signatories have agreed, for now, to emphasize monitoring, research, and assessment, deferring emissions reduction strategies for later. Fourth, although the signatories to the ozone and climate change treaties acknowledge the importance of trust and confidence, they have not been tested by attempts to impose strong verification or compliance measures. Until a permanent staff and stable financial network to fund INC activities come into place, there will be little confidence in the INC's ability to enforce the obligations of the Framework Convention, nor confidence in its ability to reduce the threat of global warming.

EMERGING ISSUES: ESTABLISHING CONFIDENCE IN NEW INSTITUTIONS

The FCCC, formulated by INC, is the first international agreement negotiated under General Assembly auspices since the Atmospheric Nuclear Test Ban Treaty of 1963. As shown in Figure 12-2, the framework convention organization comprises a COP, a secretariat, and subsidiary bodies to provide scientific and technical information and other assistance. Financial resources for achieving the convention's objectives are provided by the GEF.

Since the Framework Convention's commitments are general, leaving each signatory free to determine its own emissions reduction strategy, it is probable that subsequent protocols will establish targets for carbon dioxide stabilization, energy efficiency, and reversing deforestation. The Framework Convention charges the Subsidiary Body for Implementation with monitoring progress toward the establishment of a greenhouse gas inventory. Some means of

Figure 12–2
Institutions Established by the United Nations Framework Convention on Climate Change, 1992

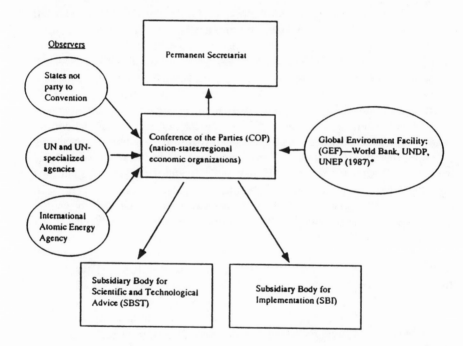

Observers

States not party to Convention

UN and UN-specialized agencies

International Atomic Energy Agency

Permanent Secretariat

Conference of the Parties (COP) (nation-states/regional economic organizations)

Global Environment Facility: (GEF)—World Bank, UNDP, UNEP (1987)*

Subsidiary Body for Scientific and Technological Advice (SBST)

Subsidiary Body for Implementation (SBI)

*Established under Montreal Protocol but incorporated into Framework Convention on Climate Change in June, 1992.

determining the relative contributions of greenhouse gases by countries will eventually be developed.

For the INC to implement the requirements of the convention—and to achieve follow-on protocols—it will have to win the confidence of signatories. This will require a durable organizational structure with norms, rules, and decision-making practices viewed as legitimate by both developing and developed countries, an adequate budget to perform these functions, and a means to verify signatory compliance.

Durable Structure and Comparable Voice

The UN Framework Convention places the burden for reducing greenhouse gases on the shoulders of industrialized countries. Article 4 calls upon all signatories to develop and publish inventories of anthropogenic emissions not covered by the Montreal Protocol (i.e., all emissions except CFCs and halon compounds) and to undertake "environmental assessments" of new projects potentially affecting climate (such as energy, agriculture reclamation, and water projects). But only Organization for Economic Cooperation and Development (OECD) countries, CIS, and the nations of Eastern Europe are required to limit emissions and protect and enhance "sinks and reservoirs" that absorb greenhouse gases. In addition, developed countries must provide "new and additional" financial resources, training and public education, and the systematic collection of climate data.

It is not clear how the treaty can implement these goals. The central authoritative mechanism of the climate convention is COP, established under Article 7, which comprises 154 signatory countries and several regional economic organizations. Each signatory state has one vote, although regional economic organizations have as many votes as they have signatory states—unless those states choose to vote independently (United Nations General Assembly, 1992:L.14/Add.8).

The COP is supposed to function as both General Conference (legislature) and Board of Governors (executive) of the convention. Its role is to examine signatory obligations and recommend actions to fulfill them—drawing upon advice provided by the Subsidiary Body for Scientific and Technological Advice and the Subsidiary Body for Implementation. It also has the authority to mobilize financial resources, settle disputes (by itself or through the International Court of Justice), and approve protocols to the convention.

Although the COP must meet once a year, it can be called into special session at the request of any signatory if supported by one-third of the COP members. This effectively means that G-77 countries can call for special sessions of the COP whereas developed countries cannot do so without some G-77 support. Although this would appear to work in favor of developing nations anxious to hold developed countries to their obligations, it is far from clear that this will be the result. G-77 countries are divided in their support for greenhouse gas emission limits. During INC framework convention negotiations, conservative oil-producing states (Saudi Arabia, Venezuela, and Kuwait) aligned themselves with the United States in resisting firm emission limits. They also warned of the scientific uncertainties associated with global warming.

Three developing country blocs are identifiable: those supporting the U.S. position; those, such as Papua New Guinea, Vanuatu, and other AOSIS members (35 countries total), that favor immediate, significant reductions in greenhouse gases; and the so-called Group of 24 led by China, India, and Brazil, which emerged during the December 1991 INC negotiations. This last group favors developing nations undertaking "feasible measures to address climate change issues." But it is opposed to firm commitments or timetables and favors massive aid transfers to developing countries for "climate-related measures" on preferential and favorable terms (Petesch, 1992:20). In short, these policy differences hinder the ability of developing countries to speak with a unified voice so as to leverage assistance from developed nations. Since developing countries cannot create an entirely new regime, they must develop coherence within this existing framework if they are to acquire resources for adaptation (Krasner, 1985:28).

Achieving consensus on climate change is also difficult because stabilizing greenhouse gases encompasses a wider range of potential policy options than does protecting the ozone layer, including emission and fuel taxes, emission trading schemes, mandatory energy efficiency standards, and reforestation-afforestation efforts (Nitze, 1990; Grubb, 1990). Recognizing this problem, the COP has invited the IAEA and UN specialized agencies to serve as COP observers and to offer advice on measures for achieving—and verifying—these objectives.

Adequate Budgets

Article 21 of the Framework Convention vests financial authority for climate management in the GEF, jointly administered by the World Bank, UNDP, and UNEP. The GEF exemplifies the iterative character of the climate regime. Originally established in 1990 as an Interim Multilateral Fund to help developing countries find substitutes for ozone-depleting halon compounds, its structure and funding base has been modified to fulfill the more complex obligations of the climate convention.

During INC negotiations, developing countries criticized the GEF for Northern Hemisphere control of most of its assets. Three alternatives to GEF were debated: (1) an independent "green" fund whose assets would be shared by developed and developing nations, (2) a large-scale debt reduction plan to free up investment capital, and (3) the use of special consultative groups to bring together donor and recipient countries on a case-by-case basis (Petesch, 1992:77).

Stating that equity should be the touchstone of all proposals on a convention, and that firm commitments to technology transfer and financial resources should be provided, India proposed the Green Fund at the third INC meeting. This fund was endorsed by China, Vanuatu, and Senegal ("Climate Change Convention Equity Concerns," 1992:3). Pakistan's chief negotiator and chairman of the G-77 bloc urged that this fund be used to compensate developing countries for limiting fossil fuel use in favor of solar, renewables, and biomass. The fund would also pay for national greenhouse gas inventories (Weisskopf, 1992).

The debt-reduction plan was also introduced during INC's third meeting. To assist developing countries in meeting the incremental costs associated with climate change adaptation, Bangladesh demanded that new energy and environmental protection technologies be provided on preferential, no-strings-attached terms ("Climate Change Convention Equity Concerns," 1992:3). It also urged that debt-for-nature swaps be used to compensate for the "ecological and social losses" caused by colonialism and foreign investment. This same point was stated at a preparatory meeting for the Earth Summit held in Paris in December 1991 ("Alternative 'Agenda 21,'" 1991).

The "consultative group" idea (advanced by the United Nations University) proposed an ongoing evaluation of the environmental performance of projects by developing and donor countries. Gradual reform of existing financial institutions would alleviate the adverse impacts of new projects (Petesch, 1992:77).

As a compromise, a resolution to restructure the GEF was accepted at the Earth Summit (Pearce, 1992:27; United Nations General Assembly, 1992:add. 6). Three billion dollars are to be made available for grants and low-interest loans for projects related to ozone layer depletion, biodiversity conservation, protection of international waters, and climate change. The GEF's fourteen-member executive committee now equally represents Northern (donor) and Southern Hemisphere (recipient) nations, and all votes require a two-thirds majority—imposing a developing country veto on allocation decisions (Kimball, 1992:37). This restructuring is consistent with developing country goals to obtain more aid and control over the decision-making agenda of existing international organizations (Krasner, 1985:175).

It remains unclear, however, how this restructuring will affect actual expenditures on greenhouse gas reduction. Two emerging issues are the appropriate level of national contributions to these efforts and the verifiability of national environmental protection expenditures. Through the UNCED, developing countries demanded a variable dues structure to support the GEF.

The UNCED called for developed country Official Development Assistance to be annually levied at 0.7 percent of gross domestic product by 1995.

Only Scandinavian countries are close to achieving this contribution level. Moreover, although European Union nations are committed to this target, no agreement on a timetable has been reached. And there is no systematic way to determine how much foreign assistance is spent on environmental matters. OECD's Development Assistance Committee does not itemize environmental protection assistance programs in a manner that makes verifiable reporting possible (Petesch, 1992:56). Estimates of annual costs for all Agenda 21 actions—including the climate convention—range upwards of $125 billion, whereas all forms of official development assistance from UN agencies and bilateral and multilateral sources currently total about $62 billion (U.S.) dollars (Kimball, 1992:74).

Debate over these budgetary issues exemplifies an evolving (iterative) maturity. IAEA and other functional organizations have tried to reconcile divergent developed and developing country budget concerns for over twenty years. Despite greater time to address such concerns, IAEA's solutions have been largely ad hoc. IAEA budgetary growth has been flat for many years because, since the mid-1970s, the Group of 77 has frozen contributions allotted to IAEA safeguard activities, placing the burden of support upon developed countries. During this same period, however, the board of governors has increased the size of IAEA's technical assistance programs that disproportionately benefit less developed countries. The lesson is that developed countries are likely to accept unequal national contributions if the potential benefit is achieving universal compliance.

Verifying Compliance: Trust and Confidence

In the short term, the greatest potential for achieving functional integration under the Framework Convention lies in the Subsidiary Body for Scientific and Technological Advice (SBST) and the Subsidiary Body for Implementation (SBI) (see Figure 12-2).

The SBST comprises representatives of science and technology ministries. Membership is multidisciplinary. All COP members may attend meetings. Despite this broad-based representation, however, NGOs are excluded. This is significant because NGO participation was critical to the achievement of earlier climate management efforts and NGO exclusion could weaken the perceived independence of the Framework Convention. SBST is charged with the preparation of scientific assessments on policy issues and periodic reports to the COP on the general state of scientific knowledge pertaining to climate issues. SBST is also committed to establishing a detailed research agenda for monitoring greenhouse gases.

SBI's central purpose is to develop verification instruments to ensure signatory compliance with the convention. This function is shared with the UN Commission on Sustainable Development, an independent organization established by separate treaty at Rio. The commission's fifty-three-member secretariat is charged with assessing progress toward all the objectives of Agenda 21, including the Climate Change and Biodiversity Conventions. Its immediate objective is to provide periodic reports to the UN General Assembly and the Economic and Social Council (ECOSOC).

With experts on climate change as its members, SBI has the difficult task of monitoring national progress toward the development of inventories of greenhouse gases and methods for stabilization. Over time, SBI may serve to focus the COP's agenda by prescribing emissions stabilization and technology transfer programs. Like the negotiations that led to the Framework Convention, however, this task is likely to be a daunting one.

At the third session of the INC held in fall 1991, it was agreed that the Framework Convention should defer harmonization of national inventories to later agreement by COP signatories assisted by the SBI (United Nations General Assembly, 1992:add. 2). This was a direct result of U.S. rejection of calls for commitments to specific reduction targets, timetables, or financing mechanisms. Instead, the United States urged reliance upon national means of verification, compliance, and monitoring and rejected calls for new enforcement institutions until their necessity is demonstrated (National Climate Program Office, 1991).

For functional integration of verification to be achieved, SBI must develop compliance mechanisms that minimize economic intrusiveness (i.e., require little on-site inspection) and rely on an emissions index that accounts for the global warming potential of all emissions from human activities. Such an index would weigh emissions reduction and sequestering efforts—thus rewarding national efforts to reduce greenhouse gas emissions by whatever means.[2]

CONCLUSION

A successful FCCC must encourage widespread participation, inspire confidence, contain precise commitments, and make the reopening of negotiations easy. Prospects for achieving success hinge upon the extent to which underlying power relationships in these new organizations are directly tied to formal participation mechanisms. In short, economic power must be linked to political authority (Krasner, 1985:263). Although it is impossible to predict success, the neorealist and liberal-reformist theoretical stances posit different obstacles facing the Framework Convention. The latter optimistically argues that durable institutions will emerge with the power to manage climate change. The former posits the opposite. Both ignore the fact that international cooperation is inhibited by the ambivalent roles played by risk perception and national interest.

According to neorealist Stephen Krasner, the behavior of signatory states to agreements is a function of their relative power. Developing countries lack money or authority to influence superpower decisions. Extrapolating this argument to climate change would mean that (1) rich states will seek to dominate new global institutions through control of finances, exclusion of NGOs in subsidiary bodies concerned with compliance and verification issues, and resistance to massive resource transfers; and (2) less developed countries will seek to use treaty organizations to air long-standing grievances about the need for mitigating climate change impacts, to embarrass wealthier countries, and to obtain a new international economic order through reallocation of finances. Developing countries desire many of the same economic and political goals as developed states, but they are more likely to pin their hopes on international instruments that equalize access to common property and increase their representation in fora that redistribute resources (Krasner, 1985:4-7).

The evolution of climate change institutions partially conforms to this prediction. Wealthy states have agreed to changes in the financial component of the climate change regime, but they have not made firm commitments of new resources. Developing countries have made it clear through the INC that they cannot reduce greenhouse gas emissions without outside help. Nevertheless, optimism concerning an iterative functional approach is warranted because, as the Montreal, IPCC, and INC processes show, countries' views on climate issues have gradually evolved toward a preference for prudent, preventive measures.

The liberal-reformist approach—exemplified by Robert McNamara (formerly of the World Bank) and Maurice Strong (UNCED chair) presumes that signatory states are mostly concerned with achieving justice (Krasner, 1985). This view is especially pervasive in the less developed nations, according to whom the burden for reducing greenhouse gases should be placed on industrialized countries. The developing nations' ability to acquire foreign assistance and favorable credit—to continue industrializing while reducing greenhouse gases—should be made easier.

If structural changes in the international economic order hoped for by developing nation signatories to the Framework Convention are brought about, this expectation may come to pass. In the short term, however, the prognosis is unlikely for two reasons. First, the liberal-reformist approach assumes that the environment is the paramount national concern in climate change negotiations. But domestic stability and economic growth are at least as critical in the eyes of nation-states. This is evidenced in two ways. First, the most divisive issues in climate change negotiations—such as refugee and resettlement policies, technology transfer, and verification of national compliance activities—were deliberately excluded from INC consideration at Rio because it was recognized that impasse over these tough issues would make any agreement impossible. Second, agreement over what constitutes justice in the global sphere is neither universal nor a sound basis for political unity among poorer nations. As we have seen, G-77 countries are divided over targets and timetables for limiting emissions and even over how to pay for a compliance regime.

Nevertheless, iterative functionalism may continue to shape future negotiations. INC's efforts at formulating a framework convention suggest that national behavior toward climate issues is shaped partly by concerns over power *and* equity. The most important factor guiding the course of negotiations has been perception of risk. Because climate change is a problem of unknown probability but potentially catastrophic consequence, both developed and developing country signatories agree that the potential hazards from climate change muddle the notion of "winners" or "losers." This is why limited, ambiguous engagement in an iterative negotiating process has made sense to both industrialized and developing countries—even those opposed to specific mitigation measures.

Although the Framework Convention's commitments are rather vague, this vagueness may be an asset. It has kept short-term expectations modest, has encouraged broad national participation through nonpolitical bodies that perform vital risk reduction tasks, and has eased reopening of negotiations when new information has been acquired. These tasks include updating science, analyzing policies, assessing indexing efforts, and resolving disputes. Neorealism will continue to dominate on tough fiscal issues, and liberal-reformist rhetoric will likely prevail at COP general conferences, but the vital technical tasks noted above will continue to be pursued through an iterative functional approach, making the resolution of more complex problems (such as verification and compliance) eventually easier to achieve.

Iterative functionalism's significance for international organizations and environmental policy is threefold. First, iterative functionalism is a learning process in which nation-states and other international actors gradually acquire the ability to resolve technical problems, such as cooperative research and sharing and standardizing environmental data. If these fundamental tasks are effectively performed, then these new institutions may move onto more ambitious tasks such as verification of national behavior and compliance with commonly articulated goals. The key to effectiveness is that these organizations must use the best available scientific knowledge. Second, iterative functionalism suggests that nation-states may allow negotiations to shape perceptions—rather than coming to negotiations with preformed agendas. This explains their encouragement of input from nongovernmental sources in order to broaden policy choices. This openness comes with a price, however. Scientific and environmental NGOs must sustain policymakers' issue attentiveness: the latter have neither the time nor the interest to do so themselves. Third, iterative functionalism is forcing national security to be redefined in terms of long-term ecological security, protection of common goods, and promotion of intergenerational justice. This represents a considerable change from classic realist views of foreign policy agenda building centered upon narrowly defined strategic goals. Such a change in definition of security demands that national energy and environmental programs be opened to international scrutiny.

NOTES

1.   ICSU was a coorganizer of the Second World Climate Conference (October/November 1990) which formulated elements of IPCC's research agenda, including suggestions for strengthened international actions on energy, agriculture, afforestation, and technology transfer (United Nations General Assembly, 1990).

2. Sequestering is the long-term conversion of carbon dioxide, methane, and other greenhouse gases to carbon or methane storage or reduction. This can be done by planting trees, raising fewer cattle or other livestock that generate methane, or substituting non-rice crops for rice. These have been proposed as means of permitting countries to "take credit" for lessening their contributions of greenhouse gas emissions.

13

Forum Shopping: Issue Linkages in the Genetic Resources Issue

Robin Pistorius

The last two decades have witnessed an increasing number of multilateral negotiations on the protection of the global commons. Well-known examples are the lengthy negotiations conducted on the access to the high seas and space, such as those concerning the United Nations Conventions on the Law of the Sea (UNCLOS). A relatively recent negotiation process involves the conservation and use of genetic resources. Since the United Nations Conference on Environment and Development (UNCED 1992, Rio de Janeiro), the conservation and use of genetic resources has become subject to the Biodiversity Convention.

As with other commons, the negotiations on the draft texts of the Biodiversity Convention are complex and lengthy, and, until now, have not been subject to any scholarly analysis. This chapter highlights one aspect of modern "bio-diplomacy," namely the increasing interaction and overlap of a rapidly growing number of international organizations dealing with the same commons.

As the number of multilateral environmental agreements continues to grow, the number of international organizations that occupy themselves with environmental issues likewise grows. Indeed, the more that international environmental politics becomes embedded in other international issues, the more organizations previously without an environmental mandate start to play a role in multilateral environmental decisionmaking.

Another tendency is that "new" environmental issues offer opportunities for developing countries to play a role in environmental issue areas they previously were not involved with. Stephen Krasner (1985:233, 245-46) has described the lengthy negotiations on the drafting and (unsuccessful) implementation of UNCLOS (1982) to illustrate how the UN was "used" by the Group of 77 to assert unilateral control over contiguous ocean areas, with the deep seabed outside the twelve-mile zone to become part of the "common heritage of mankind." But the negotiations on UNCLOS not only showed the new opportunities for developing countries in international negotiations on global commons within the UN, but also demonstrated that the industrialized countries are able to walk away from negotiations that oppose their interests.

Indeed, many multilateral negotiations on global commons have not been successful. The signing of the Biodiversity Convention by the Clinton administration can be considered an important exception in this respect, especially when taking into consideration the lengthy controversy over what has become known as the "genetic resource issue."

Why did the industrialized countries not terminate the negotiations when considering the controversies surrounding the genetic resource issue? In attempting to explain this phenomenon, analysts have referred to international public pressure on the governments of industrialized countries, particularly the United States, not to cause a failure of the UNCED, of which the Biodiversity Convention was an important pillar. This explanation starts from two misinterpretations. The first is that the UN representatives from industrialized countries—after a decade of intense international negotiations—succumbed to public pressure at the eleventh hour. Second, it assumes that the genetic resource issue is addressed only within one political arena, namely that of environmental protection.

In order to understand why both industrialized and developing countries could agree on the Biodiversity Convention, in spite of structural controversies, an analysis involving more than the political arena is necessary. The analysis of the plant genetic resource issue can serve as an example for an increasing number of global environmental issues such as deforestation, desertification, ozone layer, and global warming, which are dealt with in different and sometimes competing arenas, sometimes represented by organizations with completely different mandates.

ISSUE LINKAGES BETWEEN DIFFERENT POLITICAL ARENAS

The more the value of genetic resources is understood, the more international fora—representing different political arenas—occupy themselves with this issue, albeit with different agendas. The fact that the plant genetic resource issue is dealt with by three different political arenas—food production, environmental protection, and free trade—has serious implications for the countries involved in the multilateral negotiation process on the plant genetic resource issue.

I hypothesize that issue linkages can help a political actor (most often a state) to choose among political arenas, causing a specific issue to be dealt with differently in each arena. According to Ernst Haas and some other New Institutionalists, "issue-linkages" usually take place *within one* political arena. In Haas's definition, "[I]ssue-linkage refers to bargaining that involves more than one issue," for example, when the nuclear test ban is discussed in conjunction with limits on strategic weapons (E. Haas, 1990:76). I suggest that issue linkages can also be considered as linkages between *different* political arenas (represented by different political fora) involving more than one issue. This adapted concept is useful because it offers inroads for describing a spillover of one specific issue from one political arena to another. Understanding a spillover helps to detect the benefits accruing to political actors who promote a spillover of one issue through issue linkages between several political arenas. Furthermore, such an analysis of the genetic resource issue will show that developing countries are less able than industrialized countries to benefit from spillovers.

In order to judge the consensus within one political arena, it is important that other arenas in which the issue is treated should be analyzed simultaneously. In the genetic resource issue, for instance, this approach helps to describe how industrialized countries, in accordance with their interests, are better able than developing countries to create issue linkages between the three political arenas.

THE PLANT GENETIC RESOURCE ISSUE IN THREE POLITICAL ARENAS

As was illustrated by the debates before and during the UNCED negotiation process, the concern for the genetic resource issue stems from both agricultural (economic) and environmental interests. This involves three different fora dealing with the same issue. This chapter considers (1) the resulting competition between the Food and Agriculture Organization (FAO) of the United Nations, the United Nations Environment Programme (UNEP), and the General Agreement on Tariffs and Trade (GATT), and (2) the efforts of powerful (mostly industrialized) countries to benefit from this competition in accordance with their agricultural (economic) interests. The three fora are chosen because of their importance for the plant genetic resource issue, as well as their status as major "representatives" of three important political arenas:

1. FAO represents the political arena of food production, promoting a program aiming at an equal division of food resources and therefore a fair and equal access to plant genetic resources of all countries.
2. UNEP represents the political arena of environmental protection, aiming at the preservation of plant genetic resources for the "well-being of future generations."
3. GATT represents the political arena of free trade, aiming at the reduction of distortions of international trade with regard to plant genetic resources, genetic material, and taking into account the need to promote effective and adequate protection of intellectual property rights (mostly on improved genetic material) resting on some of these resources.

The Political Arena of Food Production

The political arena of food production was the first in which the plant genetic resource issue was discussed. The plant genetic resource issue within this arena often focuses on the problem that (a) the north is "gene poor" while the south is "gene rich" and (b) the north is "technology rich" while the south is "technology poor."

The political awareness of the plant genetic resource issue within the arena of food production grew rapidly in the late 1970s and early 1980s. At that time, it became clear that industrialized countries could utilize an increasing array of technologies (notably genetic engineering and other forms of biotechnology) to exploit genetic resources originating from the centers of diversity, often located in developing countries. The rising awareness of "the gene" as a valuable tool for agricultural progress led several critical social scientists[1] and politicians to question what has become known as the "toll-free gene drain" going from south to north. Central to their analysis was the notion that the agro-industry in the industrialized world increasingly depends on a regular infusion of genetic resources from the south to "refresh" the resources already in stock for agricultural (biotech) research, and the developing countries often are not compensated for the export of their genetic resources. Industrialized countries, throughout botanical history, have considered plants and plant genetic resources as common heritage and thus freely available.

The south's awareness of its richness in (plant) genetic resources offered many developing countries new opportunities to strengthen their position in international negotiations on agricultural and related food issues. The whole conflict about the control over plant genetic resources would have been settled much earlier if the south had been completely dependent on resources from the north. But a rapid settlement of the conflict through power play did not happen because of the interdependence between the north and south with respect to plant genetic resources: industrialized countries need the genetic resources from developing countries, whereas developing countries increasingly buy seeds with improved genetic characteristics from industrialized countries in order to escape food shortages. Also, several advanced developing countries (notably the South and Central American and Southeast Asian countries) are eager to import biotechnologies to strengthen their own agro-industry. This interdependence can be considered an important explanation for the handling of the plant genetic resource issue within three political arenas instead of one.

FAO, in the early 1980s, was the first forum to deal with the plant genetic resource issue. It had been dealing with conservation and other scientific and agricultural matters regarding plant genetic resources almost since its establishment in 1945. For industrialized countries, however, FAO was not the best forum. The majority of developing countries in the FAO council offered room for taking action against northern dominance in international agricultural research. Among other resolutions, this opposition resulted in the support by the Group of 77 for the FAO International Undertaking on Plant Genetic Resources in 1983. The FAO Undertaking had the objective "...to ensure that plant genetic resources...will be explored, preserved, evaluated and made available...based on the universally accepted principle that plant genetic resources are a heritage of mankind and consequently should be available without restriction" (FAO Commission on Plant Genetic Resources, 1991:art. 1).

So far, most industrialized and developing countries could agree on the FAO Undertaking. However, Article 2.1 of the Undertaking explicitly included "special genetic stocks."[2] Because this inclusion would harm the commercial interests of countries with an advanced agro-industry, it received opposition from such countries as Australia, Canada, Japan, and the United States.[3] Some industrialized countries (for example, the Nordic countries and the southern European countries) did support the Undertaking, although with reservations. Since 1983, 127 countries, mostly from the south, have signed the Undertaking.

A second (related) conflict dealt with Article 6 of the Undertaking, which aims at establishing an International Fund for Plant Genetic Resources. This fund was meant "to channel intergovernmental and non-governmental organizations, and private industries and individuals, to fulfil their common responsibility to maintain the world's plant genetic diversity" (Esquinas Alcázar, 1990:4). A controversial issue in relationship to the fund was the taxing of seed companies on their sales value. As yet, however, the funding mechanisms are still unclear. Even more controversial was the concept of channeling the fund's revenues to Third World farmers, as a reward for domesticating, safeguarding, and developing many crops before they were imported to the north. The acknowledgement of the so-called farmer's rights at the international level would serve as a basis for this reward. The budgets would be used to generate the collection, use, and conservation of genetic resource programs in the countries of origin.

A third conflict lay in the establishment of a central international gene bank under the auspices of FAO. The major argument for the establishment of this gene bank was the unclear mandate of the existing gene bank network of the International Board for Plant Genetic Resources (IBPGR)—a quasi-UN organization financed mainly by industrialized countries. The developing nations, with Mexico in the lead, feared that the IBPGR network would decrease their control over genetic resources. Most industrialized countries, however, particularly the United States, were convinced that the existing network was reliable enough to maintain control over the resources, arguing that a nationalization would stimulate politicization and harm IBPGR's functioning. Most developing countries, however, felt that as IBPGR freely distributed existing collections to gene banks under national control in industrialized countries, the "use for present and future generations" would not be guaranteed (De Groot, 1989).

The fourth source of controversy between developing and industrialized countries lay in the establishment of the FAO Commission on Plant Genetic Resources in 1983. The commission was meant to cope with problems concerning the use and accessibility of genetic resources.[4] As such, it was the first and only international governmental body through which governments could assemble to talk about the issue of the control of plant genetic resources. Because the United States feared that the commission, as an official political body, would influence or even set IBPGR policies,[5] the United States argued unsuccessfully that, for "budgetary reasons," it was necessary to cancel the establishment of the commission. As the commission's budget is only a fraction of the total FAO budget, this argument was understood as an attempt to eliminate the commission. As of 1993, 104 (mainly developing) countries are members of the commission. The United States and Canada are not. A high-ranking U.S. State Department official confided that the real reason for opposing the establishment of the commission had to do with the fact that the UN as a "super-democracy" could not be trusted (Fowler et al., 1988:260).

In spite of these controversies, the FAO Commission has been able to act as a forum for discussions on the control of plant genetic resources. In the late 1980s, however, there emerged alternative fora that also started to deal with plant genetic resource issue in a global context, overlapping the mandate of the FAO Commission. The first forum causing such overlap was UNEP.

The Political Arena of Environmental Protection

The 1972 United Nations Conference on the Human Environment held in Stockholm, at which UNEP was established, was the first conference through which the global concern for the preservation of living resources (plants, animals, and living organisms) generated worldwide preservation projects and programs in and outside the UN. But it was only during the second half of the 1980s that the plant genetic resource issue, in tandem with discussions within FAO on plant genetic resources, was considered a new global issue comparable with other global issues such as global economic change and global warming.[6]

UNEP's mandate to protect the environment involved an emphasis on the preservation of as much plant genetic resources as possible, with minimal attention to their agricultural value. This approach contrasted with the FAO conservation programs that focused on the agricultural value of plant genetic resources to strengthen global food security. Because the UNEP programs, at least initially, were not focused on the use (and implicitly also not on the ownership of plant genetic resources), UNEP was not as susceptible to political controversy as FAO.

With the popularization of the plant genetic resources issue during the 1980s, the FAO and UNEP mandates started to overlap. After 1987 an Ad Hoc Working Group on Biodiversity prepared the UNEP Biodiversity Convention designed to be used as a global legal instrument for the conservation and preservation of biological diversity, which became the basis for the Convention on Biological Diversity signed during UNCED (July 1992).

FAO officials—aware that the UNEP Biodiversity Convention, if accepted at UNCED, would overrule the Undertaking—initially received the UNEP initiative with certain misgivings (Rosendal, 1991). FAO officials suspected that the convention would merely bind the developing countries into surrendering their plant genetic resources for free. This anxiety was connected to the notion that a UNEP treaty would merely aim at the preservation of genetic resources for environmental protection regardless of their agricultural or economic value. Also, a shift of the plant genetic resource discussion toward UNEP would offer industrialized countries an opportunity to deal with the transfer of plant genetic resources from developing countries to industrialized countries without having to deal with politicized issues, notably the use of, access to, and ownership of plant genetic resources as within the forum provided by FAO. The mistrust of FAO officials turned out to be justified.

During its first meeting (Geneva, November 1989), the UNEP Working Group stated that "other relevant international programs (e.g., the FAO Undertaking) could not adequately meet the aim of conserving biological diversity on a global level" (Rosendal, 1991). But whereas the first meeting had been held behind closed doors, the second meeting (February 1990) was open to nongovernmental organizations (NGOs) which, almost inevitably, led to the politicization of the discussions on the content of the UNEP Convention. An important consequence was that the FAO successfully proposed to add elements of the FAO Undertaking to the UNEP Convention. In accordance with the interpretation of the FAO Undertaking, the working group agreed that "access" in the UNEP Convention would not imply "free access" or "access without payment."

After this event, industrialized countries, including the United States, the United Kingdom, and the Netherlands, began to express their skepticism of the UNEP Convention. Nevertheless, the UNEP Convention was more acceptable to the industrialized countries than the FAO Undertaking because such issues as intellectual property rights were not (yet) discussed. NGOs and officials within FAO speculate that the preference for UNEP as a forum may also be found in the strong role of the United States within UNEP.[7] The United States, to date, has refused to pay its yearly contribution to FAO for many years.

The intensification of the discussion of the more controversial elements of the plant genetic resource issue within UNEP motivated FAO to regain ground. At the third session of the UNEP ad hoc working group (Geneva, July 1990), FAO presented its International Convention on the Conservation and Utilization of Biological Diversity. In this new convention, both ecological interests (with regard to the conservation of plant genetic resources) and agricultural interests (with regard to the utilization of plant genetic resources) seemed to be treated in harmony by linking the two items through the term "sustainable use."[8] The FAO Convention, however, still defined conservation in a much narrower sense. Besides, it was not the intention of FAO to let the new convention replace the FAO Undertaking.

Within the UNEP working group, the FAO proposal was received with mixed feelings. The governmental representatives from Norway, Sweden, and Denmark, together with the United Kingdom, France, Canada, and many developing (especially Latin American) countries, supported the proposal, but Germany, the Netherlands, and the United States refused to accept FAO's narrow focus on conservation.

In spite of the last minute efforts of FAO, it became clear that the UNEP Convention was to serve as a framework for the UNCED Biodiversity Convention. Nevertheless, there still was a highly controversial element of the plant genetic resource issue that had to be dealt with in order to receive global support, namely, intellectual property rights. In fact, this subject was not dealt with until July 1992, during the UNCED, much to the detriment of many developing countries which were confronted with the United States' refusal to sign the Biodiversity Convention. In order to understand why the United States refused for a time to sign such an important treaty, the third issue (international trade), as dealt within the framework of GATT, should be considered.

The Political Arena of International Trade

The plant genetic resource issue has recently emerged as an item of the multilateral trade negotiations in the GATT Uruguay Round. One of the GATT negotiating groups has been set up to design a worldwide agreement on Trade Related Intellectual Property Rights (TRIPs). The TRIPs agreement aims at "reducing distortions and impediments to international trade . . . taking into account the need to promote effective and adequate protection of intellectual property rights" (Acharya, 1992:7).

If approved, the direct effect of the TRIPs agreement will be that developing countries (when they are members of GATT) have the obligations to recognize patents on microorganisms and to adopt a plant variety protection system (Van Wijk and Junne, 1992). A direct consequence of the TRIPs agreement is that developing countries are expected to adopt intellectual property rights on improved genetic material in new varieties.[9] The United States especially, through trade sanctions, has put great pressure on several developing countries (Taiwan, South Korea, Brazil, Mexico, Thailand, India, and China) to accept intellectual property rights. Developing countries and agricultural NGOs fear that, by granting patent protection to new varieties, royalties will have to be paid to the inventor (often a multinational company with headquarters in industrialized countries), which in turn will impede the development of new varieties on the basis of local "landraces"[10] as well as the exchange of these varieties on a local or national scale.

GATT, however, still regards genetic material that has not been improved by scientific techniques (notably biotechnology) as "common heritage" and therefore freely available. Many developing countries and critical NGOs argue that this position is a deliberate attempt to maintain free access to the world's genetic material on which Western agro-industry depends for the development of new varieties.

THE PLANT GENETIC RESOURCE ISSUE ACROSS THREE POLITICAL ARENAS

The above treatment of the plant genetic resource issue within three political arenas illustrates that the issue, although in general terms consisting of the same elements, is not treated in the same way in each political arena because each element receives a different amount of attention in each arena (see Figure 13-1). These elements can be divided into three large categories:

1. Ownership: all elements of the issue that relate to the use and intellectual ownership of plant genetic resources (most significantly within the GATT TRIPs negotiations).
2. Conservation: all elements that relate to the use of plant genetic resources for improving food security (most significantly within the FAO mandate).
3. Preservation: all elements that relate to the long-term environmental protection of plant genetic resources (most significantly within UNEP).

The fact that FAO, UNEP, and GATT are differently involved in the plant genetic resource issue has implications for the relative strength of the member countries. This political strength relates not only to the ability of a country to control the decisionmaking within one political arena, but also to the extent to which it, in accordance with its interests, is able to establish linkages between or across the political arenas.

Issue Linkages between FAO and UNEP

First, Article 2.1 of the FAO Undertaking, based on the assumption that plant genetic resources are a "common heritage" including commercially valuable "special genetic stocks," was unacceptable to most industrialized countries (principally Australia, Canada, Japan, and the United States). In the

Figure 13-1
Rank Order of the Different Aspects
of the Plant Genetic Resources Issue

Issue Areas

Food protection (FAO)	Environmental protection (UNEP)	International trade liberalization (GATT)
1 conservation	1 preservation	1 ownership
2 ownership	2 conservation	2 conservation
3 preservation	3 ownership	3 preservation

Under
discussion
since:
1983   1989   1990

reactions of governmental representatives at the UNEP working group session, there was strong support of many industrialized countries for replacing "common heritage" in the UNEP Convention (having a large overlap with the FAO Undertaking) with the much looser formulation of "common concern" and to cancel the inclusion of "special genetic stocks." The use of the phrase "common concern" would liberate many industrialized countries from the obligation to compensate the existing free transfer of unimproved genetic material from developing to industrialized countries with improved commercially valuable genetic material. In other words, the FAO officials' suspicion that the initial version of the UNEP Convention would merely bind the developing countries into surrendering their germ plasm for free was justified.

Second, the establishment of the FAO International Fund for Plant Genetic Resources, to channel money from intergovernmental organizations (IGOs) and NGOs, private industries, and individuals to Third World farmers, was not acknowledged in the initial UNEP Convention. Most industrialized countries considered the fund to be infeasible because it would only overlap with other existing international financial support for the conservation of plant genetic resources (such as via IBPGR). The initial version of the UNEP Convention offered the opportunity to opt for a more general interpretation of plant genetic resource funding. It implied that "the benefits derived from utilization and the cost of conservation of biological diversity should be shared." This meant that not only Third World farmers would benefit from a possible new fund, but so would all actors involved in the improvement of crops, including (Western) private companies and international organizations. In this respect, the concept of farmers' rights laying the basis for the FAO Fund was seriously blurred to the disadvantage of the local farmers in many (especially gene-rich) developing countries.

Third, the norm of free access in the FAO Undertaking is connected to the rule that genetic resources are not automatically free of charge. The initial version of the UNEP Convention, however, under pressure from most industrialized countries, explicitly states that "access" to plant genetic resources should be dealt with in "mutual agreements." This preference for a bilateral treatment of the access to plant genetic resources could lead to a wide variety of deals between individual developing and industrialized countries, in which access to genetic resources would be exchanged for technological expertise (such as on biotechnology) or other resources. Although this construction in itself was not considered a bad idea, developing countries feared that the outcome of such deals would largely depend on the economic and political strength of the developing and the industrialized country involved. Consequently, only a very limited category of developing countries with large stocks of plant genetic resources and sufficient agricultural know-how would benefit (e.g., Argentina, Brazil, Colombia, Costa Rica, Indonesia, India, Malaysia, and Mexico).

The overall tendency in the issue linkages between FAO and UNEP can be summarized by the following observation: issues connected to access (points 1 and 3), and finance (point 2), which were generally regarded as controversial issues in the FAO Undertaking, did also receive attention in the first versions of the UNEP Convention, but in much less politicized terms. This explains why the UNEP Convention received much more support from most industrialized countries.

Issue Linkages between UNEP and GATT

As discussed above, the UNEP Convention and the FAO Undertaking during 1990 and 1991 increasingly started to overlap. Most important was that the UNEP working group agreed that access in the UNEP Convention would not imply "free access" or access without payment (as defined within the FAO Undertaking). In due course, the industrialized countries (namely, the United States, the United Kingdom, and the Netherlands) started to express their skepticism toward the UNEP Convention.

The skepticism of the industrialized countries toward the UNEP Convention grew simultaneously with the approach of UNCED, as the Biodiversity Convention was framed on the UNEP Convention. The initial United States refusal to sign the UNCED convention was a serious setback for a settlement of the plant genetic resource issue. Although the direct reason for the United States' refusal to sign (i.e., the protection of the U.S. biotechnology industry) was extensively discussed in the media, it has never been analyzed in a broader context. Why did President Bush refuse to sign the UNCED Biodiversity Convention, even though the U.S., like many other industrialized countries, depends on the south-north gene drain? The answer can be connected to the issue linkage between the UNEP-UNCED Convention and negotiations within the GATT on the control of plant genetic resources with regard to the nucleus of the controversy on the whole plant genetic resource issue: the application of intellectual property rights on plant genetic resources.

During UNCED, William Reilly, head of the U.S. delegation, stated, "We have negotiated in the Uruguay Round of the GATT to try to protect intellectual property rights. We're not about to trade away here in an environmental treaty [i.e., the UNCED Convention] what we worked so hard to protect there" (Pistorius, 1992:8). In other words, the U.S. expected to benefit much more from an arrangement of the intellectual property rights question within the TRIPs negotiations than through the UNCED Biodiversity Convention.[11] The implementation of the TRIPs agreement would form a much better tool for the United States and other industrialized countries eager to protect new (genetically engineered) varieties and other living organisms with a commercial value.[12]

ISSUE LINKAGE BETWEEN POLITICAL ARENAS

Most developing countries, despite possessing over two-thirds of the world's genetic resources and representing a majority in the UN organizations, are not able to enlarge their influence in international decisionmaking on the plant genetic resource issue. As this chapter reveals, this conclusion is not only related to the defeat of developing countries within the political arena of food production, but also to their performance within the political arenas of environmental protection and international trade. Put differently, their defeat lies in their incapacity to let the plant genetic resource issue spill over to other political arenas in a way that can serve their interests. The industrialized countries (increasingly with the approval of the more advanced developing countries) were more successful in this respect: the longer the plant genetic resource issue was discussed, the more they were able to "push" controversial elements of the discussion from one political arena to another.

This explanation suggests that the industrialized countries were acting according to their interests. Indeed, both within the FAO and UNEP (and later in the context of UNCED), the industrialized countries were not able to determine the outcome directly by simply using their political power. But when looking at the course of the treatment of the plant genetic resource issue across the FAO, UNEP, and GATT, stronger states (notably the United States) did determine the outcome of the issue, although in an indirect way. This "forum shopping" offered industrialized countries (as "gene consumers") the opportunity to secure their dominant position in the multilateral decisionmaking on plant genetic resources.

On the basis of this finding, I suggest two hypotheses which could be of use in further analyses of international environmental organizations:

1. The outcome of decisionmaking on a certain (environmental) issue should not only be attributed to a state's political power within an international organization, but also to the state's ability to push an issue from one political arena to another.
2. Different mandates of international organizations lead to different issue linkages. Since policymaking on environmental issues is often guided by considerations that are less related to environmental matters but instead inspired by stands on other policy issues, these different linkages can lead to different policy outcomes on the same issue in different international organizations.

CONCLUSION

In a world in which global political issues increasingly overlap, issue linkages between political arenas deserve more attention. The behavior of different states regarding a particular issue in international negotiations cannot be judged by focusing only on one particular political arena or one international organization.

In this case, an analysis based on one political arena would have offered a rather static view of the plant genetic resource issue in general and the related north-south conflict within this issue in particular. Analyzing more political arenas offers greater insight into the phenomenon that some states react differently to the same issue in different political arenas. That offers a better insight into the bargaining strength of states in each political arena and their ability to create tactical issue linkages across political arenas. A related drawback of the one-political arena approach is that it offers a limited focus on the relative bargaining strengths of actors. An analysis of the plant genetic resource issue that focused only on the political arena of food production, or only on environmental protection, would have overestimated the negotiation power of the developing countries.

NOTES

1. Notably Pat Roy Mooney (1979) and Frederick Buttel (1992).

2. "Special genetic stocks" are genetic materials that have been improved to serve certain agricultural purposes, for example, resistance to diseases or pests. These materials have a higher commercial value than unimproved genetic material.

3. The Undertaking ran counter to existing plant breeders' rights in several industrialized countries, in general, and the Plant Variety Protection Act of the United States in particular.

4. More specifically, the commission was to monitor the international Undertaking, review the FAO activities in crop and plant genetic resources, and arrange the legislation on seed and plant breeding in relation to the international exchange of plant genetic resources (see, for example, Fowler et al., 1988).

5. The official position of the United States considered the IBPGR the primary coordinating body at the international level for plant genetic resources (Fowler et al., 1988:20-21).

6. Another global issue was "the population bomb," a notion from population biology and demography, codified in popular terms by Paul Ehrlich and the "Limits of Growth," a notion put forward by the Club of Rome. Buttel notes that the "rainforest connection" (a connection between the loss of rainforests and biodiversity) has helped the plant genetic resource issue to become anchored in the environmental movement ideology (1992:20).

7. UNEP receives relatively large voluntary contributions from the United States.

8. The FAO Convention stated that conservation and utilization of biological diversity and sustainable development of mankind must be closely interrelated.

9. This regulation focuses not only on plant varieties but on all living organisms.

10. "Landraces" are varieties, breeds, or cultivars of a crop species associated with traditional agricultural systems, often highly adapted to local conditions.

11. The draft TRIPs agreement leaves member countries free to decide whether they include not only single plants, but also whole plant varieties and animals in their patent laws. Under this patent law, all unauthorized commercial use of patented plant material in breeding programs may be refused or restricted by the patent holder. If agreed upon, the TRIPs draft will form a powerful tool for patent holders, especially the holders of biotechnology patents covering a large number of genes, to control the current worldwide exchange of plant genetic resources (Van Wijk and Junne, 1992:85).

12. The critique by the United States of the UNCED Convention can be opposed by referring to Article 16(2) of the convention which states, "In the case of technology subject to patents and other intellectual property rights . . . access and transfer shall be provided on terms *which recognize and are consistent with the adequate and effective protection of intellectual property rights*" (emphasis added). In other words, according to the convention, access of developing countries to technology in industrialized countries would not harm any commercial interests (Pistorius, 1992:9).

14

Do We Need a New Theory of International Organizations?

Madhu Malik

The nature and scope of international politics are significantly different today than was true during most of the post-World War II years. New international realities have emerged that require new ways of describing, explaining, and analyzing. Changing global conditions of particular significance are, first, the increasing salience and seriousness of global environmental problems and, second, more active participation by international organizations in international politics, particularly in addressing global environmental problems. Existing theories of international politics are inadequate to account for or explain these phenomena, and the question therefore arises whether new or alternative "theories" and perspectives are required to keep pace with changing global conditions.

Many of the problems threatening and endangering the world today are substantively different from the continuing though changing problems of war and invasion. There is a threat of nuclear disaster, to be sure, but there are also emerging problems of environmental degradation, nationally and globally, that are just as serious. Given the complexity and transnational nature of such environmental problems as transboundary pollution, climate change, loss of genetic diversity, the greenhouse effect, and stratospheric ozone depletion, most states have recognized the necessity of facilitating international cooperation to address these problems. They have also recognized the instrumental role that international organizations can play in providing the necessary fora for gathering reliable and valid scientific information, in building consensus about the nature of environmental problems and the solutions required, and in fostering the cooperation and participation of states required to formulate and implement a global response to environmental problems.

International organizations, in particular international environmental organizations, have been in existence for more than a century (Caldwell, 1972). What makes international organizations so significant for international environmental cooperation in the 1990s is that many are breaking out of the molds made at the time of their creation and are reinterpreting their catalytic and coordinative mandates in more action-oriented terms. Moreover, many new international organizations are being created with environmental missions (see Chapter 8). In the last several decades, formal organizations have been called upon increasingly by the international community to deal with environmental problems, reflecting the need for concerted, comprehensive, and cross-national cooperation to preserve and restore environmental quality. International organizations have long played crucial roles in global environmental protection and management by sponsoring conferences, providing extension services, conducting research, and funding developmental projects, among other things. International organizations are now playing an even more active and assertive role in creating worldwide awareness of global environmental problems and in coordinating and undertaking international activities to address such problems. No longer are they, if they ever were, merely passive entities in the processes of international politics, means to be used by nations for national self-interest.

But our ability to analyze meaningfully how international environmental policy is made, to understand the structure and functioning of international environmental politics, and to evaluate and understand the participation of formal international organizations in international environmental policy and politics remains limited. Although many scholars recognize the significance of international organizations in addressing global environmental problems, most do not utilize any theoretical perspective or framework for analyzing the participation of international organizations in international environmental policy and politics. Only passing reference, or sometimes none at all, is made to scholarly literature or theories of international politics that might provide an understanding of the capabilities and limitations of international organizations in international politics in general or to international environmental politics more specifically. On the other hand, inadequacies and weaknesses of existing theoretical perspectives on international organizations have become obstacles to fuller understanding among policymakers and scholars about the nature and potential of such organizations in addressing global environmental problems.

Past theoretical developments in international relations have been unable to explain adequately the emerging realities of the 1990s, in particular the active participation of international organizations in managing and addressing complex environmental problems of a global nature. In order to understand more fully the contributions of international organizations to international environmental policy and politics, we need to move beyond traditional theories and perspectives. A policy perspective can enhance understanding of the range of policy processes and activities undertaken collectively by policy actors, including international organizations, in addressing common areas of concern such as global environmental problems. Recent international environmental literature has begun to make strides in a policy direction by examining some policy processes, such as agenda setting and implementation. A comprehensive policy framework, however, can place these processes in a larger iterative context. Placing individual policy processes in a broader perspective also illustrates the complex political and economic realities within which international organizations interact with other policy actors and within which global environmental problems are addressed.

THEORETICAL DEVELOPMENTS IN INTERNATIONAL RELATIONS

The study of international organizations has traditionally fallen under the field of international organization, which emerged as a distinct and systematic field of study and scholarship in the 1920s after the creation of the League of Nations. Initially, international organization scholars were preoccupied with the structures, roles, goals, objectives, and hoped-for effects of international organizations (Rochester, 1986; Gallarotti, 1991). Gradually, the focus shifted away from the structure of international organizations toward the processes of multilateral arrangements and broader forms of institutionalized behavior (Kratochwil and Ruggie, 1986). The international organization field gradually deteriorated as a field of study in the 1970s—ironically just as the numbers, roles, and importance of international organizations were growing substantially.

By the 1980s, the field of international organization lost its identity as a distinct area of study, and it became subsidiary to the study of international politics with its primary focus on patterns of international conflict and cooperation and concepts of power and security (Rochester, 1986). Since then the study of international organizations has relied upon theories of international politics for theoretical and methodological guidance. Inherent limitations of existing theoretical perspectives in international politics, however, have constrained the use of theory in the study of international organizations. International relations theorists, too, have distanced themselves from the study of international law and its potential for the analysis of cooperation in general and the concept of regimes in particular (see Chapter 9). We need to examine, then, the extent to which these theoretical developments in international relations have been unable to explain adequately the emerging realities of the 1990s, in particular the active participation of international organizations in managing and addressing complex environmental problems of a global nature.

Realism and International Organizations

Also known as the "power politics" school, realism perceives world politics as being concerned primarily with the struggle for power among states

(Morgenthau, 1967; Carr, 1964). According to the fundamental premises and assumptions of the realist perspective, international organizations of all types might aspire to the status of independent actors, but would be unable to achieve this. By this view, international organizations such as the United Nations (UN) or the North Atlantic Treaty Organization (NATO) cannot be independent actors, being composed of sovereign, independent, and autonomous states who determine the agendas, functions, and capabilities of these organizations. Realists are interested in the "balance of power" in the international system and in those organizations with a part in it, rather than organizations that are engaged in promoting "collective security" and carrying out economic, social, and welfare tasks. The creation of international organizations presupposed the mitigation and minimization of international conflicts (Morgenthau, 1967).

Although Rheinhold Niebuhr, an early realist, realized the potential of international organizations in providing mechanisms to bridge various segments of the world separated by divisive issues, he also discussed several opposing forces operating simultaneously that limited the integration of the world community—economic disparities among states and the lack of common convictions on particular issues (Niebuhr, 1949). Neither was Morgenthau eager to overstate the role of international organizations in facilitating harmonious interstate relations. International organizations were merely the instruments of states empowered to acquire power and control in the international system with little independent initiative and effectiveness (Morgenthau, 1967). This view of international organizations has not changed considerably among later realists.

Realists' conceptions of international politics and of the roles of international organizations fail to capture the increasingly complex pattern of social and economic interaction characteristic of the international system, which joins diverse actors into a loose global network. Realists ignore actors and issues not related to the maintenance of state security. Non-state actors such as international organizations are excluded, downplayed, or trivialized. Realists accept the status quo in international relations based on power relationships and do not acknowledge the potential of international organizations to play a positive role in creating a different world. This dismissive treatment of international organizations by the realist perspective, particularly in light of the growth of international organizations and international nongovernmental organizations (INGOs) in the 1980s and 1990s, raises doubts about the accuracy of its predictive powers and its claim to realism. The resolution of even fairly simple pollution problems requires more than a few half-hearted efforts by leading industrial nations; it requires cooperation and accommodation between the polluters and the affected nations and groups, within a legitimate international forum. Nor is the power assumption of realism as relevant in the complex, interdependent environment of the 1990s as it might have been during earlier periods. Not all international phenomena and issues can be expressed in terms of military components, technical resources, or the ability to move the behavior of another actor in a desired direction. Environmental policy developments, particularly since the 1970s, are difficult to explain using only such concepts as power, conflict, and security.

The realists' neglect of economic, social, cultural, and ecological issues is an even greater omission in light of the increasing appearance of environmental issues on national and international agendas. Increased popularity of green parties, particularly in Europe, is one indication of the salience given to ecological concerns along with political and economic concerns at the national level. Environmental issues also made their way to the top of the agenda at the 1991 World Economic Summit. The 1992 UN Conference on Environment and Development held in Brazil was devoted entirely to a wide range of environmental problems, from ozone depletion to deforestation, and to their interrelatedness with economic and developmental concerns.

Despite the various criticisms levied against realism, understanding the general principles of state action and the practices of governments can provide useful insights by highlighting potential problems that international organizations may confront in formulating and implementing environmental policy and administration. Realism, as a framework of questions and initial hypotheses, can be valuable in estimating the capabilities of international organizations to achieve stated goals and objectives. Furthermore, states will not necessarily discontinue their own adherence to the state-centric and power-oriented view of the world, even when it is neither theoretically nor practically useful (Soroos, 1986:24). States continue to pursue self-help strategies and to guard national sovereignty even in the face of complex environmental problems that demand transnational problem solving.

In sum, realism lacks much utility as a theoretical base for analyzing the role of international organizations in environmental policy and administration in the 1990s. Its state-centric and power assumptions render it incapable of recognizing global environmental problems as key issues of global politics, of acknowledging international organizations as significant actors, or of providing much guidance in regulating the variety of expectations, practices, and institutions necessary to address environmental problems.

Neorealism and International Organizations

Keohane and Nye (1977), major proponents of the neorealist perspective, saw international organizations as emerging actors in international politics particularly with the increased level of transnational activity in the decades following World War II. They gave these organizations an important position in a complex interdependence model of world politics. In this model, not only do international organizations foster multilevel linkages among a variety of state and non-state actors, but they are also instrumental in international regime dynamics (the creation, maintenance, and the transformation of regimes). In addition, international organizations facilitate political bargaining, activate political coalitions, and enable weak and small states to pursue linkage strategies in a world characterized by multilevel issues. Furthermore, they set the international agenda and act as catalysts for coalition formation and as arenas for political initiatives (Keohane and Nye, 1977).

Neorealists identify several consequences of the growth of international interactions and of international organizations in the conduct of interstate relations (Keohane and Nye, 1971). First, attitudes among citizens are changing toward a more pluralistic world. Second, an increase in international pluralism is evident through an increase in "the linking of national interest groups in transnational structures, usually involving transnational organizations for the purpose of coordination" (Keohane and Nye, 1971:xviii). As a result of increased linkages, there is increased dependence and interdependence among the various actors in the world system. Independent non-state actors have emerged with their own policies that may deliberately challenge existing state policies. Neorealists are also concerned with a range of social, economic, and ecological issues.

Thus, in contrast to the realist perspective of international organizations as peripheral to world politics, international organizations are seen by neorealists as more than merely arenas within which sovereign states interact. They are seen as independent actors in their own right who have considerable influence in setting the international agenda. Given an increasingly interdependent world economy, the potential is increased for transnational actors such as international organizations, INGOs, and multinational corporations (MNCs) to play a role in political bargaining and coalition building. Consequently, such non-state actors cannot be dismissed as being of marginal importance.

Neorealists, however, tend not to distinguish between different types of non-state actors, such as international organizations, multinational corporations, and nongovernmental organizations (NGOs), each of which are structurally and functionally distinct types of institutions. Nor do they distinguish between different types of transnational relations in which non-governmental actors participate. Neorealists are quick to dismiss new developments in the international system as superficial and thus they are ill-equipped to recognize major global changes. For neorealists, the more things change, the more they stay the same. Furthermore, the structural explanation of world politics offered by neorealists gives priority to the international system and its structure in explaining state behavior at the expense of accounting for the attributes of and interactions between individual units (Waltz, 1979). Issues outside the military and security areas are still downgraded or ignored in the structural explanation of the international system.

Despite these shortcomings, neorealists have provided insights into several dimensions of transnational politics, and they have shifted attention away from purely governmental actors in interstate relations to some focus on non-state actors such as international organizations. Although neorealism does attribute a substantial role to non-state actors in social, economic, and ecological issues, it is nonetheless inadequate for explaining the full role of international organizations in addressing international environmental problems and developments.

Globalism and International Organizations

During the late 1960s and early 1970s, globalist ideals had already begun to challenge state-centric and power-oriented realist and neorealist approaches toward world politics. According to the globalist perspective, the starting point of analysis was the overall structure of the international system, or the global context within which states and non-state actors interact. It started with a world centricism that placed decreasing emphasis on the nation-state as the only global political actor. Globalism represented a "whole world" approach that stressed not the discrete requirements of individuals, groups, or states, but the well-being of the global ecosystem in which they function. A primary concern of this approach was the survival and efficient functioning of the planet (Brown, 1972; Falk, 1972). In deemphasizing the state as the only dominant actor in global politics, the globalists challenged the core of the realist paradigm.

Concerning the global atmosphere, the oceans, and the world's weather systems, matters to which pretensions of national sovereignty have no relevance, Ward and Dubos (1972) perceived the immediate need for a common policy and coordinated action. Although institutional frameworks and organizational structures were not very well developed, the authors did propose the establishment of a network of functionally based organizations that could take up much of the work currently not done by national governments. Globalism thus viewed international organizations as playing a dominant role in the vision of a global community based on protection against war and environmental destruction. It was a vision that stressed unity and common cause rather than disagreement and confrontation.

Globalism, however, was criticized for being too idealistic in a cynical world, too structural in a complex world, and too impractical in its institutional and organizational suggestions. Despite attributing a major role to international organizations in global politics and environmental protection, globalists remained immersed in value preferences and normative considerations. Some of their strategies were dismissed as "globaloney" because of their inadequate recourse to scientific methods of analyses and to current reality (Rochester, 1986). Their failure to consider adequately political and security concerns of the international system detracted from globalism's descriptive, explanatory, and predictive capabilities as a theory of international politics. Furthermore, globalist scholars tended to overemphasize the goals and objectives of international institutions with relatively less attention given to the organizational capabilities of meeting these objectives.

Regimes and International Organizations

Although derived from the neorealist tradition, regime analysis seeks to transcend the state-centric assumptions that neorealists continue to adhere to. Regime analysis shifts the focus away from patterns of institutionalized behavior to specific issues at hand and seeks to identify key problems, variables, and actors relevant to the particular issue under consideration. Most regime theorists view international organizations as part of a network of actors that cooperate and interact with each other through various types of institutional arrangements to address shared interests, concerns, and problems. The fate of such organizations is intimately connected with the dynamics of regime creation, maintenance, and dissipation. Viewing international organizations as explicit organizational arrangements accompanying regimes raises a host of research questions pertaining to the autonomy of such organizations vis-à-vis other actors in the international system, their rules and procedures, personnel, budget, location of physical facilities, and their function (Young, 1980).

In the view of regime theorists, the functions performed by international organizations are best understood in the context of the regimes of which they are a part. These functions vary from collecting resources and providing collective goods (Young, 1989b), to coordinating behavior according to set standards (Ruggie, 1975), to implementing and securing adherence to rules and procedures (Krasner, 1982). Taking a more policy-making perspective, Ruggie (1975) developed a threefold classification of tasks performed by international organizations within a regime framework: facilitative tasks, whereby an international organization assists in the planning of regime functions but does not participate in decisionmaking and implementation; enabling tasks, whereby it participates in planning and decisionmaking functions of the regime but not implementation; and operational tasks, whereby it performs all three tasks of planning, decisionmaking, and implementation.

Although international organizations can be viewed and understood as the organizational arrangements that institutionalize cooperative national behavior among members of regimes (Young, 1980), not all regimes are accompanied by explicit and extensive organizational arrangements. Puchala and Hopkins (1982) contend that international organizations and regimes are independent of each other and do not necessarily require the presence of the other to exist and operate effectively in global politics. Not all regimes are formally institutionalized and accompanied by international organizations, and similarly, not all international organizations are an institutionalization of regimes. Instead of creating new institutional arrangements with their own personnel, budget, and facilities, it is often preferable for regimes to utilize existing institutional arrangements.

International regime analysis has the potential to produce better understanding of the participation of international organizations in global politics. It can be particularly useful in the context of global environmental problems since the nature of these problems varies to such an extent as to demand different sets of actors and processes. Furthermore, a regime can be an especially attractive unit of analysis if we characterize global politics as being issue specific, and as a domain of political action in which both power and process often differ dramatically from issue to issue (Donnelly, 1990).

Despite the usefulness of regime analysis, it has several definitional and conceptual problems that undermine its utility for understanding the participation of international organizations in global politics, including international environmental policy. The most serious criticism that may be leveled against regime analysis is the ambiguous, umbrella-like nature of its definition. Conceptually, it may be difficult to determine the boundaries of any given regime or between different regimes, or the relationship between its four component parts (principles, norms, rules, and decision-making procedures), or the locus of any authoritative control. In addition, liberal and mercantilist regime theorists view the creation and emergence of international organizations as the result of hegemonic decisions to reduce the hegemon's share of responsibility in the international system and as reflecting patterns of hegemony, respectively (E. Haas, 1982). Neither views international organizations as autonomous entities that can participate meaningfully in international politics.

Reconsideration

Critiques of the realist, neorealist, globalist, and regimes perspectives thus illustrate the limited utility of these conventional theories alone, or combined where possible, for understanding the participation of international organizations in international politics and the emergence of international environmental issues in global politics. Also ignored to some extent by this scholarship in international politics is a significant feature of world politics: a substantial body of international public policy and a range of policy processes by which it is formulated and implemented (Soroos, 1986). Environmental policy developments, particularly since 1972, present a challenge to existing explanations of international politics, given that dynamics of international environmental policy can be only inadequately captured in the language of conflict, cooperation, security, power, nation-states, principles, norms, rules, and decision-making procedures.

Alternative theoretical perspectives (or new interpretations of classical theories) are necessary if such issues are ever to be better understood and effectively addressed.   As global conditions become more complex and interdependent, and as the international system is confronted by challenging environmental issues that defy simple solutions, there emerges a greater need for coordinated problem solving on a global scale. Globalism alone, however, is not adequately equipped to provide the theoretical and analytical framework for such problem solving. Policy-making approaches and models can shed much needed insight into the procedures and processes used by the international community in formulating and implementing responses to global environmental problems.

What is needed to explain the processes by which international organizations participate in international environmental policy and politics are more theoretically based, policy-oriented approaches that recognize international organizations as key actors in international politics, that are concerned with actual or potential responses to global environmental problems, and that analyze the policy processes that generate such responses. Such approaches can foster productive scholarly inquiry and informed public discussion about international organizations and international environmental policy.

POLICY APPROACHES

What are policy-oriented or policy approaches? To begin with, there is no one approach that constitutes *the* policy approach.   Rather, a variety of orientations, frameworks of analysis, and ways of thinking that focus on some policy processes or policy developments can be viewed as policy approaches. Bührs and Bartlett (1993) identify three types of policy models, theories, and perspectives commonly used in public policy analysis: analycentric, policy process, and meta-policy, each offering a distinct analytical framework for studying public policy.

The analycentric approach to policy analysis is primarily concerned with analyzing data and information, formal models, or simulations in order to better understand the complexities and intricacies of policy developments in a particular area of concern, for instance, environmental problems.   International environmental policy research in the analycentric tradition—as in the case of domestic policy research—involves the use of quantitative techniques for sophisticated mathematical modeling; cost-benefit analysis; risk assessment; technical details of measurement of specific environmental problems such as pollution of air, water, and land, the nature and causes of acid rain, ozone depletion, and global warming; and simulation and forecasting models of climate change, ecosystems, and so on. Such research does not require background or understanding of the political dimension of policy—or even much knowledge of most other analycentric work.   In sheer quantity and salience, analycentric research dominates the literature on international environmental policy and international organizations, overshadowing research based on the policy process and meta-policy approaches.

The policy process approach, although similar to the analycentric approach in its multidisciplinary nature, is an attempt to focus attention on the decision-making dimensions of policy which are, for the most part, neglected by the analycentric approach. Deriving its inspiration from the policy sciences that are concerned with "knowledge of" and "knowledge in" the policy process (Lasswell, 1950), the policy process approach sees policymaking as involving several phases over time. Although the identified number of phases may vary, all policy cycles progress through four broad phases consisting of problem definition and agenda setting, policy formulation and selection, implementation, and evaluation (Bührs and Bartlett, 1993).

The global policy framework, developed by Marvin Soroos (1986), applies the policy process model to developments and processes occurring at the international and global levels of interaction and cooperation. It consists of three elements which constitute a framework for examining responses to individual policy problems as well as a model for understanding how policies are negotiated and implemented in the context of international organizations. The global agenda concerns the nature of global problems that are prominent on international policy agendas and the factors responsible for bringing such problems to the policy agenda and maintaining them there. Global policy processes focus on the primary policy actors involved in addressing global problems, the procedures and steps undertaken in global policymaking, and the arenas within which these policy-making processes are conducted. The global response examines the products of the policy-making processes (outputs), enforcing these outputs, ensuring their compliance, and strategies for evaluating their effectiveness (Soroos, 1986:27).

For international environmental policy, understanding the significance of each of these phases, especially the politics that suffuses each stage of policymaking, is critical to appreciate the roles international organizations may and do legitimately play. As in purely domestic policymaking, a variety of factors such as the state of the economy at a particular point in time, lobbying by environmental organizations and other interest groups, and the coverage by the news media all come into play in the salience of a policy issue and the nature of the rhetoric that frames the discussion about it. These in turn determine whether the issue gets on an international agenda and, equally significant, how it is defined (see Chapters 4 and 7). Policy formulation is also a process marked by negotiation and coordination among different policy actors, a phase in which intense bargaining and compromise may lead eventually to agreement—at least enough agreement for a policy to come into effect. Where the analycentric approach's view of policy formulation is based on assumptions of "decisionism" and rationality (Majone, 1986, 1989), the policy process stage recognizes that the multiple participants involved in the formulation of policy have differing objectives, and any consensus is through a highly political process of persuasion and negotiation. Moreover, such consensus is at best temporary, and the adopted policy is influenced by the institutional mechanisms that shape the implementation (and hence the interpretation) of policies and their quality (see, for example, Dryzek, 1987).

Policy implementation, like the other stages of policymaking, has its own set of political dimensions. The political complexities that accompany the agenda setting and policy formulation stages are likely to spill over into this phase. Policy implementation is shaped and molded by the implementors who interpret policy from their own standpoint or that of the organizations they represent. Indeed, the implementation of a policy is determined primarily by the way the issue has been defined during the early stages of the policy process (see Chapters 6 and 13). The extent to which multilateral international law prescribes new or existing international organizations depends largely on the importance of noncontroversial implementation as a route to policy success. For example, the "public good" characteristic of the services provided by the World Meteorological Organization (WMO), unhampered by problems of free riders or an unwillingness on the part of industrialized countries to shoulder a bulk of the costs involved, has allowed WMO to acquire the status of a highly effective international organization (see Chapter 5).

It is in the third kind of policy research, meta-policy, that there is a paucity of literature dealing with international environmental policy. Unlike the other two approaches, meta-policy analysis focuses on the broader context within which policy analysis occurs and within which policy research is conducted and policy knowledge is created. It analyzes, for instance, the role and significance of policy analysis in policymaking, how policy analysis influences decisionmaking, and the similarities or differences between policy analysis and policymaking. Meta-policy can offer an analysis of knowledge systems, worldviews, and belief patterns that affect the nature of the policy system. With its focus on values, education, and culture, it may result in bringing about institutional changes and changes in ways of policymaking.

One feature of all policy approaches is that they are concerned with some aspect of policy, ranging from identifying issues on the policy agenda to evaluating policy responses, or with other policy developments in a particular area of concern. A second common characteristic of policy approaches is that they tend to use a variety of disciplines in their attempts to comprehend complex reality, including political science, economics, statistics, law, sociology, and others. In other words, policy approaches are multidisciplinary. Most policy approaches also have a normative component that makes them human oriented; that is, these approaches are concerned with the promotion of values and with the effect of policy developments on human values.

For the most part, policy approaches have been confined to an analysis of policy occurring at the national or subnational level. But there is no reason that these policy theories and models cannot be applied to the supranational levels to analyze policy developments at the regional, international, or global levels. It is more the limited use of policy approaches by scholars rather than an inherent inadequacy within the approaches themselves that has precluded their application to the international or global levels. Recent developments in international environmental literature, making an implicit use of policy approaches, have begun to remedy this shortcoming.

STATE OF THEORY

Scholarship is generating new insight into international environmental policy and politics and has begun to explain the role of international organizations in addressing global environmental problems. Although a new "theory" of international organizations has not emerged from this literature, foundations have been laid: recognition of international organizations as relevant actors in international environmental policy, identification of the roles and functions that international organizations perform in addressing global environmental problems, analysis of structural and procedural factors that influence the capability and effectiveness of international organizations, and the explanation of linkages that are formed between international organizations and other participants, state and non-state, in addressing and responding to issues on the global agenda.

Although a policy perspective, in general, and the global policy framework, in particular, do not constitute a new theory for international organizations, they do promote more productive inquiry and informed discussion about international organizations in international environmental policy and in the context of a comprehensive policy framework that enables us to comprehend the complexities accompanying policy processes and developments and to discern recognizable patterns of behavior by international organizations in these processes. As noted earlier, much of the recent literature in international environmental policy makes an implicit use of a policy approach by analyzing one or two policy processes such as agenda setting, the negotiation process, or implementation of international environmental agreement. The nature and scope of involvement of international organizations in international environmental policy, however, can be better understood in the context of a comprehensive policy framework that links a range of policy processes together into a larger process and thus links a variety of actors to each other in the course of that process. Such a framework provides a larger common political and economic context within which individual policy processes could be located and gives a sense of continuity to these processes.

The global policy approach goes one step farther toward identifying the parameters of this comprehensive framework. A global policy approach has the potential to promote better understanding of the participation of international organizations in international environmental policy and politics in several ways. First, the global policy approach goes beyond a focus on the structure and process of international organizations per se (as emphasized by international organization scholars), on power politics (as emphasized by realists), or on cooperative arrangements designed to address specific transnational issues (as emphasized by regime analysts). It illustrates the complex dimensions of international policymaking and politics that cannot be adequately explained by emphasizing these other factors alone.

Second, the global policy approach highlights the role of international organizations as significant and relevant actors in international environmental politics. Using a policy perspective enables us to capture in more detail the specific tasks and functions performed by international organizations in addressing global environmental problems. It promotes a more comprehensive understanding of the myriad roles played by international organizations in their interactions with other policy actors as they seek to formulate and implement agreements on managing environmental problems. Whereas international organization scholars, international relations theorists, and regime analysts tend to view international organizations as dependent, independent, or intervening variables, respectively, the global policy approach does not limit their role to one or the other.

The global policy approach provides a framework of analysis for examining the performance of each of these three roles by international organizations but at different stages of the policy process. International organizations can be viewed as the arenas within which representatives of national governments negotiate with each other and make decisions in the form of resolutions or treaties (dependent variables). The outcomes of these decision-making processes conducted by representatives of states are influenced, to some extent, by the nature of the arena within which they are being conducted (intervening variables). And, some international organizations are endowed with a "legal personality" at creation which allows their officials to participate actively and directly in the decision-making processes being conducted by representatives of states, and to conclude agreements with them and other international organizations (independent variables) (Soroos, 1986:82).

One serious limitation, however, of the global policy approach is its predictive power; it is unable to foretell, for instance, at what stages of the policy process international organizations will be performing a dependent, intervening, or independent role. Nonetheless, the global policy approach sheds important light on the functions, tasks, and operations performed by international organizations, and it also provides much needed insight into their relationships with other policy actors, the influence of organizational leadership and resource constraints on the performance of international organizations, and their limitations in formulating, implementing, and evaluating global responses designed to address global environmental problems.

We need to ask whether we really need a new theory for international organizations at all, and whether such a theory is even possible. The picture that emerges of international environmental policy and politics is a complex, multidisciplinary, and normative one. None of the predominant theoretical perspectives in international politics—realism, neorealism, globalism, and regime theory—is adequate to explain this rich complexity. Nor do policy approaches constitute an adequate new theory for international organizations or environmental politics. But policy approaches do facilitate theoretical thinking about the role of international organizations in addressing environmental problems, the processes involved in the multilateral management of environmental problems, and the broader context within which policy processes occur. Given the complex reality of environmental problems and the context within which these problems are addressed, explaining policy processes and developments by a single or even several simple theoretical perspectives is a dubious prospect. Still better understanding of the roles of international organizations in these processes may be fostered by relying on a multitude of theoretical and disciplinary perspectives—not haphazardly, but within the structure provided by a comprehensive policy framework.

Bibliography

Abbott, Kenneth W. 1989. "Modern International Relations Theory: A Prospectus for International Lawyers." *Yale Journal of International Law* 14 (Summer):335-411.

Acharya, Rohini. 1992. "Intellectual Property, Biotechnology and Trade: The Impact of the Uruguay Round." *Biopolicy International Series.* Issue no. 4. Nairobi: African Centre for Technology Studies.

Adler, Emanuel. 1989. *The Power of Ideology.* Berkeley: University of California Press.

Agarwal, Bina. 1992. "The Gender and Environment Debate: Lessons from India." *Feminist Studies* 18 (1):119-58.

Agesta Group AB. 1982. *Twenty Years of Stockholm 1972-1992: A Report on the Implementation of the Stockholm Action Plan and Institutional Arrangements for the 1980s.* Berlin: Erich Schmidt Verlag.

Aggarwal, Vinod. 1983. "The Unraveling of the Multi-Fiber Arrangement, 1981: An Examination of International Regime Change." *International Organization* 37 (Autumn):617-45.

"Alternative 'Agenda 21' Produced by NGOs for Earth Summit." 1991. *Diversity* 7(4):5-7.

Ascher, William, and Robert Healy. 1990. *Natural Resource Policymaking in Developing Countries.* Durham, N.C.: Duke University Press.

Ashby, Eric and Mary Anderson. 1981. *The Politics of Clean Air.* Oxford, England: Clarendon Press.

Ashley, Richard K. 1986. "The Poverty of Neorealism." In *Neorealism and its Critics,* edited by Robert O. Keohane, pp. 255-300. New York: Columbia University Press.

Atwood, Wallace W. 1959. "The International Geophysical Year in Retrospective." *Department of State Bulletin* 40 (11):682-89.

Atwood, Wallace W. 1956. "The International Geophysical Year: A Twentieth-Century Achievement in International Cooperation." *Department of State Bulletin* 35 (910):880-86.

Axelrod, Robert. 1984. *The Evolution of Cooperation*. New York: Basic Books.

Badgikian, Ben. 1974. "Congress and Media: Partners in Propaganda." *Columbia Journalism Review* (January/February):3-10.

Baldock, David. 1989. Personal communication with Senior Fellow, Institute for European Environmental Policy.

Bandow, Doug. 1989. "What's Still Wrong with the World Bank?" *Orbis* 33 (1):73-89.

Barratt-Brown, Elizabeth P. 1991. "Building a Monitoring and Compliance Regime under the Montreal Protocol." *Yale Journal of International Law* 16 (Summer):520-70.

Barrett, Jill. 1991. "The Negotiation and Drafting of the Climate Change Convention." In *International Law and Global Climate Change*, edited by R. Churchill and D. Freestone, pp. 183-200. London: Graham and Trotman.

Bartlett, Robert V. 1990. "Ecological Reason in Administration: Environmental Impact Assessment and Administrative Theory." In *Managing Leviathan: Environmental Politics and the Administrative State*, edited by Robert Paehlke and Douglas Torgerson, pp. 81-96. Lewiston, N.Y.: Broadview Press.

Bartlett, Robert V. 1986a. "Ecological Rationality: Reason and Environmental Policy." *Environmental Ethics* 8:221-39.

Bartlett, Robert V. 1986b. "Rationality and the Logic of the National Environmental Policy Act." *The Environmental Professional* 8:105-11.

Benedick, Richard E. 1993. "Perspectives of a Negotiation Practitioner." In *International Environmental Negotiation*, edited by Gunnar Sjostedt, pp. 219-243. Newbury Park, Calif: Sage.

Benedick, Richard E. 1991a. "Protecting the Ozone Layer: New Directions in Diplomacy." In *Preserving the Global Environment: The Challenge of Shared Leadership*, edited by Jessica T. Mathews, pp. 112-53. New York: W.W. Norton.

Benedick, Richard E. 1991b. *Ozone Diplomacy: New Directions in Safeguarding the Planet*. Cambridge, Mass: Harvard University Press.

Bergesen, Helge O., Magnar Nordenhaug and Georg Parmann, eds. 1992. *Green Globe Yearbook 1992*. Oxford, England: Oxford University Press.

Bierly, Eugene W. 1988. "The World Climate Program: Collaboration and Communication on a Global Scale." *Annals of the American Academy of Political and Social Sciences* 495:106-16.

Birnie, Patricia W., and Alan E. Boyle. 1992. *International Law and the Environment*. Oxford, England: Clarendon Press.

Birnie, Patricia W. 1992. "International Environmental Law." In *The International Politics of the Environment*, edited by Andrew Hurrell and Benedict Kingsbury, pp. 51-84. Oxford, England: Clarendon Press.

Birnie, Patricia W. 1988. "The Role of International Law in Solving Certain Environmental Conflicts." In *International Environmental Diplomacy: The Management and Resolution of Transfrontier Environmental Problems*, edited by James E. Carroll, pp. 95-121. Cambridge: Cambridge University Press.

Biswas, Asit K., ed. 1979. *The Ozone Layer*. Oxford, England: Pergamon/UNEP.

Boardman, Robert. 1981. *International Organization and the Conservation of Nature*. Bloomington: Indiana University Press.

Bobrow, Davis, and John Dryzek. 1987. *Policy Analysis by Design*. Pittsburgh: University of Pittsburgh Press.

Boxer, Baruch. 1983. "The Mediterranean Sea: Preparing and Implementing a Regional Action Plan." In *Environmental Protection: The International Dimension*, edited by David Kay and Harold K. Jacobson, pp. 267-309. Totowa, N.J..: Allanheld, Osmun.

Brennan, Timothy. 1989. *Salman Rushdie and the Third World: Myths of the Nation*. New York: St. Martin's Press.

Brown, Lester D. 1972. *World without Borders*. New York: Knopf.

Brown-Weiss, Edith, Paul C. Szasz, and Daniel Magraw, eds. 1992. *International Environmental Law Basic Instruments and References*. New York: Transnational Publishers.

Brownlie, Ian. 1990. *Principles of Public International Law*. 4th ed. Oxford, England: Clarendon Press.

Brownlie, Ian. 1983. *Basic Documents In International Law*. 3rd ed. Oxford: Clarendon Press.

Bruce, James P. 1991. "The World Climate Programme: Achievements and Challenges." In *Climate Change: Science, Impacts, and Policy*, edited by J. Jäger and H. L. Ferguson, pp. 149-155. Proceedings of the Second World Climate Conference. Cambridge, England: Cambridge University Press.

Bryner, Gary C. 1993. *Blue Skies, Green Politics: The Clean Air Act of 1990*. Washington, D.C.: CQ Press.

Buckley, James L. 1982. "The United Nations Environment Programme: A Ten-Year Retrospective." *Environmental Law* 3 (Winter):4-6.

Bührs, Ton, and Robert V. Bartlett. 1993. *Environmental Policy in New Zealand: The Politics of Clean and Green?* Auckland, New Zealand: Oxford University Press.

Buttel, Frederick. 1992. "Biodiversity Conservation: Socioeconomic and Ethical Implications." Paper presented at the conference on Environment and Development, University of Wisconsin, Madison, March 1992.

Cain, Melinda L. 1983. "Carbon Dioxide and the Climate: Monitoring and a Search for Understanding." In *Environmental Protection: The International Dimension*, edited by David Kay and Harold K. Jacobson, pp. 75-99. Totowa, N.J.: Allanheld, Osmun.

Caldwell, Lynton K. 1990a. *Between Two Worlds: Science, the Environmental Movement and Policy Choice*. Cambridge, England: Cambridge University Press.

Caldwell, Lynton K. 1990b. *International Environmental Policy: Emergence and Dimensions*. 2nd ed. Durham, N.C.: Duke University Press.

Caldwell, Lynton K. 1988. "Beyond Environmental Diplomacy: The Changing Institutional Structure of International Cooperation." In *International Environmental Diplomacy*, edited by James E. Carroll, pp. 13-27. Cambridge: Cambridge University Press.

Caldwell, Lynton K. 1972. *In Defense of Earth: International Protection of the Biosphere*. Bloomington: Indiana University Press.

Campbell, Laura. 1993. Interview with the Deputy Coordinator, Secretariat of the Vienna Convention and Montreal Protocol, United Nations Environment Programme, Nairobi, Kenya, May 1993.

Carr, Edward H. 1964. *Twenty Years' Crisis, 1919-1939*. New York: Harper and Row.

Centre for Our Common Future. 1992a. "The Role of NGOs in the Post-Rio Era." *Network*, no. 21 (November).

Centre for Our Common Future. 1992b. "General Assembly Creates CSD." *Network*, no. 21 (November):1,4.

Centre for Our Common Future. 1992c. "Progress towards ICPD '94: The United Nations Conference on Population and Development." *Network*, no. 21 (November):2.

Chayes, Abram, and Antonia H. Chayes. 1991. "Adjustment and Compliance Processes in International Regulatory Regimes." In *Preserving the Global Environment*, edited by Jessica T. Mathews, pp. 280-308. New York: W.W. Norton.

Chen, Lung-Chu. 1989. *An Introduction to Contemporary International Law*. New Haven, Conn: Yale University Press.

Claude, Inis. 1984. *Swords into Plowshares: The Problems and Progress of International Organization*. 4th ed. New York: Random House.

Claude, Inis. 1957. *Swords into Plowshares: The Problems and Progress of International Organization*. New York: Random House.

"Climate Change Convention Equity Concerns." 1992. *Climate-Related Impacts International Network Newsletter* 7 (2):3.

Cohen, Bernard C. 1963. *The Press and Foreign Policy*. Princeton, N.J.: Princeton University Press.

Cohen, M., J. March, and J. Olsen. 1972. "A Garbage Can Model of Organization Choice." *Administrative Science Quarterly* 17 (March):1-25.

Colorado Journal of International Law and Policy. 1993. Vol. 4 (1):whole issue.

Commission of the European Communities. 1990a. *Environmental Policy in the European Community*. Luxembourg: Office for Official Publications of the European Communities.

Commission of the European Communities. 1990b. "Monitoring the Implementation of Community Law on the Environment." Information Memo, pp. 1-4, February 8.

Commission of the European Communities. 1988. "Communication to the Council: The Greenhouse Effect and the Community, Commission World Programme concerning the Evaluation of Policy Options to Deal with the Greenhouse Effect and Draft Council Resolution on the Greenhouse Effect and the Community." *COM* (88):656.

Conable, Barber. 1987. "Address to the World Resources Institute." Washington, D.C.: World Bank, 5 May.

Cook, Timothy E. 1989. *Making Laws and Making News*. Washington, D.C.: Brookings Institution.

"Copenhagen Revisions." 1992. Fourth meeting of the Parties to the Montreal Protocol on Substances That Deplete the Ozone Layer, Copenhagen, Denmark. UNEP/Oz.L.Pro.4/15.

Council on Environmental Quality. 1989. *Environmental Quality: Twentieth Annual Report*. Washington, D.C.: Council on Environmental Quality.

Council on Environmental Quality. 1985. *Environmental Quality: Sixteenth Annual Report*. Washington, D.C.: Council on Environmental Quality.

Cox, Robert W. 1981. "Social Forces, States, and World Orders: Beyond International Relations Theory." *Millenium* 10 (Summer):126-55.

Cox, Robert W., and Harold K. Jacobson. 1973. *The Anatomy of Influence: Decision-Making in International Organizations*. New Haven, Conn.: Yale University Press.

Craig, Gordon A., and Alexander L. George. 1990. *Force and Statecraft*. 2nd ed. New York: Oxford University Press.

Crockett, Tamara Raye, and Cynthia B. Schultz. 1991. "The Integration of Environmental Policy and the European Community: Recent Problems of Implementation and Enforcement." *Columbia Journal of Transnational Law* 29 (1):169-91.

Cronon, William. 1993. "The Uses of Environmental History." *Environmental History Review* 17 (3):1-22.

Cyert, R. M. and J. G. March. 1963. *A Behavioral Theory of the Firm*. Englewood Cliffs, N.J.: Prentice-Hall.

Dahlberg, Kenneth A., Marvin S. Soroos, Anne T. Feraru, James E. Harf, and B. Thomas Trout. 1985. *Environment and the Global Arena: Actors, Values, Policies, and Futures*. Durham, NC: Duke University Press.

Daltrop, Anne. 1986. *Politics and the European Community*. New York: Longman.

D'Anieri, Paul. 1993. "Distributive Issues in International Environmental Cooperation." Paper presented at the annual meeting of the International Studies Association, Acapulco, Mexico, 24-27 March.

Dasmann, Raymond F. 1988. "Toward a Biosphere Consciousness." In *The Ends of the Earth: Perspectives on Modern Environmental History*, edited by Donald Worster, pp. 277-88. New York: Cambridge University Press.

Davies, Sir Arthur. 1990. *Forty Years of Progress and Achievement: A Historical Review of WMO*. Geneva: WMO Publication no. 731.

De Groot, Cocky. 1989. "The International Debate on the Consequences of Biotechnology." Master's Thesis, University of Nijmegen, the Netherlands.

Deutsch, Karl W. 1966. *The Nerves of Government*. New York: Free Press.

Diesing, Paul. 1982. *Science and Ideology in the Policy Sciences*. Hawthorne, N.Y.: Aldine.

Diesing, Paul. 1962. *Reason in Society: Five Types of Decisions and Their Social Conditions*. Urbana: University of Illinois Press.

Dluhy, M. J. 1990. *Building Coalitions in the Human Services*. Newbury Park, Calif: Sage Publications.

Doniger, David D. 1988. "Politics of the Ozone Layer." *Issues in Science and Technology* 4 (3):86-92.

Donnelly, Jack. 1990. "Global Policy Studies: A Skeptical View." *Journal of Peace Research* 27 (2):221-30.

Donnelly, Jack. 1986. "International Human Rights: A Regime Analysis." *International Organization* 40 (Autumn):599-642.

Donoghue, Joan E. 1992. "Legal Dimensions of Compliance and Dispute Resolution in a Global Climate Regime." Paper presented the annual conference of the International Studies Association, Atlanta, Georgia, 31 March-4 April.

Dotto, Lydia, and Harold Schiff. 1978. *The Ozone War*. Garden City, N.Y.: Doubleday.

Downie, David L. 1995. Understanding International Environmental Regimes: The Origins, Creation and Expansion of the Ozone Regime. Ph.D. diss. University of North Carolina.

Dryzek, John S. 1987. *Rational Ecology*. New York: Basil Blackwell.

Dunlap, Thomas. 1988. *Saving America's Wildlife*. Princeton, N.J.: Princeton University Press.

Ehrenfeld, David. 1981. *The Arrogance of Humanism*. New York: Oxford University Press.

Ellul, Jacques. 1964. *The Technological Society*. Translated by John Wilkinson. New York: Alfred A. Knopf.

Elsom, Derek. 1987. *Atmospheric Pollution*. Oxford, England: Basil Blackwell.

Environment. 1992. Vol. 34 (8):whole issue.

"Environmental Concerns Set Global Regulatory Trend." 1990. *Transnationals: Quarterly Newsletter of the United Nations Centre on Transnational Corporations* 2 (4):1-2, 6.

Environmental Policy and Law. 1992. Vol. 22 (4):whole issue.

Environmental Protection Agency. 1990. "Policy Options for Stabilizing Global Climate Change." Report to Congress, Office of Policy, Planning, and Evaluation, Washington, D.C.

Erbring, Lutz, Edie Goldenberg, and Arthur Miller. 1980. "Front-Page News and Real World Cues: A New Look at Agenda Setting by the Media." *American Journal of Political Science* 24 (1):16-49.

Esquinas Alcázar, José. 1990. "FAO Global System on Plant Genetic Resources." Results of the third session of the FAO Commission on Plant Genetic Resources, Rome, Italy.

Etheredge, L. S. 1979. *Government Learning*. Cambridge, Mass.: Center for International Studies, Massachusetts Institute of Technology.

European Communities. 1988a. "Decision 540/88 of 14 October 1988 Concerning the Conclusion of the Vienna Convention for the Protection of the Ozone Layer and the Montreal Protocol on Substances That Deplete the Ozone Layer." *OJ: Official Journal of the European Communities* L397 (31 October):8.

European Communities. 1988b. "Regulation 3322/88 of 14 October 1988 on Certain Chlorofluorocarbons and Halon which Deplete the Ozone Layer." *OJ: Official Journal of the European Communities* L297 (31 October):1.

European Communities. 1988c. "Resolution of 14 October 1988 for the Limitation of Use of Chlorofluorocarbons and Halons." *OJ: Official Journal of the European Communities* C285 (9 November):1.

European Communities. 1982. "Decision 82/795 of 15 November 1982 on the Consolidation of Precautionary Measures Concerning Chlorofluorocarbons in the Environment." *OJ: Official Journal of the European Communities* L329 (25 November):29.

European Communities. 1980. "Decision 80/372 of 26 March 1980 Concerning Chlorofluorocarbons in the Environment." *OJ: Official Journal of the European Communities* L90 (3 April):45.

European Communities. 1978. "Council Resolution of 30 May 1978 on Chlorofluorocarbons in the Environment." *OJ: Official Journal of the European Communities* C133 (7 June):1.

Falk, Richard A. 1972. *This Endangered Planet: Prospects and Proposals for Survival.* New York: Random House.

Falloux, François, and Lee Talbot. 1992. *Crise et opportunité: Environnement et développement en Afrique.* Paris: Maisonneuve et Larose.

Falloux, François. 1989. "Land Information and Remote Sensing for Renewable Resource Management in Sub-Saharan Africa." World Bank Technical Paper no.108, Washington, D.C.

FAO Commission on Plant Genetic Resources. 1991. *The International Undertaking on Plant Genetic Resources.* Rome: FAO.

Farman, Joseph C., et al. 1985. "Large Losses of Total Ozone in Antarctica Reveal Seasonal ClOx/NOx Interaction." *Nature* 315 (16 May):207-10.

Feld, Werner J., and Robert S. Jordan with Leon Hurwitz. 1988. *International Organizations: A Comparative Perspective.* New York: Praeger.

Feldman, David L. 1991. "International Decision Making for Global Climate Change." *Society and Natural Resources* 4 (4):379-96.

Ferretti, Janine. 1993. *Elements of an Effective North American Commission on the Environment.* Toronto, Ontario: Pollution Probe.

"Final Statement of the Second World Climate Conference, Geneva, Switzerland, 29 October-7 November 1990." 1991. *Environmental Conservation* 18 (1):62-66.

Finger, Matthias. 1991. "The Role of Environmental NGOs in the UNCED Process." Paper presented at the seminar on International Environmental NGOs, The Great Lakes and Beyond. School of Natural Resources, University of Michigan, 18-19 October.

Fisher, Roger. 1981. *Improving Compliance with International Law.* Charlottesville: University of Virginia Press.

Fowler Cary, et al. 1988. "The Laws of Life: Another Development and the New Biotechnologies." *Development Dialogue* 1-2:1-350.

Foy, George, and Herman Daly. 1989. "Allocation, Distribution and Scale as Determinants of Environmental Degradation: Case Studies of Haiti, El Salvador and Costa Rica." World Bank Environment Department Technical Paper no. 19, Washington, D.C.

"Framework Convention on Climate Change." 1992. *International Legal Materials* 31:849-73.

Franck, Thomas. 1990. *The Power of Legitimacy among Nations.* New York: Oxford University Press.

Freestone, David. 1991. "European Community Environmental Policy and Law." *Journal of Law and Society* 18 (1):135-54.

French, Hillary F. 1992. *After the Earth Summit: The Future of Environmental Governance.* World Watch Paper 107. Washington, D.C.: Worldwatch Institute.

Gallarotti, Giulio M. 1991. "The Limits of International Organization: Systematic Failure in the Management of International Relations." *International Organization* 45 (2):183-220.

Gehring, Thomas. 1990. "International Environmental Regimes: Dynamic Sectoral Legal Systems." In *Yearbook of International Environmental Law*, edited by Gunther Handl, vol 1, pp. 35-56. London: Graham and Trotman.

General Accounting Office. 1992. *International Environment: International Agreements Are Not Well Monitored*. Washington, D.C.: General Accounting Office.

George, Stephen. 1985. *Politics and Policy in the European Community*. Oxford, England: Clarendon Press.

Glantz, Michael H. 1990. "Assessing the Impacts of Climate: The Issue of Winners and Losers in a Global Context." In *Changing Climate and the Coast*, NCAR 0101/90-4. Washington, D.C.: Environmental Protection Agency.

Goldemberg, J. 1990. "How to Stop Global Warming." *Technology Review* 93 (8):25-31.

Goldie, L. F. E. 1962. "Special Regimes and Pre-Emptive Activities in International Law." *International Law and Comparative Quarterly* 11 (July):670-700.

Goodland, Robert. 1992. "Environmental Priorities for Financing Institutions." *Environmental Conservation* 19 (1):9-21.

Goodland, Robert. 1991. "The World Bank's Environmental Assessment Policy." *Hastings International and Comparative Law Review* 14 (4):811-30.

Goodland, Robert. 1990. "New Environmental Assessment Unit Promotes Operational Directive to Share 'Best Practice' Experience." *Environment Bulletin* 2 (2):6-7.

Goodland, Robert, Anastacio Juras, and Rajendra Pachauri. 1992. "Can Hydroreservoirs in Tropical Moist Forests Be Made Environmentally Acceptable?" *Energy Policy* 20 (6):507-15.

Gore, Al. 1992. *Earth in the Balance: Ecology and the Human Spirit*. New York: Houghton Mifflin.

Grieco, Joseph M. 1988. "Anarchy and the Limits of Cooperation: A Realist Critique of the Newest Liberal Institutionalism." *International Organization* 42 (Summer):485-507.

Grubb, Michael. 1990. *The Greenhouse Effect: Negotiating Targets*. London: The Royal Institute of International Affairs.

Grunberg, Isabelle. 1990. "Exploring the 'Myth' of Hegemonic Stability." *International Organization* 44 (Autumn):431-77.

Haas, Ernst B. 1990. *When Knowledge Is Power: Three Models of Change in International Organizations*. Berkeley: University of California Press.

Haas, Ernst B. 1982. "Words Can Hurt You: Or Who Said What to Whom About Regimes." *International Organization* 36 (2):23-59.

Haas, Ernst B. 1968. *The Uniting of Europe: Political, Social and Economic Forces, 1950-1957*. Stanford, Calif.: Stanford University Press.

Haas, Ernst B. 1964. *Beyond the Nation-State: Functionalism and International Organization*. Stanford, Calif: Stanford University Press.

Haas, Peter M., Robert O. Keohane, and Marc A. Levy, eds. 1993. *Institutions for the Earth: Sources of Effective International Environmental Protection*. Cambridge, Mass: Massachussetts Institute of Technology Press.

Haas, Peter M. 1992a. "Banning Chlorofluorocarbons: Epistemic Community Efforts to Protect Stratospheric Ozone." *International Organization* 46 (1):187-224.

Haas, Peter M. 1992b. "Introduction: Epistemic Communities and International Policy Coordination." *International Organization* 46 (1):1-36.

Haas, Peter M., ed. 1992c. "Knowledge, Power and International Policy Coordination." *International Organization* 46 (1):whole issue.

Haas, Peter M. 1990. *Saving the Mediterranean: The Politics of International Environmental Cooperation.* New York: Columbia University Press.

Haas, Peter M. 1989. "Do Regimes Matter? Epistemic Communities and Mediterranean Pollution Control." *International Organization* 43 (Summer):377-403.

Haggard, Stephan, and Beth A. Simmons. 1987. "Theories of International Regimes." *International Organization* 41 (3):491-517.

Hagland, Paul. 1991. "Environmental Policy." In *The State of the European Community*, edited by Leon Hurwitz and Christian Lequesne, pp. 259-72. Boulder, Colo: Lynne Reinner.

Haigh, Nigel. 1990. Personal communication with the Director, IEEP, London, England.

Haigh, Nigel. 1989. *EEC Environmental Policy and Britain.* 2nd ed. London: Longman.

Haigh, Nigel, et al. 1986. *European Community Environmental Policy in Practice.* Vol. 1. London: Graham and Trotman.

Hampson, Fen Osler. 1989-90. "Climate Change: Building International Coalitions of the Like-Minded." *International Journal* XLV (Winter):36-74.

Handl, Gunther, ed. 1991. *Yearbook of International Environmental Law.* Vol. 2. London: Graham and Trotman.

Hardin, Russell. 1982. *Collective Action.* Baltimore, Md: Johns Hopkins University Press.

Harvard Law Review. 1991. "Developments in the Law: International Environmental Law." 1991. *Harvard Law Review* 104 (7):1484-639.

Hayter, Teresa and Catharine Watson. 1985. *Aid: Rhetoric and Reality.* London: Pluto Press.

Hedberg, Bo. 1981. "How Organizations Learn and Unlearn." In *Handbook of Organizational Design*, edited by P. C. Nystrom and W. H. Starbuck, pp. 3-27. London: Oxford University Press.

Higgins, Rosalyn. 1993. "International Law and the Avoidance, Containment and Resolution of Disputes." In *Recueil des Cours*, pp. 23-41. Dordrecht, Netherlands: Martinus Nijhoff.

Hofferbert, R. 1974. *The Study of Public Policy.* Indianapolis, Ind: Bobbs-Merrill.

Hoffman, Stanley. 1985. "The Uses and Limits of International Law." In *International Politics: Anarchy, Force, Political Economy, and Decision Making*, edited by Robert J. Art and Robert Jervis, pp. 126-30. Boston: Little, Brown.

Holsti, Ole, et al., ed. 1980. *Changes in the International System.* Boulder, Colo: Westview Press.

Houghton, J. T., G. J. Jenkins, and J. J. Ephraums, eds. 1990. *Climate Change: The IPCC Scientific Assessment.* New York: Cambridge University Press.

Hudson, Stewart A., and Rodrigo J. Prudencio. 1993. *The North American Commission on Environmental and Other Supplemental Environmental Agreements*. Washington, D.C.: National Wildlife Federation.

Hughes, Donald J. 1975. *Ecology in Ancient Civilizations*. Albuquerque: University of New Mexico Press.

Hulm, Peter. 1983. "The Regional Seas Program: What Fate for UNEP's Crown Jewels?" *Ambio* 12 (1):2-16.

Hurrell, Andrew. 1993. "International Society and the Study of Regimes: A Reflective Approach." In *Regime Theory and International Relations*, edited by Volker Rittberger. Oxford, England: Clarendon Press.

Hurrell, Andrew, and Benedict Kingsbury. 1992a. "The International Politics of the Environment: An Introduction." In *The International Politics of the Environment: Actors, Interests, and Institutions*, edited by Andrew Hurrell and Benedict Kingsbury, pp. 1-47. New York: Oxford University Press.

Hurrell, Andrew, and Benedict Kingsbury, eds. 1992b. *The International Politics of the Environment: Actors, Interests, and Institutions*. New York: Oxford University Press.

Ingram, Helen and Anne Schneider. 1993. "Social Construction of Target Populations: Implications for Politics and Policy," *American Political Science Review* 87 (2):334-47.

Intergovernmental Panel on Climate Change. 1990. *Climate Change: The Scientific Assessment*. New York: Cambridge University Press.

International Chamber of Commerce. 1989. *Environmental Auditing: The ICC Working Party on Environmental Auditing*. Paris: International Chamber of Commerce.

IUCN-World Conservation Union Bulletin. 1992. Vol. 23 (3):whole issue.

Iyengar, Shanto. 1991. *Is Anyone Responsible? How Television Frames Political Issues*. Chicago: University of Chicago Press.

Izrael, Uri. 1991. Personal interview, Moscow, December 2.

Jachtenfuchs, Markus. 1990. "The European Community and the Protection of the Ozone Layer." *Journal of Common Market Studies* 28 (March):261-77.

Jacobson, Harold K. 1984. *Networks of Interdependence: International Organizations and the Global Political System*. 2nd ed. New York: Alfred A. Knopf.

Jacobson, Harold K. 1979. *Networks of Interdependence: International Organizations and the Global Political System*. New York: Alfred A. Knopf.

Jaeger, Jill. 1988. "Developing Policies for Responding to Climate Change." WMO/TD-225. A Summary of Workshops at Villach, October 1987, and Bellagio, November 1987, World Meteorological Organization, Geneva, Switzerland.

Jaycox, Edward V. K. 1992. *The Challenges of African Development*. Washington, D.C.: World Bank, Africa Region.

Jenkins-Smith, Hank C. 1991. "Alternative Theories of the Policy Process: Reflections on Research Strategy for the Study of Nuclear Waste Policy." *PS: Political Science and Politics* 24 (2):157-66.

Johnson, S. P. and G. Corcelle. 1989. *The Environmental Policy of the European Communities*. London: Graham and Trotman.

Kaelberer, Matthias. 1992. "State Power and International Environmental Cooperation: A Comparison of Collaborative Efforts on Global Warming and Ozone Layer Depletion." Paper prepared for the International Studies Association Convention, Atlanta, Georgia, 31 March-4 April.

Kahler, Miles. 1992. "Multilateralism with Small and Large Numbers." *International Organization* 46 (3):681-708.

Kathlene, Lyn. 1990. "A New Approach to Understanding the Impact of Gender on the Legislative Process." In *Feminist Research Methods*, edited by Joyce M. Nielsen, pp. 238-260. Boulder, Colo: Westview Press.

Kathlene, Lyn. 1989. "Uncovering the Political Impacts of Gender: An Exploratory Study." *Western Political Quarterly* 42 (2):397-421.

Kay, David A., and Harold K. Jacobson, eds. 1983. *Environmental Protection: The International Dimension*. Totowa, N.J.: Allanheld, Osmun.

Kay, David A., and Eugene Skolnikoff, eds. 1972. *World Eco-Crisis: International Organizations in Response*. Madison: University of Wisconsin Press.

Kelsen, Hans. 1952. Principles of International Law. New York: Rinehart.

Kennedy, David. 1987. "The Move to Institutions." *Cardozo Law Review* 8 (April):841-988.

Keohane, Robert O. 1990. "Multilateralism: An Agenda For Research." *International Journal* 45 (4):731-64.

Keohane, Robert O. 1989. *International Institutions and State Power*. Boulder, Colo: Westview Press.

Keohane, Robert O. 1988. "International Institutions: Two Approaches." *International Studies Quarterly* 32 (4):379-96.

Keohane, Robert O. 1986. "Realism, Neorealism, and the Study of World Politics." In *Neorealism and its Critics*, edited by Robert O. Keohane, pp. 1-26. New York: Columbia University Press.

Keohane, Robert. 1984. *After Hegemony: Collaboration and Discord in the World Political Economy*. Princeton, N.J.: Princeton University Press.

Keohane, Robert. 1983. "The Demand for International Regimes." In *International Regimes*, edited by Stephen D. Krasner, pp. 141-71. Ithaca, N.Y.: Cornell University Press.

Keohane, Robert O. 1980. "The Theory of Hegemonic Stability and Changes in International Economic Regimes." In *Changes in the International System*, edited by Ole R. Holsti, et al, pp. 131-62. Boulder, Colo: Westview Press.

Keohane, Robert O., and Robert Axelrod. 1986. "Achieving Cooperation Under Anarchy: Strategies and Institutions." In *Cooperation under Anarchy*, edited by Kenneth Oye, pp. 226-54. Princeton, N.J.: Princeton University Press.

Keohane, Robert O., and Stanley Hoffman. 1991. "Institutional Change in Europe in the 1980s." In *The New European Community: Decisionmaking and Institutional Change*, edited by Robert O. Keohane and Stanley Hoffman, pp. 1-39. Boulder, Colo: Westview Press.

Keohane, Robert O., and Joseph S. Nye. 1977. *Power and Interdependence: World Politics in Transition*. Boston: Little Brown.

Keohane, Robert O., and Joseph S. Nye. 1971. *Transnational Relations and World Politics*. Cambridge, Mass.: Harvard University Press.

Kerr, Robert A. 1988. "Stratospheric Ozone is Decreasing." *Science* 239 (4847):1489-91.

Kevles, D. J. 1992. "Some Like It Hot." *New York Review of Books* (26 March): 31-34, 36-39.

Kimball, Lee A. 1992. *Forging International Agreement: Strengthening Intergovernmental Institutions for Environment and Development.* Washington, D.C.: World Resources Institute.

King, Alexander, and Bertrand Schneider. 1991. *The First Global Revolution: A Report by the Council of the Club of Rome.* New York: Pantheon Books.

Kingdon, John W. 1984. *Agendas, Alternatives, and Public Policy.* Boston: Little, Brown.

Kiss, Alexandre. 1991. "Present Limits to the Enforcement of State Responsibility for Environmental Damage." *International Responsibility for Environmental Harm*, edited by F. Francioni and T. Scovazzi, pp. 3-14. London: Graham and Trotman.

Kiss, Alexandre, and Dinah Shelton. 1991. *International Environmental Law.* New York: Transnational Publishers.

Klein, M. W., and N. Maccoby. 1954. "Newspaper Objectivity in the 1952 Campaign," *Journalism Quarterly* 31:285-96.

Köhler, A. 1988. "WMO's Activities on Background Atmospheric Pollution and Integrated Monitoring and Research." *Environmental Monitoring and Assessment* 11:253-68.

Korten, David C. 1991. "Sustainable Development." *World Policy Journal* 9 (1):157-90.

Koskenniemi, Martti. 1993. "Breach of Treaty of Non-Compliance? Reflections on the Enforcement of the Montreal Protocol." *Yearbook of International Environmental Law* 3:123-62.

Kramer, Ludwig. 1987. "The Single European Act and Environmental Protection: Reflections on Several New Provisions in Community Law." *Common Market Law Review* 24 (4):659-688.

Krasner, Stephen D. 1991. "Global Communications and National Power: Life on the Pareto Frontier." *World Politics* 43 (3):336-66.

Krasner, Stephen D. 1988. "Sovereignty: An Institutional Perspective." *Comparative Political Studies* 21 (1):66-94.

Krasner, Stephen D. 1985. *Structural Conflict: The Third World against Global Liberalism.* Berkeley: University of California Press.

Krasner, Stephen D., ed. 1983a. *International Regimes.* Ithaca, N.Y.: Cornell University Press.

Krasner, Stephen D. 1983b. "Regimes and the Limits of Realism: Regimes as Autonomous Variables." In *International Regimes*, edited by Stephen D. Krasner, pp. 355-68. Ithaca, N.Y.: Cornell University Press.

Krasner, Stephen D. 1983c. "Structural Causes and Regime Consequences: Regimes as Intervening Variables." In *International Regimes*, edited by Stephen D. Krasner, pp. 1-21. Ithaca, N.Y.: Cornell University Press.

Krasner, Stephen D. 1982. "Structural Causes and Regime Consequences: Regimes as Intervening Variables." *International Organization* 36 (Spring):185.

Krasner, Stephen D. 1976. "State Power and the Structure of International Trade." *World Politics* 28 (April):317-43.

Kratochwil, Friedrich V. 1989. *Rules, Norms and Decisions.* Cambridge, England: Cambridge University Press.

Kratochwil, Friedrich, and John G. Ruggie. 1986. "International Organization: A State of the Art or an Art of the State." *International Organization* 40 (4):753-75.

Kuwabara, Sachiko. 1984. *The Legal Regime of the Protection of the Mediterranean Against Pollution from Land-Based Sources.* Dublin, Ireland: Tycoon International Publishing.

Lang, Winfried. 1993. "Diplomacy and International Environmental Law-Making: Some Observations." *Yearbook of International Environmental Law* 3:108-22.

Lasswell, Harold D. 1950. "The Policy Orientation." In *The Policy Sciences,* edited by David Lerner and Harold D. Lasswell, pp. 9-15. Stanford, Calif.: Stanford University Press.

Leonard, H. Jeffrey, ed. 1989. *Environment and the Poor: Development Strategies for a Common Agenda.* Washington, D.C.: Overseas Development Council.

Le Prestre, Philippe. 1989. *The World Bank and the Environmental Challenge.* Selinsgrove, Pa.: Susquehanna University Press.

Le Prestre, Philippe. 1986. "The Problematique of International Organizations." *International Social Science Journal* 38 (1):127-38.

Lewis, H. L. 1960. "The Cuban Revolt Story: AP, UPI, and 3 Papers," *Journalism Quarterly* 37:573-78.

Liberatore, Angela. 1991. "Problems of Transnational Policymaking: Environmental Policy in the European Community." *European Journal of Political Research* 19:281-305.

Lindberg, Leon. 1963. *The Political Dynamics of European Economic Integration.* Stanford, Calif.: Stanford University Press.

Linsky, Martin. 1986. *Impact: How the Press Affects Federal Policymaking.* New York: W. W. Norton.

Linstone, H. A. 1984. *Multiple Perspectives for Decision-Making: Bridging the Gap between Analysis and Action.* New York: Elsevier.

Lipson, Charles. 1991. "Why Are Some International Agreements Informal?" *International Organization* 45 (Autumn):495-538.

Liska, George. 1957. *International Equilibrium.* Cambridge, Mass: Harvard University Press.

List, Martin, and Volker Rittberger. 1992. "Regime Theory and International Environmental Management." In *International Politics of the Environment,* edited by Andrew Hurrell and Benedict Kingsbury, pp. 85-109. Oxford, England: Clarendon Press.

"London Revisions to the Montreal Protocol on Substances That Deplete the Ozone Layer." 1991. *International Legal Materials* 30 (6):1594-1623.

Lovelock, James E. 1986. "The Earth As a Living Organism." In *Biodiversity,* edited by E.O. Wilson, pp. 486-89. Washington, D.C.: National Academy Press.

Lowe, Philip. 1989-90. Personal communication with Lecturer in Countryside Planning, University College, London, England.

Lowi, Theodore J. 1972. "Four Systems of Policy, Politics, and Choice." *Public Administration Review* 32:298-310.

Machiavelli, Niccolo. 1518. *Discourses on the First Ten Books of Titus Livy.* Book 3, chapter 9.

Mackie, T. T. 1990. *Europe Votes 3.* Aldershot, England: Dartmouth.

MacKuen, Michael, and Steven Coombs. 1981. *More than News: Media Power in Public Affairs.* Newbury Park, Calif.: Sage.

MacNeill, Jim, Pieter Winsemius, and Taizo Yakushiji. 1991. *Beyond Interdependence: The Meshing of the World's Economy and the Earth's Ecology.* New York: Oxford University Press.

Magrath, William B., and John B. Doolette. 1990. "Strategic Issues for Watershed Development in Asia." Environment Working Paper no. 30. World Bank, Environment Department, Washington, D.C.

Majone, Giandomenico. 1989. *Evidence, Argument, and Persuasion in the Policy Process.* New Haven, Conn.: Yale University Press.

Majone, Giandomenico. 1986. "Analyzing the Public Sector: Shortcomings of Current Approaches. Part A. Policy Science." In *Guidance, Control, and Evaluation in the Public Sector,* edited by Franz-Xaver Kaufmann, Giandomenico Majone, and Vincent Ostrom, pp. 61-70. New York: Walter de Gruyter.

Malone, Thomas P. 1992. Personal interview, Raleigh, North Carolina, 25 March.

Malone, Thomas P. 1986. "Mission to Planet Earth." *Environment* 28 (8):6-11, 39-42.

Manno, Jack. 1992. *Advocacy and Diplomacy in the Great Lakes: A Case History of NGO Participation in World Environmental Politics.* Syracuse, N.Y.: Great Lakes Research Consortium, Sunny College of Environmental Science and Policy.

Mansfield, W. H. 1993. Interview with the Special Representative of the Executive Director, United Nations Environment Programme, Nairobi, Kenya, 4 May.

Margulis, L. and James E. Lovelock. 1974. "Biological Modulation of the Earth's Atmosphere." *Icarus* 21:471-489.

Markham, J. W. and G. H. Stempel III. 1957. "Analysis of Techniques Measuring Press Performance." *Journalism Quarterly* 34:187-90.

Martin, Lisa L. 1992. "Interests, Power, and Multilateralism." *International Organization* 46 (4):767-792.

Mathews, Jessica Tuchman, ed. 1991. *Preserving the Global Environment.* New York: W. W. Norton.

Maxwell, James H., and Sanford L. Weiner. 1993. "Green Consciousness or Dollar Diplomacy? The British Response to the Threat of Ozone Depletion." *International Environmental Affairs* 5 (Winter):19-41.

McCombs, Maxwell E., and Donald L. Shaw. 1972. "The Agenda-Setting Function of Mass Media." *Public Opinion Quarterly* 36:176-184.

McCormick, John. 1995. *The European Union: Politics and Policies.* Boulder, Colo.: Westview.

McCormick, John. 1991. *British Politics and the Environment.* London: Earthscan.

McCormick, John. 1989a. *Acid Earth: The Global Threat of Acid Pollution.* London: Earthscan.

McCormick, John. 1989b. *Reclaiming Paradise: The Global Environmental Movement*. Bloomington: Indiana University Press.

McCully, Patrick. 1992. "The Most Arrogant Institution in the World." *Econet* (web:en.unced.news) June 5.

McDougal, Myres S., and Harold D. Lasswell. 1959. "The Identification and Appraisal of Diverse Systems of Public Order." *American Journal of International Law* 53 (January):1-29.

McKay, Gordon A. and Henry Hengeveld. 1990. "The Changing Atmosphere." *Planet Under Stress* edited by Constance Mungall and Digby J. McLaren, pp. 46-79. New York: Oxford University Press.

Merchant, Carolyn. 1980. *Death of Nature: Women, Ecology, and the Scientific Revolution*. San Francisco: Harper and Row.

Mikesell, Raymond F., and Larry Williams. 1992. *International Banks and the Environment*. San Francisco: Sierra Club Books.

Miller, Susan. 1978. "Congressional Committee Hearings and the Media: Rules of the Game." *Journalism Quarterly* (Winter):657-663.

Mitrany, David. 1966. *A Working Peace System*. Introduction by Hans J. Morgenthau. Chicago: Quadrangle Books.

Mitrany, David. 1946. *A Working Peace System*. Chicago: University of Chicago Press.

Mitrany, David. 1943. *A Working Peace System*. London: Royal Institute of International Affairs.

Miyazawa, Kiichi. 1992. "Creating a Policy Framework for the Rio Process." *Earth Summit Times*, 14 September, p. 10.

Molina, Mario J., and F. Sherwood Rowland. 1974. "Stratospheric Sink for Chlorofluoromethanes: Chlorine Atomic Catalyzed Destruction of Ozone." *Nature* 249 (28 June):810-12.

"Montreal Protocol on Substances That Deplete the Ozone Layer." 1987. *International Legal Materials* 26 (6):1541-61.

Mooney, Pat Roy. 1979. *Seeds of the Earth: A Private or a Public Resource?* Ottawa, Ontario: Inter Paris.

Morel, Pierre. 1991. "Overview of the World Climate Research Programme." *Climate Change: Science, Impacts, and Policy*, edited by J. Jäger and H. L. Ferguson, pp. 9-12. Proceedings of the Second World Climate Conference. Cambridge, England: Cambridge University Press.

Morgenthau, Hans J. 1973. *Politics among Nations: The Struggle for Power and Peace*. 5th ed. New York: Alfred A. Knopf.

Morgenthau, Hans J. 1967. *Politics among Nations: The Struggle for Power and Peace*. 4th ed. New York: Alfred A. Knopf.

Morrisette, Peter M. 1991. "The Montreal Protocol: Lessons for Formulating Policies for Global Warming." *Policy Studies Journal* 19 (Spring):152-161.

Morse, Bradford, and Thomas Berger. 1992. *Sardar Sarovar: Report of the Independent Review*. Washington, D.C.: World Bank.

Nadelmann, Ethan A. 1990. "Global Prohibition Regimes: The Evolution of Norms in International Society." *International Organization* 44 (Autumn):479-526.

Nagel, Stuart S., ed. 1991. *Global Policy Studies: International Interaction toward Improving Public Policy*. New York: St. Martin's Press.

NASA. 1988. "Executive Summary of the Ozone Trends Panel." NASA, Office of Management, Scientific and Technical Information Division, Washington, D.C., 15 March.

National Climate Program Office. 1991. *Climate Issues: Synopsis of First Negotiating Session of the INC for a Framework Convention on Climate Change and U. S. Institutional Involvement*. Vol. 2, no. 2. Washington, D.C.: NCPO.

Nelson, B. J. 1984. *Making an Issue of Child Abuse*. Chicago: University of Chicago Press.

Ness, Gayl D., and Steven R. Brechin. 1988. "Bridging the Gap: International Organizations as Organizations." *International Organization* 42 (2):245-273.

New York Times. 14 April 1992.

New York Times. 15 November 1993.

Niebuhr, Rheinhold. 1949. "The Illusion of World Government." *Foreign Affairs* 27:379-88.

Nitze, W. 1990. *The Greenhouse Effect: Formulating a Convention*. London: Energy and Environmental Programme, Royal Institute of International Affairs.

Nye, Joseph S. 1971. "Comparing Common Markets: A Revised Neo-functionalist Model." In *Regional Integration: Theory and Research*, edited by Leon N. Lindberg and Stuart A. Scheingold, pp. 192-231. Cambridge, Mass.: Harvard University Press.

Olson, Mancur. 1965. *The Logic of Collective Action: Public Goods and the Theory of Groups*. Cambridge, Mass.: Harvard University Press.

Ophuls, William, and A. Stephen Boyan, Jr. 1992. *Ecology and the Politics of Scarcity Revisited*. New York: W. H. Freeman.

Organ, D. W. 1971. "Linking Pins between Organizations and Environment." *Business Horizons* 14:73-80.

Orr, David W. 1992. *Ecological Literacy: Education and the Transition to a Postmodern World*. Albany, N.Y.: State University of·New York Press.

Orr, David W. 1979. "Modernization and the Ecological Perspective." In *The Global Predicament: Ecological Perspectives in World Order*, edited by David W. Orr and Marvin S. Soroos, pp. 75-89. Chapel Hill: University of North Carolina Press.

Ostrom, Eleanor. 1986. "An Agenda for the Study of Institutions." *Public Choice* 48:2-25.

Oye, Kenneth A., ed. 1986a. *Cooperation Under Anarchy*. Princeton, N.J.: Princeton University Press.

Oye, Kenneth A. 1986b. "Explaining Cooperation Under Anarchy: Hypotheses and Strategies." In *Cooperation Under Anarchy*, edited by Kenneth A. Oye, pp. 1-24. Princeton, N.J.: Princeton University Press.

Padbry, Peter. 1993. "Non-Governmental Organization Alternative Treaties at the 1992 Global Forum." *Associations Transnationals* 4:193-99.

Paehlke, Robert C. and Douglas Torgerson, eds. 1990. *Managing Leviathan: Environmental Politics and the Administrative State*. Peterborough, Ontario: Broadview Press.

Palmer, Geoffrey. 1992. "New Ways to Make International Environmental Law." *American Journal of International Law* 86 (April):259-83.

Pearce, Fred. 1992. "Last Chance to Save the Planet?" *New Scientist* 134 (1823):24-28.

Peterson, M. J. 1992. "Whalers, Cetologists, Environmentalists, and the International Management of Whaling." *International Organization* 46 (1):147-86.

Petesch, Patti L. 1992. *North-South Environmental Strategies, Costs, and Bargains.* Policy Essay no. 5. Washington, D.C.: Overseas Development Council.

Petsonk, Carol A. 1990. "Recent Developments in International Organizations: The Role of the United Nations Environment Programme (UNEP) in the Development of International Environmental Law." *American University Journal of International Law and Policy* 5 (2):351-91.

Pistorius, Robin. 1992. "Was the US' Refusal to Sign the Biodiversity Convention Necessary?" *Biotechnology and Development Monitor* 12 (September):8-9.

Plant, Glen. 1991. "Institutional and Legal Responses to Global Warming." In *International Law and Global Climate Change*, edited by R. Churchill and D. Freestone, pp. 165-81. London: Graham and Trotman.

Plant, Glen. 1990. "Institutional and Legal Responses to Global Climate Change." *Millennium* 19 (3):413-28.

Porter, Gareth, and Janet W. Brown. 1991. *Global Environmental Politics.* Boulder, Colo.: Westview Press.

Prins, Gwyn. 1990. "Politics and the Environment." *International Affairs* 66 (4):711-30.

Protocol to the 1979 Convention on Long Range Trans-Boundary Air Pollution. 1986. Sofia, Yugoslavia, October 31.

Puchala, Donald J., and Raymond F. Hopkins. 1982. "International Regimes: Lessons from Inductive Analysis." *International Organization* 36 (Spring):246-67.

Redclift, Michael. 1987. *Sustainable Development: Exploring the Contradictions.* New York: Methuen.

Reisman, W. Michael. 1992. "International Law in Policy-Oriented Perspective." *Proceedings of the American Society of International Law*, 1-3 April 1992, pp. 101-20. Washington, D.C.

Rixecker, Stefanie. 1994. "Expanding the Discursive Context of Policy Design: A Matter of Feminist Standpoint Epistemology." *Policy Sciences* 27 (2-3):119-42.

Roan, Sharon L. 1989. *Ozone Crisis: The 15-Year Evolution of a Sudden Global Emergency.* Chichester, England: John Wiley and Sons.

Robinson, Nicholas, Parvez Hassan, and Françoise Burhenne-Guilmin, eds. 1992. *Agenda 21 and UNCED Proceedings.* 5 vols. Dobbs Ferry, N.Y.: Oceana Publications.

Rochester, John M. 1986. "The Rise and Fall of International Organization as a Field of Study." *International Organization* 40 (4):777-813.

Rogers, Everett M., and James W. Dearing. 1988. "Agenda-Setting Research: Where Has It Been, Where Is It Going?" *Communication Yearbook* 11:555-94.

Rosendal, Kristin G. 1991. *International Conservation of Biological Diversity: The Quest for Effective International Solutions.* Lysaker, Norway: Fridtjof Nansens Institute.

Rowlands, Ian, and Malory Greene. 1991. *Global Environmental Change and International Relations.* Basingstoke, England: Macmillan.

Royal Commission on Environmental Pollution. 1984. Annual Report. London: Her Majesty's Stationery Office.

Rubin, Jeffrey Z. 1993. "Third Party Roles: Mediation in International Environmental Disputes." In *International Environmental Negotiation*, edited by G. Sjostedt, pp. 275-90. Newbury Park, Calif.: Sage.

Ruggie, John G. 1979-80. "On the Problem of 'The Global Problematique': What Roles for International Organizations?" *Alternatives* 5 (4):517-50.

Ruggie, John G. 1975. "International Responses to Technology: Concepts and Trends." *International Organization* 29 (Summer):557-84.

Ruster, B., B. Sima, and M. Bock, eds. 1975- . *International Protection of the Environment: Treaties and Related Documents.* Dobbs Ferry, N.Y.: Oceana Publications.

Sabatier, Paul A. 1991. "Political Science and Public Policy." *PS: Political Science and Politics* 24 (2):147-56.

Sabatier, Paul A. 1988. "An Advocacy Coalition Framework of Policy Change and the Role of Policy-Oriented Learning Therein." *Policy Sciences* 21:129-68.

Sagoff, Mark. 1991. "Nature versus the Environment." *Philosophy and Public Policy* 11 (3):5-8.

Sand, Peter H. 1991a. "International Cooperation: The Environmental Experience." In *Preserving the Global Environment*, edited by Jessica T. Mathews, pp. 236-79. New York: W. W. Norton.

Sand, Peter H. 1991b. "Institutions For Global Change: Whither Environmental Governance?" *Policy Studies Journal* 19 (2):93-102.

Sanford, Jonathan E. 1982. *U.S. Foreign Policy and Multilateral Development Banks.* Boulder, Colo.: Westview Press.

Sarma, K. M. 1993. Interview with the Coordinator, Secretariat of the Vienna Convention and Montreal Protocol, United Nations Environment Programme, Nairobi, Kenya, 3 May.

Sbragia, Alberta. 1991. "The European Commission and Implementation: Environmental Policy in Comparative Perspective." Paper presented at the 1991 annual meeting of the American Political Science Association, Washington, D.C., 29 August-1 September.

Schachter, Oscar. 1991. *International Law in Theory and Practice.* Dordrecht, Netherlands: Martinus Nijhoff Publishers.

Schachter, Oscar. 1968. "Towards a Theory of International Obligation." *Virginia Journal of International Law* 8 (2):300-22.

Schattschneider, E. E. 1975. *The Semi-Sovereign People.* Hinsdale, Ill.: Dryden Press.

Schechter, Michael G. 1993. "The New Haven School of International Law, Regime Theorists, Their Critics and Beyond." Paper presented at the annual meeting of the International Studies Association, Acapulco, Mexico, 23-27 March.

Schechter, Michael G. 1990. "Intergovernmental Organization Executive Heads as Change Agents: A Comparative Inquiry." Paper presented at the annual meeting of the International Studies Association, Washington, D.C., 10-14 April.

Scheinman, Lawrence. 1987. *The International Atomic Energy Agency and World Nuclear Order.* A Resources for the Future Book. Washington, D.C.: Johns Hopkins Press.

Schelling, Thomas C. 1960. *The Strategy of Conflict.* Cambridge, Mass.: Harvard University Press.

Schildhauer, Johannes. 1985. *The Hanse: History and Culture.* Translated by Katherine Vanovitch. Leipzig, Germany: Edition Leipzig.

Schlozman, Kay Lehman, and John T. Tierney. 1986. *Organized Interests and American Democracy.* New York: Harper and Row.

Schnieder, Anne, and Helen Ingram. 1993. "Social Construction of Target Populations: Implications for Politics and Policy." *American Political Science Review* 87 (2):334-47.

Schön, Donald A. 1983. "Organizational Learning." *Beyond Method: Strategies for Social Research,* edited by Gareth Morgan, pp. 114-28. Beverly Hills, Calif.: Sage.

Schultz, Cynthia B., and Tamara Raye Crockett. 1991. "Developing a Unified European Environmental Law and Policy." *Boston College International and Comparative Law Review* 14 (2):301-19.

Sebenius, James K. 1991. "Designing Negotiations toward a New Regime: The Case of Global Warming." *International Security* 15, 4 (Spring):110-47.

Selznick, Philip. 1957. *Leadership in Administration: A Sociological Interpretation.* Evanston, Ill: Row, Peterson.

Sen, Gita, with Caren Grown. 1985. *Development, Crisis, and Alternative Visions: Third World Women's Perspectives.* New Delhi: DAWN.

Serageldin, Ismail. 1991. *La protection des forêts tropicales ombrophiles de l'Afrique.* Washington, D.C.: Banque Mondiale.

Shiva, Vandana. 1988. *Staying Alive: Women, Ecology, and Survival.* New Delhi: Kali for Women.

Sjostedt, Gunnar, ed. 1993. *International Environmental Negotiation.* Newbury Park, Calif.: Sage.

Snidal, Duncan. 1990. "IGOs, Regimes, and Cooperation: Challenges for International Relations Theory." In *The United States and Multilateral Institutions: Patterns of Changing Instrumentality and Influence,* edited by Margaret P. Carns and Karen Mingst, pp. 321-350. Boston: Unwin Hyman.

Soroos, Marvin S. 1993. "From Stockholm to Rio: The Evolution of Global Environmental Governance." In *Environmental Policy in the 1990s,* edited by Norman J. Vig and Michael E. Kraft, 2nd ed., pp. 299-321. Washington, D.C.: CQ Press.

Soroos, Marvin S. 1991. "The Atmosphere as an International Common Property Resource." *Global Policy Studies: International Interaction toward Improving Public Policy,* edited by Stuart S. Nagel, pp. 188-220. London: Macmillan.

Soroos, Marvin S. 1986. *Beyond Sovereignty: The Challenge of Global Policy.* Columbia: University of South Carolina Press.

Spears, John. 1988. "Containing Tropical Deforestation: A Review of Priority Areas for Technological and Policy Research." World Bank Environment Department, Working Paper no. 10, Washington, D.C.

Statement of the Meeting of Legal and Policy Experts. 1989. *Protection of the Atmosphere: International Meeting of Legal and Policy Experts.* Ottawa, Ontario, February 20-22.

Stein, Arthur A. 1990. *Why Nations Cooperate.* Ithaca, N.Y.: Cornell University Press.

Stein, Arthur A. 1983. "Coordination and Collaboration: Regimes in an Anarchic World." In *International Regimes*, edited by Stephen D. Krasner, pp. 115-40. Ithaca, N.Y.: Cornell University Press.

Steinbruner, J. 1974. *The Cybernetic Theory of Decision: New Dimensions of Political Analysis.* Princeton, N.J.: Princeton University Press.

Stern, Paul C., Oran R. Young, and Daniel Druckman. 1992. *Global Environmental Change: Understanding the Human Dimensions.* Washington, D.C.: National Academy Press.

Stevens, William K. 1993. "Scientists Startled by a Drop in Ozone-Killing Chemicals." *New York Times*, 26 August.

Stevens, William K. 1992. "Rio Raises Environment Issue to Lasting World-Class Status." *International Herald Tribune*, 15 June, p. 2.

Stevis, Dimitris, Valerie J. Assetto, and Stephen P. Mumme. 1989. "International Environmental Politics: A Theoretical Review of the Literature." In *Environmental Politics and Policy: Theories and Evidence*, edited by James P. Lester, pp. 289-313. Durham, N.C.: Duke University Press.

Stewart, J. 1991. "Policy Models and Equal Educational Opportunity." *PS: Political Science and Politics* 24 (2):167-173.

Stewart, Milton D. 1943. "Importance in Content Analysis." *Journalism Quarterly* 20:286-93.

Stoel, Thomas B., Jr. 1983. "Fluorocarbons: Mobilizing Concern and Action." In *Environmental Protection: The International Dimension*, edited by David Kay and Harold K. Jacobson, pp. 45-74. Totowa, N.J.: Allanheld, Osmun.

Stone, Deborah. 1988. *Policy Paradox and Political Reason.* Glenview, Ill: Scott, Foresman.

Strange, Susan. 1983. "Cave! Hic Dragones: A Critique of Regime Analysis." *International Regimes*, edited by Stephen D. Krasner, pp. 337-354. Ithaca, N.Y.: Cornell University Press.

Studlar, Donley, and Zig Layton-Henry. 1990. "Non-white Minority Access to the Political Agenda in Britain." *Policy Studies Review* 9 (2):273-93.

Szell, Patrick. 1993. "Negotiations on the Ozone Layer." In *International Environmental Negotiation*, edited by G. Sjostedt, pp. 31-47. Newbury Park, Calif.: Sage.

Taylor, Serge. 1984. *Making Bureaucracies Think.* Stanford, Calif.: Stanford University Press.

Thacher, Peter S. 1993. "The Mediterranean: A New Approach to Marine Pollution." In *International Environmental Negotiation*, edited by Gunnar Sjostedt, pp. 110-34. Newbury Park, Calif.: Sage.

Thacher, Peter S. 1991. "Multilateral Cooperation and Global Change." *Journal of International Affairs* 44 (2):433-55.

Thacher, Peter. 1988. "Stratospheric Ozone Depletion: A Background Note on UNEP Activities Leading Up to the 1977 World Action Plan on the Ozone Layer." Prepared for the National Academy of Sciences, National Science Foundation, Washington, D.C.

Thomas, Caroline. 1992. *The Environment in International Relations*. London: Royal Institute of International Affairs.

Tietenberg, Tom H. 1991. "Managing the Transition: The Potential Role for Economic Policies." In *Preserving the Global Environment*, edited by Jessica T. Mathews, pp. 187-226. New York: W. W. Norton.

Toennies, Ferdinand, ed. 1971. *On Sociology: Pure, Applied, and Empirical*. Edited and with an introduction by Werner J. Cahnman and Rudolf Heberle. Chicago: University of Chicago Press.

Tolba, Mostafa K. 1992. "Facing Facts." Address to the Open-Ended Working Group of the Parties to the Montreal Protocol, UNEP mimeo, Geneva, Switzerland, 6 April.

Tolba, Mostafa K. 1990. "Consensus to Commitment." Statement to the second meeting of the Open-Ended Working Group of the Parties to the Montreal Protocol, UNEP mimeo Na. 90-8157, Geneva, Switzerland, 26 February.

Tolba, Mostafa K. 1989. "The Tools to Build a Global Response: Financial Mechanisms for the Montreal Protocol." Statement to the Working Group of Parties to the Montreal Protocol, UNEP mimeo, Nairobi, Kenya, 21 August.

Tolba, Mostafa K. 1987. "Nowhere To Hide." Statement to the Ad Hoc Working Group for the Preparation of a Protocol on CFCs, Third Session, UNEP mimeo, Geneva, Switzerland, 27 April.

Tolba, Mostafa K. 1979. "Preface." In *The Ozone Layer*, edited by A.K. Biswas. Oxford, England: Pergamon/UNEP.

Triggs, Gillian D., ed. 1987. *The Antarctic Treaty Regime: Law, Environment and Resources*. Cambridge, England: Cambridge University Press.

Underdal, Arild. 1990. "Designing Politically Feasible Solutions: Notes on the Political Engineering of International Cooperation." Ninth triennial convention of the Nordic Political Science Association, Reykjavik, Iceland, August.

UNEP/GC.15/Inf.2. 1989. "Register of International Treaties and Other Agreements in the Field of the Environment." Nairobi, Kenya, May.

UNEP/GC/10. 1982. "United Nations Environment Programme, Report of the Governing Council (Session of a Special Character and Tenth Session)." General Assembly, Official Records, Thirty-Sixth Session, Supplement no. 25 (A/37/25).

UNEP/GC/9. 1981. "United Nations Environment Programme, Report of the Governing Council on the Work of Its Ninth Session, 13-26 May 1981." General Assembly, Official Records, Thirty-Sixth Session, Supplement no. 25 (A/36/25).

UNEP/IG.53/4. 1985. "Final Report of the Ad Hoc Working Group of Legal and Technical Experts for the Elaboration of a Global Framework Convention for the Protection of the Ozone Layer," 28 January.

UNEP/OzL.Pro.4/15. 1992. "Report of the Fourth Meeting of the Parties to the Montreal Protocol on Substances That Deplete the Ozone Layer." Copenhagen, Denmark, 23-25 November.

UNEP/OzL.Pro.2/3. 1990. "Report of the Second Meeting of the Parties to the Montreal Protocol on Substances That Deplete the Ozone Layer." London, England, 27-29 June.

UNEP/OzL.Rat.24. 1993. "Status of Ratification," 30 April.

UNEP/WG.172/2. 1987. "Report of the Ad Hoc Working Group of Legal and Technical Experts for the Preparation of the Protocol on Chlorofluorocarbons to the Vienna Convention for the Protection of the Ozone Layer." Third session, Geneva, Switzerland, 27-30 April.

UNEP/WG/167/INF.1 and Add.1. 1987. "Ad Hoc Scientific Meeting to Compare Model-Generated Assessments of Ozone Layer Change for Various Strategies for CFC Control." Warzburg, Germany, 9-10 April.

UNEP/WG.167/2. 1987. "Report of the Ad Hoc Working Group of Legal and Technical Experts for the Preparation of the Protocol on Chlorofluorocarbons to the Vienna Convention for the Protection of the Ozone Layer." Second session, Vienna, Austria, 23-27 February.

UNEP/WG.110/4. 1984. "Report of the Working Group on Its Work at the First Part of Its Fourth Session." Geneva, Switzerland, 22-26 October.

UNEP/WG.94/10. 1984. "Report of the Ad Hoc Working Group of Legal and Technical Experts for the Elaboration of a Global Framework Convention for the Protection of the Ozone Layer." Third session, Vienna, Austria, 16-20 January.

UNEP/WG.94/5. 1983. "Report of the Ad Hoc Working Group of Legal and Technical Experts for the Elaboration of a Global Framework Convention for the Protection of the Ozone Layer." Third session, Geneva, Switzerland, 17-21 October.

UNEP/WG.78/13. 1983. "Report of the Ad Hoc Working Group of Legal and Technical Experts for the Elaboration of a Global Framework Convention for the Protection of the Ozone Layer." Second part of second session, Geneva, Switzerland, 11-15 April.

UNEP/WG.78/11. 1983. "Possible contents of annexes and/or protocols." 5 April.

UNEP/WG.78/8. 1983. "Report of the Ad Hoc Working Group of Legal and Technical Experts for the Elaboration of a Global Framework Convention for the Protection of the Ozone Layer." Second session, Geneva, Switzerland, 10-17 December 1982.

UNEP/WG.69/10. 1982. "Report of the Ad Hoc Working Group of Legal and Technical Experts for the Elaboration of a Global Framework Convention for the Protection of the Ozone Layer on its First Session." Stockholm, Sweden, 20-29 January.

UNEP/WG.7/25/Rev.1. 1977. "Report of the UNEP Meeting of Experts Designated by Governments, Intergovernmental and Non-governmental Organizations on the Ozone Layer." Washington, D.C., 1-9 March.

UNEP Environmental Effects Panel. 1991. *Environmental Effects of Ozone Depletion: 1991 Update*. Nairobi, Kenya: UNEP.

UNGA Resolution 47/191. 1993. *International Legal Materials* 32 (2):254.

United Nations. 1993. "Report of the United Nations Conference on Environment and Development at Rio de Janeiro, June 1992." Proceedings of the conference, vol. 2, New York: United Nations.

United Nations. 1992a. *Convention on Biological Diversity* (Final Text for Information Media--Not an Official Record). New York: UN Department of Public Information.

United Nations. 1992b. *Earth Summit: Press Summary of Agenda 21* (Final Text). New York: UN Department of Public Information.

United Nations. 1992c. *Earth Summit: Rio Declaration and Forest Principles* (Final Text). New York: UN Department of Public Information.

United Nations. 1992d. "The Global Partnerships for Environment and Development: A Guide to Agenda 21." New York: United Nations Publications 92-1-1:482-2.

United Nations. 1992e. *United Nations Framework Convention on Climate Change* (Final Text for Information Media--Not an Official Record). New York: UN Department of Public Information.

United Nations Environment Programme. 1990. *UNEP Profile*. Nairobi, Kenya: UNEP.

United Nations Environment Programme. 1989. *Action on Ozone*. Nairobi, Kenya: UNEP.

United Nations Environment Programme. 1988. *System-Wide Medium Term Environment Programme for the Period 1990—1995*. Nairobi, Kenya: UNEP.

United Nations Environment Program. 1977. "Draft Report of the United Nations Environment Programme Meeting of Experts Designated by Governments, Intragovernmental, and Nongovernmental Organizations on the Ozone Layer, Washington, D.C. 1-9 March 1977." In *The Ozone Layer*, edited by Asit K. Biswas, pp. 369-73. Oxford, England: Pergamon/UNEP.

United Nations Environment Programme, World Meteorological Organization, and International Council of Scientific Unions. 1985. *An Assessment of the Role of Carbon Dioxide and of Other Greenhouse Gases in Climate Variations and Associated Impact*. Geneva: WMO.

United Nations General Assembly. 1992. "Completion of a Framework Convention on Climate Change, Draft Proposed by the Chairman." A/AC.237/L.14/Add.1-10. Intergovernmental Negotiating Committee for a Framework Convention on Climate Change, fifth session, second part, New York, NY, April 30—May 8.

United Nations General Assembly. 1990. A/Conf.151/PC/5, New York, N.Y., June.

United States Congress. 1992. "Trade and Environment." Hearing before the Subcommittee on International Trade of the Committee on Finance, Senate, 102d Congress, Session 1, Washington, D.C.

United States Congress. 1991. "GATT: Implications on Environmental Laws." Hearings before the Subcommittee on Health and Environment of the

Committee on Energy and Commerce, House of Representatives, 102d Congress, Session 1, Washington, D.C.

Untawale, Mukund G. 1990. "Global Environmental Degradation and International Organizations." *International Political Science Review* 11 (3):371.

Urwin, Derek. 1991. *The Community of Europe.* London: Longman.

Usher, Peter E. 1993. Interview with the Coordinator, Climate Unit, United Nations Environment Programme, Nairobi, Kenya, 30 April.

Van Wijk, Jeroen, and Gerd Junne. 1992. *Intellectual Property Protection and Advanced Technology: Changes in the Global Technology System: Implications and Options for Developing Countries.* Amsterdam: University of Amsterdam.

Vandermeersch, Dirk. 1987. "The Single European Act and the Environmental Policy of the European Economic Community." *European Law Review* 12 (5):407-29.

Vasquez, John A., and Richard W. Mansbach. 1983. "The Issue Cycle: Conceptualizing Long-term Global Political Change." *International Organization* 37 (2):257-79.

"Vienna Convention for the Protection of the Ozone Layer." 1987. *International Legal Materials* 26 (6):1516-40.

Vogel, David. 1986. *National Styles of Regulation.* Ithaca, N.Y.: Cornell University Press.

Walker, K. J. 1989. "The State in Environmental Management: The Ecological Dimension." *Political Studies* 37:25-38.

Waltz, Kenneth N. 1979. *Theory of International Politics.* Reading, Mass.: Addison-Wesley.

Wapenhans, Willi A. 1992. "Oral Briefing of the JAC on the Report of the World Bank's Portfolio Management Task Force" (Wapenhaus Report). World Bank, Washington, D.C., 22 June.

Ward, Barbara, and Rene Dubos. 1972. *Only One Earth: The Care and Maintenance of a Small Planet.* New York: Norton.

Weisskopf, Michael. 1992. "Global Warming Rift Threatens Treaty: UN Talks Close with Industrialized Nations, Third World at Odds." *Washington Post,* 27 February.

Westbrook, David A. 1991. "Environmental Policy in the European Community: Observations on the European Environment Agency." *Harvard Environmental Law Review* 15 (1):257-73.

Westing, Arthur H. 1984. *Environmental Warfare: A Technical, Legal, and Policy Appraisal.* London: Taylor and Francis.

Westing, Arthur H. 1976. *Ecological Consequences of the Second Indochina War.* Stockholm: Almquist and Wiksell International.

White, Gilbert F. 1987. "SCOPE: The First Sixteen Years." *Environmental Conservation* 14 (1):7-13.

White, Robert M. 1979. "Climate at the Millennium." *Environment* 20 (3):31-33.

Wijkman, Per Magnus. 1982. "Managing the Global Commons." *International Organization* 36 (3):511-36.

Williamson, Richard. 1990. "Building the International Environmental Regime: A Status Report." *Inter-American Law Review* 21 (Summer):679-760.

Woods, Lawrence T. 1993. "Nongovernmental Organizations and the United Nations System: Reflecting upon the Earth Summit Experience." *International Studies Notes* 18 (1):9-15.

World Bank. 1993a. *Annual Report 1993*. Washington, D.C.: World Bank.

World Bank. 1993b. *The World Bank and the Environment. Fiscal 1993*. Washington, D.C.: World Bank.

World Bank. 1992a. "World Bank as a Development and Environment Institution." *Environment Bulletin* (Environment Department) 4 (2):1.

World Bank. 1992b. *World Development Report 1992: Development and the Environment*. Washington, D.C.: World Bank.

World Bank. 1991a. *Annual Report 1991*. Washington, D.C.: World Bank.

World Bank. 1991b. *Issues Facing National Environmental Action Plans in Africa*. Washington, D.C.: World Bank (AFTEN).

World Bank. 1991c. *The World Bank and the Environment: A Progress Report, Fiscal 1991*. Washington, D.C.: World Bank.

World Bank. 1990a. *National Environmental Action Plans in Africa*. Washington, D.C.: World Bank (AFTEN).

World Bank. 1990b. *The World Bank and the Environment: First Annual Report, Fiscal 1990*. Washington, D.C.: World Bank.

World Bank. 1985. *Annual Report 1985*. Washington, D.C.: World Bank.

World Commission on Environment and Development. 1987. *Our Common Future*. New York: Oxford University Press.

World Meteorological Organization et al. 1991. *Scientific Assessment of Ozone Depletion: 1991*. Geneva, Switzerland: WMO.

World Meterological Organization. 1990. *The WMO Achievement: 40 Years in the Service of International Meteorology and Hydrology*. Document no. 729. Geneva, Switzerland: WMO.

World Meteorological Organization et al. 1986. *Atmospheric Ozone 1985*. (Global Ozone Research and Monitoring Project, Report no. 16). 3 volumes. Geneva, Switzerland: WMO.

World Resources 1992-93. 1992. New York: Oxford University Press.

Worster, Donald. 1993. *The Wealth of Nature: Environmental History and the Ecological Imagination*. New York: Oxford University Press.

Yost, Nicholas C. 1992. "Rio and the Road Beyond." *Environmental Law* 11 (4):1-6.

Young, Oran R. 1993a. "International Organizations and International Institutions: Lessons Learned from Environmental Regimes." In *Environmental Politics in the International Arena*, edited by Sheldon Kamieniecki, pp. 145-164. Albany, N.Y.: SUNY Press.

Young, Oran R. 1993b. "Perspectives on International Organizations." In *International Environmental Negotiation*, edited by Gunnar Sjostedt, pp. 244-61. Newbury Park, Calif.: Sage.

Young, Oran R. 1992. "Understanding International Regimes: Contributions from Law and the Social Sciences." Paper presented at the annual conference of the American Society of International Law, Washington D.C., 1-3 April.

Young, Oran R. 1990. "Global Environmental Change and International Governance." *Millenium* 19 (Winter):337-46.

Young, Oran R. 1989a. *Compliance and Public Authority: A Theory with International Applications*. A Resources for the Future Book. Baltimore, Md: Johns Hopkins University Press.

Young, Oran R. 1989b. *International Cooperation: Building Regimes for Natural Resources and the Environment*. Ithaca, N.Y.: Cornell University Press.

Young, Oran R. 1989c. "The Politics of International Regime Formation: Managing Resources and the Environment." *International Organization* 43 (Summer):349-75.

Young, Oran R. 1980. "International Regimes: Problems of Concept Formation." *World Politics* 32 (April):331-56.

Index

About the Contributors

Robert V. Bartlett is an Associate Professor of Political Science at Purdue University. He has published numerous scholarly articles and book chapters on environmental policy and politics. He is the author or editor of several books, including *The Reserve Mining Controversy: Science, Technology, and Environmental Quality* (1980) and *Policy through Impact Assessment: Institutionalized Analysis as a Policy Strategy* (1989). In 1990 he was a Fulbright Scholar and in 1992 a Visiting Fellow at the Centre for Resource Management at Lincoln University, New Zealand. Most recently he is the author (with Ton Bührs) of *Environmental Policy in New Zealand: The Politics of Clean and Green?* (1993) and editor (with James N. Gladden) of *Environment as a Focus of Public Policy* (1995).

M. Leann Brown is an Assistant Professor of Political Science at the University of Florida. She served as Program Coordinator for the International Studies Association, was a Leverhulme USA/Commonwealth Fellow at the University of Keele, England, and Visiting Professor at the University of Warwick, England. She has contributed articles to the *International Journal of the Canadian Institute of International Affairs* and the *Journal of Modern African Studies*. Her monograph, *Developing Countries and Regional Economic Cooperation*, is forthcoming.

Lynton K. Caldwell is a Professor Emeritus of Political Science and Public and Environmental Affairs at Indiana University. He holds graduate degrees from Harvard and Chicago universities, and has served on the faculties of Chicago, Syracuse, California, and Indiana universities with engagements in more than seventy-five additional institutions of higher education and research in thirty-two different countries. His publications include twelve books and 250 major articles with translations into twenty different languages. He has a long record

278 About the Contributors

of public service with, for example, the United Nations, UNESCO, the U.S. National Research Council, and numerous governmental and scientific advisory bodies. He is especially noted for his role in drafting the National Environmental Policy Act of 1969 and for his concept of the environmental impact statement.

Paul D'Anieri is an Assistant Professor of Political Science at the University of Kansas. His research focuses on theoretical approaches to international cooperation. In 1993-1994 he was a Fulbright lecturer at the University of L'viv, Ukraine. He is currently researching the problems created by Ukrainian-Russian economic interdependence.

David Leonard Downie is an Assistant Professor of Political Science and International Affairs at Columbia University and Co-Director of Environmental Policy Studies at Columbia's School of International and Public Affairs. His research interests include international organization and regimes, international environmental institutions, the foreign policy of environmental issues, and U.S. and comparative environmental politics.

David Lewis Feldman is a Senior Research Associate in the Energy, Environment and Resources Center, University of Tennessee. His publications have appeared in *Policy Studies Journal*, *Policy Sciences*, *Global Environmental Change*, *Society and Natural Resources*, *Journal of Public Policy*, *Environmental Professional*, *Policy Currents*, *Political Psychology*, *World Resources Review*, and in several books. He is the author of *Water Resources Management: In Search of an Environmental Ethic* (1991) and *Global Climate Change and Public Policy* (1994).

Lynne M. Jurgielewicz teaches in the Political Science Department and coaches the women's tennis team at Albright College, Reading, Pennsylvania. She holds a JD from the Catholic University of America (1988) and a Ph.D. (1994) from the London School of Economics and Political Science.

Priya A. Kurian is a Dissertation Scholar with the Women's Studies Program at the University of California, Santa Barbara, and a doctoral candidate in the Department of Political Science at Purdue University. Her current research is on the World Bank's environmental policies and the interconnections of gender and environmental impact assessment.

Philippe G. Le Prestre is a Professor of Political Science at the Université du Québec à Montréal. He has a Ph.D. in political science from Indiana University and advanced degrees in Ecology from the University of Paris. His current research interests include foreign environmental policy, national impacts of international environmental cooperation, and environmental security. He is the author of *The World Bank and the Environmental Challenge* (1989) and articles on international environmental politics and U.S. foreign policy.

Madhu Malik is an instructor with the Department of History and Political Science at Purdue University Calumet in Hammond, Indiana, and a doctoral candidate in Political Science at Purdue University in West Lafayette, Indiana. Her primary areas of research are international environmental policy, international organizations, environmental impact assessment, and the politics of sustainable development. She has published in *The Environmental Professional* and has presented papers at major professional meetings.

John McCormick is an Assistant Professor of Political Science at Indiana University-Purdue University Indianapolis (IUPUI). He worked for international environmental groups during the 1980s (including the World Wide Fund for Nature) and was a consultant for several UN specialized agencies (including UNEP and FAO). His recent publications include *British Politics and the Environment* (1991) and *Reclaiming Paradise: The Global Environmental Movement* (2nd ed., 1995).

Elena N. Nikitina is a senior researcher with the Institute of World Economy and International Relations of the Russian Academy of Sciences in Moscow. She has published widely in Russian and English on international environmental and resource policies as well as on the environmental situation in her native country. She is the author of a book published in Russian on the World Meteorological Organization. In recent years, she has participated in several Western research projects on global environmental security and international responses to environmental problems.

Robin Pistorius currently works as a Ph.D. student at the Department of International Relations and Public International Law of the University of Amsterdam. His thesis focuses on international conflicts on the control and use of plant genetic resources. He has been editor of the *Biotechnology and Development Monitor* and currently is working on a book describing the history of conservation strategies in plant genetic resources since the beginning of this century.

Marvin S. Soroos is a Professor and the Head of the Department of Political Science and Public Administration at North Carolina State University. He is the author of *Beyond Sovereignty: The Challenge of Global Policy* (1986) and numerous other publications on international environmental politics and policy, especially on the use of global commons. His current research is on the atmosphere as global commons, in particular the regimes that address the problems of long-range transport of air pollutants, ozone depletion, and climate change.

Dimitris Stevis is an Associate Professor in the Department of Political Science at Colorado State University where he teaches courses in international political economy, law, and environmental politics. His current research focuses on comparing the international environmental and labor movements and on environmental and natural resource politics in less industrialized countries. His most recent work has appeared in the *Policy Studies Journal, International Journal of Urban and Regional Research,* and *Latin American Research Review.*

Clifton Wilson is a Professor Emeritus of Political Science at the University of Arizona. His interests are in international law, international organization, and world order. He has published on the subjects of diplomatic privileges and immunities, international law and politics, and international organization and environment.

ISBN 0-313-29623-5

90000>

EAN

9 780313 296239

HARDCOVER BAR CODE